PRENTICE HALL

Language Teaching Methodology Series

Applied Linguistics

General Editor: Christopher N. Candlin

Learner Strategies for Learner Autonomy

Other titles in this series include

ELLIS, Rod
Classroom second language development

ELLIS, Rod
Classroom language acquisition in context

KENNEDY, Chris
Language planning and English language teaching

KRASHEN, Stephen
Second language acquisition and second language learning

KRASHEN, Stephen
Principles and practice in second language acquisition

KRASHEN, Stephen
Language acquisition and language education

KRASHEN, Stephen and TERRELL, Tracy
The natural approach

MARTON, Waldemar
Methods in English language teaching: frameworks and options

McKAY, Sandra
Teaching grammar

NEWMARK, Peter
Approaches to translation

NUNAN, David
Understanding language classrooms

NUNAN, David
Language teaching methodology

PECK, Antony
Language teachers at work

ROBINSON, Gail
Crosscultural understanding

STEVICK, Earl
Success with foreign languages

SWALES, John
Episodes in ESP

TOMALIN, Barry and STEMPLESKI, Susan
Video in action

WENDEN, Anita and RUBIN, Joan
Learner strategies in language learning

YALDEN, Janice
The communicative syllabus

Learner Strategies
for Learner Autonomy

Planning and implementing learner training
for language learners

ANITA WENDEN
York College, City University of New York

ENGLISH LANGUAGE TEACHING

PRENTICE HALL

NEW YORK   LONDON   TORONTO   SYDNEY   TOKYO   SINGAPORE

First published 1991 by
Prentice Hall International (UK) Ltd
66 Wood Lane End, Hemel Hempstead
Hertfordshire HP2 4RG
A division of
Simon & Schuster International Group

Typeset in 10/12 pt Times
by MHL Typesetting Ltd, Coventry.

Printed and bound in Great Britain
at the University Press, Cambridge.

Library of Congress Cataloging-in-Publication Data

Wenden, Anita.
    Learner strategies for learner autonomy: planning and
    implementing learner training for language learners/Anita L.
    Wenden.
        p.   cm.
    Includes bibliographical references.
        ISBN 0-13-529603-X
1. Language and languages — Study and teaching.   I. Title.
P51.W45   1991
418'.007—dc20   90-48131
                                                              CIP

British Library Cataloguing in Publication Data

Wenden, Anita
    Learner strategies for learner autonomy: planning and
    implementing learner training for language learners.
    (Language teaching methodology series)
    I. Title   II. Series
    418.007

    ISBN 0-13-529603-X

---

1 2 3 4 5 95 94 93 92 91

This book is dedicated to my mother, Anne Lanthier — who inspired me to be a teacher

Contents

General Editor's Preface

One of the most important outcomes of the movement towards more communicatively oriented language learning and teaching has been the enhancement of the role of the learner in the language learning process. Old adages that teachers teach and learners learn (and the increasing recognition through empirical research that learners regularly don't learn what teachers teach), have compelled both classroom researchers and curriculum developers to focus their attention on the process of learning. Since one cannot empirically observe learning in action, the necessary indirectness of such attention has, in turn, encouraged teachers as well as researchers to take the issue to the learners themselves, to attempt, albeit vicariously, to experience through them what the nature of this process might be. This shift of orientation of research and teaching does not, of course, exist in some curricular vacuum, it is itself part and parcel of concurrent changes to the curriculum itself towards more learner-centered and participative models. If you focus on the learner, you at the same time focus on the curriculum itself and the practices of the classroom.

In particular, the traditional curriculum distinctions between content and methodology are no longer as sharp as they previously were. *How* and *why* learners learn (or don't learn) become as important as *what* they learn. As the early writings on the communicative curriculum presaged, the *process* of language learning becomes in part the *content* of learning. More than this, however, this focus on learning and the learner changes quite radically the typical distribution of power and authority in the classroom. How learners go about making meanings and making sense of language data becomes of central importance, and it is the learners who are the sources of information on and insight into this process. They inevitably become partners in the curriculum in quite different ways than was the case earlier.

Becoming partners, however, imposes its own responsibilities, ones which have again not traditionally been accorded to the 'recipients' of teaching. Important among these responsibilities is that of consciousness about one's own learning processes and strategies, knowing how one learns. Neither teachers nor learners can take this awareness for granted. It may be cognitively latent, but it needs to be realized into appropriate action: it needs training. Awareness, however, is not on its own enough: learners need awareness with a purpose. The idea of effective partnership depends both on learners knowing about themselves and their learning and also knowing how to act *autonomously* as learners within the structures of learning imposed by whatever institutional arrangements they participate in.

It is this twin focus on strategy and autonomy, then, which is crucial and which is at the heart of Anita Wenden's long-awaited new book in the **Language Teaching Methodology Series**. Readers of her and Joan Rubin's earlier book in the Series: *Learner Strategies in Language Learning* (1987) by now the standard introduction to the research literature in this field, will have been prepared for the particular contribution of this new volume. Research now shifts to action, in teacher education and training and towards classroom and program implementation. She sets out the key themes: of learner training, of teaching strategies for learning, of the needs to change the attitudes and beliefs of teachers and learners, to estimate the impact on the curriculum and its syllabuses, and to develop these insights into the creation of appropriate learning tasks and materials development.

What is more significant perhaps than the themes themselves is the way in which they are realized and explored within the text. This is no mere theoretical account, but a task-based curriculum for teacher development. Throughout the book the overarching themes of *strategy* and *autonomy* are applied not only to learners but also to teachers and readers of the book itself. Data from the relevant literature, from learners' classroom accounts, from teachers' lesson plans and from mini case studies are made the subject of analytical and applicational tasks specially designed to engage the teacher/reader in exploring and critiquing the themes and their associated data. Anita Wenden offers her own commentary on these themes enabling the reader to focus and see the relevance of the tasks and to suggest ideas for new tasks and new activities that they can devise for their own learners. Perhaps most importantly in this consciously crafted book is the way the reader can construct his or her own pathways through the material. It is in many ways a *resource book* for developing and exploring learner autonomy, not a linear account.

Implicit in the approach taken to the roles of the teacher and the learner in this book is that of education for change. Autonomy, like awareness, needs a goal. The problematic issue of the impact of teacher education on classroom change is, of course, well-known. There have been panaceas and wild expectations in plenty. At times it has seemed as if the most debilitating influence on educational and curriculum change has been the enthuasiasm of proponents. There is a need, then, for a measured approach and one which is firmly linked to different curriculum contexts and which goes to the heart of teaching and learning: the relationship between the teacher and the learner. Anita Wenden's book achieves this focus. It does so because it sees how close this partnership has to be. Learners need to learn how to learn, teachers how they teach, and both need to learn these things of each other. Both need the tools for description, interpretation and explanation: *what* happens, *how* it happens and most important of all *why* it happens. For that they need a critical guide. **Learner Strategies for Learner Autonomy** will become a classic in the literature in the eyes of teachers mainly, I suspect, because it is such a guide and because above all it practises what it preaches.

Professor Christopher N. Candlin
National Centre for English Language Teaching & Research
Macquarie University, Sydney, Australia

Acknowledgments

I would like to express special appreciation to Chris Candlin, the series editor. His concept of a 'task-based' teacher education series dedicated to making research findings accessible to classroom teachers inspired the methodology of the book. His comments throughout the writing have been both encouraging and helpful.

I am also very grateful to all those whose insights have helped to shape and improve the manuscript during the various stages of its writing: Joan Rubin for her perceptive and critical comments on the first and penultimate versions of the manuscript; the faculty members of the United Nations Language Program, who field tested some of the earlier chapters; Irene Dutra and Kathie Brown, who read and worked through an early version of the whole manuscript; Larry Krute, who field tested materials from the first chapters with his teacher education class at Manhattanville College; Linda Kunz, whose comments on the final version contributed to making the book more readable.

I would also like to thank the following teachers, who provided information and original documentation for the mini case studies in Chapter 9: Viljo Kohonen, Department of Teacher Education, University of Tampere, Tampere, Finland (Setting 1); Martine Guerchon and Lora Leighton, United Nations Language Training Program, New York, USA (Setting 2); Carole Broder, Kathie Brown, Barbara Foerster, Ronnie Kaufmann, Parsippany, Adult and Community Education Center, New Jersey, USA (Setting 3); Lew Barnett, Escuela Superior de Administracion y Direccion de Empresas, Barcelona, Spain (Setting 4); David Mendelsohn and Marian Tyacke, University of Toronto School of Continuing Studies, Toronto, Canada (Setting 5); Kerry O'Sullivan and Liz Parkinson, Macquarie University National Center for English Language Teaching and Research, Sydney, Australia (Setting 6).

The teachers who participated in my workshops and the ESL students at York College (City University of New York) and the American Language Program (Columbia University) who worked through the tasks and materials I devised must also be recognized. They helped me to deal with issues regarding student motivation and the methodology for learner training.

I would also like to acknowledge those colleagues whose work in the field of learner strategies and learner autonomy helped to shape my earlier thinking: Joan Rubin, Andrew Cohen, Carolyn Stanchina, Carol Hosenfeld, Anna Chamot and Michael O'Malley.

A final personal note of thanks is extended to Frans C. Verhagen, my husband, for the encouragement he has always provided me in my professional endeavors and for his patient support during the last stages of the manuscript.

Acknowledgment is made to the following for permission to reprint copyrighted material: Academic Press for an excerpt from 'The development of a learning strategies curriculum' by D. Dansereau (1978) in *Learning Strategies* edited by H. O'Neill; Association for Supervision and Curriculum Development for an excerpt from *Strategic Teaching and Learning: Cognitive Instruction in the Content Areas* edited by B.F. Jones, A.M. Palinscar, D.S. Ogle and E.G. Carr (1987); the editors of Canadian Modern Language Review for an excerpt from 'Learning behaviors of successful adult students in intensive language training', by Marjorie Wesche (1979) and an adaptation of 'Language learning on the spot' by H.H. Stern (1980); Heinle & Heinle for material from *How to be a More Successful Language Learner* by J. Rubin and I. Thompson (1982); Lawrence Erlbam Associates for an excerpt from 'Cognition and adaptation: the importance of learning to learn' by J.D. Bransford, B.S. Stein, T.S. Shelton and R.A. Owings (1981) in *Cognition, Social Behavior and the Environment* edited by J.H. Harvey; Longman Group (UK) for materials from *Listening Focus* by E. Kisslinger and M. Rost (1980); National Center for English Language Teaching and Research for an excerpt from *Learning Styles in Adult Migrant Education* by K. Willing (1987); Ontario Institute for Studies in Education for an adaptation of the findings from *The Good Language Learner* by M. Naiman, M. Frohlich, D. Stern and A. Todesco (1978); Oxford University Press for an excerpt from 'What do we want teaching materials for?' by R. Allwright (1981); Prentice Hall International for an excerpt from *Language Learning Tasks* by C. Candlin and D. Murphy (1987) and a table from an article by A. Chamot (1987) in *Learner Strategies in Language Learning* edited by A. Wenden and J. Rubin; J. Reid for 'Explanation of learning style preferences' (1984); J. Rubin for use of her classification scheme from 'How learner strategies can inform language teaching' (1989); Simon & Schuster for Figure 2.3 from *The Universe Within* by Morton Hunt (1982); M. Tyacke and D. Mendelsohn for an excerpt from 'Classroom implications of learner diversity' (1988).

Thematic groupings

Theme	Chapter
Significance of learner training	1
Content of learner training	2, 3, 4
Getting information on how students learn	2, 3, 4 and 6
Teaching strategies	2 and 7
Changing learner beliefs	3 and 8
Changing learner attitudes	4 and 8
Syllabus development	2, 3, 4, 5 and 6
Developing tasks	5, 6, 7 and 8
Materials development	5, 7 and 8
Program models	9

Introduction

Aim of the book

Give a man a fish and he eats for a day.
Teach him how to fish and he eats for a lifetime.
                    An ancient proverb

Learner Strategies for Learner Autonomy aims to help teachers acquire the knowledge and skills they need to plan and implement learning that will help language learners become more autonomous. This is a goal with which few teachers will disagree. In fact, since the early 1970s, our language teaching practices have become increasingly learner centered.

Influenced by insights from humanist and cognitive psychology, classroom teachers and language teaching methodologists have looked at how the tasks we set for our students and the materials we ask them to use can be improved or changed. Humanist psychologists have stressed the importance of self-concept and affective factors in adult learning. According to Dubin and Olshtain (1986) language teaching objectives that draw on such humanist views on learning will encompass the following:

1. Emphasize meaningful communication.
2. Place high respect and value on the learner.
3. View learning as a form of self-realization.
4. Give learners considerable say in the decision-making process.
5. Place teachers in the role of facilitator whose task is to develop and maintain a supportive class atmosphere.
6. Stress the role of other learners as a support group.

Cognitive pyschologists, on the other hand, emphasize learners' mental processes. They have recognized that learners are actively involved in the process of learning — selectively attending to incoming data, hypothesizing, comparing, elaborating, reconstructing its meaning and integrating it with previously stored information for future use. Language learning tasks on the cognitive view of learning strive to give learners the opportunity to do the following:

1. Test their hypotheses.
2. Draw upon their prior knowledge.
3. Take risks.
4. Use the language to communicate (cf. Prator and Celce-Murcia, 1979; Larsen-Freeman, 1986).

If humanist and cognitive psychology has encouraged the development of learner-centered teaching methods, new insights from sociolinguistics have led to learner-centered language content. Emphasizing the pragmatic function of language, these insights have brought to our attention the need to make learners' special purposes for learning a language a determining factor in the selection of content (cf. Munby, 1978; Hutchinson and Waters, 1987). As a result, courses and materials that focus exclusively on the needs of specific learner groups have been developed.

Teaching practices reflecting ideas from humanist and cognitive psychology and sociolinguistics can now be seen in many 'eclectic' classrooms. However, while these practices give the learner a more central role, in fact, they focus on teachers, striving to make them better by changing what they teach and how they teach.

A third set of learner-centered practices has focused on changing the learner — on making the learner a better learner. Writings describing this approach recommend that learner autonomy be included as an objective in language programs. They encourage teachers to help learners learn how to learn and outline methods for providing 'learner' training (cf. for example, Abe, Stanchina and Smith, 1975; Stanchina, 1976; Hosenfeld, 1976, 1981; Moulden, 1978, 1980; Dickinson and Carver, 1980; Holec, 1981; Sinclair and Ellis, 1985; Dickinson, 1987; Wenden and Rubin, 1987; Cohen, 1990; O'Malley and Chamot, 1990; Oxford, 1990).

Learner Strategies for Learner Autonomy advocates this third approach; its purpose is to help teachers learn how to implement it.

Overview of the content

Learner Strategies for Learner Autonomy provides teachers with tasks, data and commentary to acquire the skills and knowledge necessary to help their students become more autonomous as learners. Some of the concepts and the terms used to talk about them may be new. However, the skills will not be, for teachers already use most of them in the planning of their language classes. Working through *Learner Strategies for Learner Autonomy*, they will learn to apply these skills to learner training, and as they do, they will be able to approach the task of promoting autonomy in their classrooms more autonomously themselves. It will not be necessary to depend on pre-planned procedures from textbooks to decide what to teach (as regards learner training) and how. Teachers will be able to devise their own learning plans and evaluate those that already exist.

Chapter content

Each chapter in the book is based on a question that teachers will need to clarify as they set out to help their students become more autonomous. The intended outcome of each chapter is a planning resource or specific understandings implied by the question. Table I outlines the questions and related resource or understandings.

Information formats

Learner Strategies for Learner Autonomy provides information on the chapter content through five different kinds of formats.

Chapter overview

The first page of each chapter includes an overview of the chapter content. The *focus* question indicates the topic of the chapter in general terms. The focus questions for each chapter have

TABLE I
Overview of content

Focus	Outcome
1 Why should I help students learn how to learn?	Rationale for promoting autonomy
2 How can I help my students deal with their learning problems?	An inventory of learning strategies
3 What beliefs about language learning do students hold? What should they know about it?	Resource file of materials on language and the learning process
4 What attitudes will encourage students to take responsibility for their learning?	An understanding of two attitudes necessary for autonomous learning
5 How do I decide *what* to teach students about how to learn?	A planning guide
6 How can I find out how my students actually go about learning?	Ways of obtaining, analyzing and recording information on students' learning processes
7 How can students be helped to learn to use strategies?	Guidelines for strategy training
8 How can learner beliefs about language learning be changed? How can learners be encouraged to be more autonomous?	Guidelines for changing learner beliefs and attitudes
9 How can learner autonomy be incorporated on a program level?	Illustrations of different ways of incorporating learner autonomy into a language program

already been listed in Table I. The *process* outline shows how the topic will be developed. The *outcome* refers to what the reader is supposed to 'get out of the chapter'. These are the understandings and planning resources which are listed in Table I.

Data

Data refers to information that illustrates the concepts or themes that develop the topic of each chapter. The four kinds of data used in the book are listed in Table II.

Tasks

Tasks, the third kind of format used in each chapter, will suggest ways for working with the data. The idea of including tasks to help readers clarify some of the ideas presented in

TABLE II
Data types

Chapter(s)	Data type
1, 3, 7	*Excerpts from the literature*: brief passages from the writings of language educators and researchers, cognitive psychologists
1, 2, 3, 4, 5, 6	*Learner accounts*: learners' descriptions of how they approach their language learning in general or what they do to complete a particular language learning task
5, 7, 8	*Lesson plans*: procedures that illustrate guidelines to be used in the devising of tasks to promote autonomy
9	*Mini case studies*: descriptions of language programs that include learner autonomy as an objective in their curriculum.

a chapter or to apply them to their teaching is not new to the literature on language teaching methodology. Ordinarily, the tasks are listed at the end of each chapter and are a supplement for those who feel the need to think further about what they have read; readers may or may not do them.

In contrast, tasks are central to the methodology of *Learner Strategies for Learner Autonomy*. Their purpose is to involve readers (teachers) more intensely with the content. Of course, good readers are active readers, and, as they reflect on their reading they will initiate their own tasks. It is not intended that the tasks in *Learner Strategies for Learner Autonomy* discourage such personal initiative. However, they do provide ways of structuring reflection and of making explicit the concepts and themes that underlie the content of a chapter. Generally there are two kinds of tasks — analytic and application.

Analytic tasks encourage an inductive approach to learning about the content of each chapter. Some of these tasks will ask readers to reflect on their experience as learners and as teachers in order to elicit their prior knowledge on the subject and to initiate discussion. Others will suggest ways for working with the data that will lead to an understanding of the concepts and themes presented in the chapter. Finally, analytic tasks should prepare readers to evaluate the author's analysis of the same tasks, which follows in the commentary.

Application tasks ask readers to evaluate the planning resources they learn about in the various chapters. They will suggest ways of using these resources in a teaching/learning setting to test their usefulness. Application tasks usually follow the author's commentary.

Commentary

The author's commentary follows the data and the analytic tasks. It explains the concepts and themes that are the focus of the chapter using illustrations from the data (e.g. learner accounts, lesson plans) and making reference to the related theory and research. In Chapter 2, for example, two kinds of learning strategies are defined and classified, with examples from the two learner accounts presented at the beginning of the chapter. In Chapter 7, guidelines for strategy training are explained by referring to the lesson plan included in the chapter. In effect, the commentary is the author's response to the analytic tasks, which readers can compare with their own.

Valuable readings

At the end of each chapter there is a short annotated list of valuable readings relevant to the chapter focus for those who wish to pursue the topic further.

How to use the book

It is true that the content of the book is organized in such a way that later chapters build upon earlier ones, and, as noted earlier, there is a logic to the order in which the tasks, data and commentary are presented within a chapter. However, the time that teachers can set aside to pursue self-study may be limited. They may not be able to work through the chapters consecutively. Besides, they will probably be most interested in what is relevant to the problems or needs that their students are actually facing at any given time. Therefore, they are encouraged to work through the book according to an order that reflects these interests using the time they have available.

In other words, *Learner Strategies for Learner Autonomy* should not be approached with the same set of expectations one has when setting out to read or study most other methodology books. It may best be viewed as a set of resources for an autonomous seminar on learner autonomy. Typically, in a teacher training or professional development setting, the seminar leader is the 'expert' (the college professor, the invited workshop leader), who is expected to select and set the tasks and to determine their order and purpose. Seminar participants can turn to the leader for help in clarifying questions and for (expert) views on the topic. In *Learner Strategies for Learner Autonomy*, the book is a substitute for the expert in a seminar, but its role is somewhat different. It provides the tasks; the commentary is a synthesis of 'expert' opinion and can also be referred to for clarification. However, the teachers are the seminar leaders. They can choose the tasks and order them according to their particular needs and interests. They may turn to each other for clarification and for alternative opinions. The following suggestions take this general approach into account.

The learning group

The tasks should be done with one or more teachers. In this way it is possible to benefit from several views and different experiences. On the other hand, if for some reason it is necessary to work through the book alone, I have been assured by teachers who have used the material in this way that this can also be a valuable experience.

The learning journal

Teachers are encouraged to keep a learning journal. The journal can be a record-keeper of different kinds of information. Here are some suggestions:

- Evolving understandings and opinions about learner autonomy.
- Questions that need to be answered.
- Ideas to try in the classroom.
- Unclear concepts.
- Answers to the tasks.

Teachers can write in their journal after completing one set of tasks or a series of tasks. Alternatively, they may use it only at the outset of a chapter to briefly record a few ideas about the focus question and again at the end to summarize what has been learned. As teachers progress through the book, earlier notes in the journal can be examined and compared with later ones to see whether one's questions have been answered; to reflect on ideas one has tried out; to note how one's insights evolve. For teachers who work through the book on their own, using the journal in this way is a substitute for discussion with a learning group.

Order

Learner Strategies for Learner Autonomy addresses questions about learning that may be of particular interest to teachers as students of learning or that may deal with learning problems their students have. Therefore, to decide in which order to work through the book, it will be necessary to identify these problems and questions. Teachers can, then, examine (1) the table of contents, (2) the list of thematic groupings and (3) the overview of each chapter to find the chapter that relates to these interests and begin there. If concepts introduced in earlier chapters appear, it is possible to refer to the glossary for a short definition or to the index to locate the chapter(s) where they are discussed in more detail.

The order in which readers work through a chapter is also flexible and their approach will reflect their learning style. That is, having examined the overview, some may prefer to go directly to the commentary and then to do the tasks, ignoring some and spending more time on those which they consider more useful or interesting. Moreover, in reading the commentary, they may wish to limit themselves to the definitions and classifications and return to the analysis once the tasks are done or even at a later time. On the other hand, others may prefer to work inductively and do the tasks in exactly the order in which they are listed before reading the commentary.

Once again, I wish to emphasize that it is the reader/teacher who should decide how to work through the book. It is not necessary to start at the beginning and proceed page by page.

Procedures for completing a task

The following procedures are suggested for working through a set of tasks. They assume that teachers are working in a group of two or more and that they have set a time for meeting on a regular basis.

Data analysis tasks

Before the meeting:

1. Read and think about the tasks before meeting with your learning group.

During the meeting:

2. Do the task analysis.
3. Discuss and identify differences of opinion.
4. Reach a consensus on differences or an understanding of why there is disagreement.
5. Compare your insights with my commentary.

Teachers who are working through the tasks alone may wish to think about them or jot down their ideas in their learning journal. They can, then, compare their insights with the commentary.

Application tasks

1. Plan the application with your group.
2. Implement the applications using your whole class or selected students.
3. Implementation may be done in teams and other members of the group may be invited to observe.
4. Analyze your experience together with members of your group, comparing insights, problems and outcomes.
5. Discuss together possible revisions.
6. Make any revisions suggested by the evaluation and discussion.
7. Implement a second time.

A final note

Learner Strategies for Learner Autonomy is a task-based approach to teacher education. Its contents will not be mastered in one quick reading. Of course, teachers can look at the table of contents or the chapter overview and skim the commentary sections in each chapter. This will provide them with a theoretical notion of what the book is about. To appreciate the theory, however, they will need to work through the tasks. This will allow them to relate it to their own experience-based insights and so to deepen their understanding of its significance.

Underlying the aims of *Learner Strategies for Learner Autonomy* is the belief that teacher education is an essential ingredient in the management of educational change. In the promotion of new methods and materials, the teacher is the main change agent — not the materials or techniques in which innovations are packaged. Their acceptance and success will depend on the teacher. In other words, however teacher-proof new materials or techniques may be, they will be used inappropriately by an untrained teacher and not at all by unwilling teachers who may be unwilling because they are unaware of their relevance. Finally, because educational change is human change, the specific needs of learners and the particular learning tasks which respond to these needs will vary. The implementation of new methods and the use of new materials will depend on the creativity of a committed and informed teacher. Therefore it becomes important that opportunities be provided for teachers to educate themselves in the classroom applications of research-based educational innovations.

Certainly, when it comes to acquiring the skills and knowledge necessary to help learners become more autonomous, participating in a weekend workshop or reading through a manual of suggested techniques will not be sufficient. Teachers will need time to reflect, experiment and evaluate. *Learner Strategies for Learner Autonomy* is intended to guide such reflection and experimentation. It is a teaching resource that teachers can turn to time and time again in search of tasks that will enable them to gain insight into the questions that emerge as they do so.

Chapter 1

Reasons for promoting learner autonomy

Focus   Do you agree that helping students learn how to *learn* a language is as important as helping them learn how to *use* it?

Process   • Characteristics of autonomous language learners
               • Reasons for promoting learner autonomy

Outcome   Rationale for promoting learner autonomy

Characteristics of autonomous language learners

1.1   Describing autonomous language learners

The following are excerpts from the accounts of two language learners, Laszlo and Ilse, who were asked to talk about how they helped themselves learn English.

(a)   As you read each account, try to determine whether they are autonomous learners.

(b)   Use illustrations from the accounts to support your views.

LEARNER ACCOUNT 1.1

Laszlo immigrated to the United States from Hungary, where he had begun his English studies on his own. Once in the United States, he began to work. At the time of the interview which formed the basis for this account, he was also taking formal courses in English for seven hours a week while he continued to work.

I didn't learn English in school. I learned it in a private way, so I had problems with my spoken English and the practical way of expressing my thoughts to put the ideas into forms was my problem. I understand by reading much more than speaking. In the first [when he had arrived in the United States], I couldn't catch [what] other people said because it was very strange for my ear.

   After reading . . . it's difficult. I couldn't speak to anybody . . . my problem [is] I understand a lot of words . . . that is only the passive way of improving my knowledge . . . . But . . . here I have [the] opportunity to speak more to practise the theoretical knowledge I acquired in Hungary . . . . I had some improvement.

   In Hungary I read and I learned alone. I didn't have a good method though . . . a system. I bought a book. It's English, a verb book. Then I went through it . . . four lessons. I learned the verbs, the grammar, but one of my deficiencies was I didn't resolve the exercises. I only accumulated a great deal of the words and expressions. I didn't take the trouble. I was impatient . . . in a short time I wanted to . . . [acquire] a very large quantity of knowledge.

When you found something you didn't understand, how did you deal with it?

I looked it up in the dictionary. I had a good dictionary though it was English–Hungarian so I didn't eliminate the Hungarian language. Here I have an English dictionary . . .

Webster's . . . so the explanation of the word is in English; it's much better. I don't have to think in my native language.

I came here in March . . . so two months I spent in Ohio. I worked, I got a job . . . I was [an] aluminium polisher. I didn't have the chance to speak. I was silent all day. That was not pleasant.

After work, I had some friends . . . Americans . . . it was very good. Whenever I didn't understand anything, I asked, I inquired and they explained. I was not ashamed to ask. That was the main point. I tried to overcome this shame . . . this fear and . . . . This is the only way to learn to ask always . . . learn . . . .

What did you do after they explained it to you?

I kept it in my mind. I practised . . . I tried to keep it in my mind.

You tried to remember it?

Yes, memorize and to recollect it more times in a day . . . and to use it to build a sentence by myself and in conversation.

Did you have any other ways to figure out the meaning?

Sure . . . the word is not isolated. It's in the environment of other words. Sometimes I inferred the meaning. Sometimes I didn't ask because I found it out on my own.

What do you do when you want to say something in English? Do you plan before?

When I talk . . . I try to eliminate my native language so the idea and the word are almost simultaneous. I concentrate on what I say but I don't formulate it from the Hungarian language. It's the best. A language has to reflect the reality and not in another language.

I remember in Hungary three years ago, at the very beginning I used the method where I connect the English word to the object and not to the Hungarian word, so I made an associative relation — the objects and the English word . . . . I think of the idea, the image and not the Hungarian word.

Of course, when I talk, I always have the feeling that I'm making a mistake, so I ask my friends to correct me.

After they corrected you, what did you do?

I noticed . . . I kept it in mind. I fixed it in (my) mind. I try to remember. I think about the meaning. I never imitate without understanding. There is always movement in my mind.

Sometimes I try to figure out my mistakes myself by connecting the word or phrase to the situation where I learned it.

It's a good way to learn from those kind of mistakes . . . good because I learned by that. I became aware of my mistakes. [But] . . . that's not a good feeling to know how little I know and how much I have to improve to reach a good level . . . [but] it gave me power, it gave me energy to get over these difficulties and at the same time it was despairing how much I have to learn but usually it gave me an energy and a motivation to work [on] these problems.

What about when you don't know how to say something, for example ordering a sandwich in a restaurant? What do you do?

I hear how others ask. Not that I couldn't [ask myself] but it wouldn't sound American. My version wouldn't be the highest level. So I always pay attention to people's speech. My mind is always open to accept information about the language. I always concentrate because I have to learn.

I plan to acquire this language perhaps in another ten years.

LEARNER ACCOUNT 1.2

Ilse, who had learned English in high school in Austria, spent a year or more living and travelling in the United States shortly after completing her high school. Then she returned home.

I came here in May mostly to learn English and study the language where I can watch the culture and background.

I think it's easier to learn the language when you can watch the culture and the people and everything. I especially want to take the habits from the people when I'm in this country. I want to learn everything, all customs and everything.

I studied eight years in high school — but only one or two lessons a week. You don't profit of it 'cause most things are spoken in German; you only learn grammar.

I saw I knew very much grammar [when I came to the United States] but I couldn't speak a word. I didn't dare to speak a word . . . I couldn't express myself in the right way, so I was afraid to speak. But when you are forced to speak, it comes at that time. That's the benefit of studying in the country.

In school in your country, you can study a long time (and never learn) . . . because you have to translate everything into your language. But here, as far as I'm concerned after some time I began to think also in English.

When I first came, I spent most of my time walking. I only walked and listened to the people speaking and went to museums and interesting places. I wanted to know where I was . . . . Little by little I lost the fear of everything foreign and I became accustomed to the sound. It's very important to get the sound and to keep it and then to transfer everything to thinking.

I watched a little TV too. I didn't understand the TV news very well at the beginning . . . a few words but it didn't give me the content. It was very difficult and boring. I didn't get what they spoke. But I tried to understand to get the main idea . . . according to the few words I understood. Maybe there were more words that I knew, but the sound was difficult. It was too fast.

Maybe I didn't increase my vocabulary much, but I got used to the sound. Now I understand with the same vocabulary.

I also listened to people's conversations. Of course, some idioms, those that are very unusual, you can't understand at the beginning. But they are used very often and you ask one day what it is and what it means. Then you know it and get it into your vocabulary. But some things are hard to use because the conversation goes so fast.

Exercises in class were very useful. When the teacher notices the class didn't understand something, then we repeat it over again and I see if what I thought before was not right and then I compare it. I just don't take it as it comes. I change it in my mind. There's always a movement. You don't recognize it exactly. You only know that it becomes better.

When I read, I try to look up as little as possible. I try to avoid memorizing vocabulary. I try to get it out of the context and to get it by using it.

When I don't understand a passage, I read it more and more and I look up only the words that are really important. Then I try to remember the meaning in English and not to translate everything into German.

Sometimes I try to find other examples for it — other meanings to explain the word in English. That's what I mean by using. It's better for thinking in the language, because when you look up every word, you're always in thinking in your language . . . . But when you try to remember it and try to get it out of the context, you begin to think in English.

I think this is very important because some words don't have the same meaning in different languages. Some have only a meaning in one language. You couldn't translate it 'cause it wouldn't sound very good, so I don't try.

I'm also taking Spanish classes. That's a good way to learn because I also have the exercise in English that I told you about — listening to the people and putting the sound in my mind. I do that there too. Of course Spanish is very different from English. In Spanish you speak like you write. In English pronunciation is different from the writing. But it's not so very difficult. It's difficult but also I compare. Some words are similar in English and Spanish and completely different in German. Some words in German and Spanish are similar and completely different in English.

So when you compare those you also learn because you remember it more easily. This is also an example of using. Using is better than memorizing only.

1.2   Identifying autonomous language learners in your class

Consider the learners you are presently teaching. Are they autonomous learners?

(a)   Divide them into the following groups:
   (i) those you consider autonomous;
   (ii) those who would be open to training for autonomy;
   (iii) those who might be resistant to such training.
(b)   What criteria did you use for dividing the students?

Reasons for promoting learner autonomy

Few teachers will disagree with the importance of helping language learners become more autonomous as learners. However, while they may often give their students hints about how to learn, learner autonomy is not usually included as a main objective in their lessons plans and course outlines. In this next series of tasks you will consider whether it should be and why.

1.3   Listing your reasons for promoting learner autonomy

Should language teachers systematically include in their lesson plans activities that would help students become more autonomous as learners?

(a)   List reasons to support your opinion.
(b)   If you answered yes, state whether you consider such activities to be equal in importance with language training.

1.4   Researching reasons for promoting learner autonomy

The following excerpts are from selected writings in second language learning and cognitive psychology. Each one provides information that argues explicitly or implicitly for the educational importance of helping learners learn how to learn. As you read the excerpts identify and summarize their arguments.

EXCERPTS

From 'Learning behaviors of successful adult students in intensive language training'

When interview findings for highly successful students were compared with those for the least successful, they revealed differences between the groups of most and least successful learners in the following areas: the diversity of French practice activities reported per individual, insight into and interest in one's own ways of taking and retaining information, and personal involvement in learning the language. Highly successful learners tended to consciously expose themselves to French and to practise it in different ways. They in most cases appeared quite insightful about their ways of learning, and without exception had strong and multiple reasons for learning French . . . . On the other hand, the types of learning procedures reported were similar for both groups.

. . . results from interviews with the eleven most successful students suggested that . . . rehearsal, many types of association-making, and practice (retrieval) are important techniques in the learning of new language material . . .

The statistical analyses and interview findings both provide evidence that a number of the learning behaviors and activities investigated were indeed related to the improvement of French listening and speaking skills by these adult students in beginning level intensive French training.

[Wesche, 1979]

From 'Classroom implications of learner diversity'

Nicholas (1985: 181) contrasts: (a) learners who concentrate on meaning with those who concentrate on form; (b) those who practice extensively in the same area with those who move on to new areas immediately; (c) those who control the flow with those who prefer to react to the initiatives of others; (d) those who have a high criterion of accuracy with those who are fluently inaccurate; (e) those who explore functions and those who explore structures.

Whether it is possible to consider cognitive style without analysing personality variables remains to be seen. Each individual will have a unique way of dealing with reality and processing information. Of course, perceptive teachers have always attempted to deal with these differences without being able to analyse them precisely, but, so far, little has been done to incorporate them into programme design.

. . . Brown feels that 'The burden on the learner is to invoke the appropriate style for the context . . . . The burden on the teacher is to understand the preferred styles of each learner and to sow the seeds of flexibility in the learner' (1987: 88). This suggests . . . the burden is on the learner to adjust to the learning context. Perhaps this is the most realistic approach to take until we know more about what is going on in the learner's head . . . we know that making them more flexible is not going to do them any harm. Perhaps good learners are those who are capable of making those shifts themselves anyway.

[Tyacke and Mendelsohn, 1988]

From 'Metacognition, self-knowledge, and learning disabilities: some thoughts on knowing and doing'

A child's personal beliefs, motivations, and affect clearly influence the ways that the child addresses and solves problems. Research on self-esteem . . . has demonstrated a clear link between an individual's judgment of his or her own competence and that individual's actual performance on school-related tasks. The implication for metacognitive theory and methodology is that attention must be given to 'person variables' such as intentions, attributions, expectancies and beliefs about one's competence and learning abilities.

One area in which these variables may influence how the child approaches a problem focuses on self-perception of ability and the belief that a problem is solvable, given effort.

Self-schemata represents knowledge about one's own social and cognitive features. Both adults and children form self-schemata concerning their capabilities and limitations, their degree of personal control over academic achievement, their reasons for success and failure at different tasks, and their expectancies for the future . . . . The child's view of himself or herself as a learner is an important form of metacognition.

[Hagen *et al.*, 1982]

From 'Cognition and adaptation: the importance of learning to learn'

It seems clear that the ability to learn new information can be important for adaptation. We have focused on people's abilities to learn new information by consulting written documents and texts . . . . Our evidence suggests that academically successful and less-successful students may take different approaches to the problem of learning. The successful students seem more likely to evaluate the arbitrariness of factual content and to spontaneously activate knowledge that can make information more meaningful and significant. When less successful children are explicitly prompted to ask themselves relevant questions (e.g. what's the relationship between this fact and this activity?), their performance improves; so does their enjoyment of the tasks. Our work in the area of intervention is only preliminary, of course, but the evidence is at least consistent with the notion that the activities that underlie learning are subject to modification . . . .

[Bransford *et al.*, 1981]

From 'Comprehension monitoring: the neglected learning strategy'

As Markman (1981) states, 'The ability to monitor one's comprehension is necessary for academic excellence . . . without knowledge about comprehension, comprehension itself will suffer' (p. 81) . . . . Researchers who focus on college student's monitoring skills also come up with results which indicate that children are not the only ones deficient in such strategies (Baker, 1979).

. . . Why is this so? Why do college students lack such skills even after years of schooling? Schallert and Kleiman (1979) offer the explanation that the comprehension-monitoring function is one that teachers typically perform for their students. Teachers try to stay in tune with their students' level of understanding by watching for subtle clues (e.g. facial expressions) and by stopping at appropriate times to ask questions in order to ascertain students' weak spots. In other words, teachers are very often much more active in the learning process than are students. While this may result in very effective teaching strategies, these teaching behaviors do not necessarily help the students gain independence by developing effective comprehension-monitoring strategies of their own.

Successful students, however, learn to adopt active strategies for themselves, incorporating monitoring behaviors into their repertoire of learning skills. Less successful students apparently do not, continuing to rely on teachers for this function. This is, perhaps, why students encounter difficulty in college, where most instructors do not have the time or desire to serve this purpose for students who, by this time, are presumed to be independent learners.

[Weinstein and Rogers, 1985]

From 'The development of a learning strategies curriculum'

By not stressing learning strategies, educators in essence discourage students from developing and exploring new strategies, and, in so doing, limit students' awareness of their cognitive capabilities. For example, the results of the administration of an extensive learning strategy inventory (Dansereau *et al.*, 1975) indicate that even good college students have very little knowledge of alternative learning techniques. This lack of awareness obviously limits an individual's ability in a situation requiring new learning strategies. In addition, if the strategies that individuals have spontaneously adopted do not match their cognitive capabilities, the emotional toll may be very large. Most of us know individuals who spend inordinate amounts of time memorizing college or high school materials and are still barely 'getting by'. Such an individual's personal, intellectual, and social development must certainly suffer from the pressures created by this use of a relatively inefficient learning strategy.

[Dansereau, 1978]

From 'What do we want teaching materials for?'

. . . the analysis by highlighting the complexity of the teacher's job, also sheds light on a common problem found almost every time that teachers are observed or observe themselves. It is the problem of teacher 'overload'.

Teacher 'overload' often entails learner underinvolvement since teachers are doing work learners could more profitably do for themselves. Involvement does not just mean 'activity', however. It is not just that learners are not busy enough. 'Involvement' means something more akin to Curran's 'investment' (Curran, 1972, 1976) which suggests a deep sort of involvement, relating to the whole-person. This sort of 'whole-person involvement' should be related not simply to 'participation in classroom activities' but to participation in decision-making, and in the whole business of the management of language learning . . . . But we should not expect the learners to be already expert at the sorts of decision-making . . . involved in the management of language learning. We must therefore consider ways of conducting learner-training.

[Allwright, 1981]

From 'Learning strategies as information management'

For the past few years it has been generally acknowledged in ESL teaching circles that an increased emphasis on helping learners learn how to learn would be valuable. Every teacher has encountered students who, although intelligent and adequately exposed to apparently useful and meaningful material, nevertheless seem to learn very little. Such instances of non-learning are attributed to a number of possible causes: the student may be disoriented by the formal learning situation or by Anglo-Saxon cultural assumptions in general; there may be a clash of the student's personality with the teaching approach; the material may be perceived to be irrelevant; the student may be under excessive emotional stress; he may have poor language aptitude; and so on.

Another common way of stating the cause in many of these cases is to say that the student uses inadequate or inappropriate learning strategies . . . . Given the inevitable limitations on time and resources for teaching specific language content, it is now clear that learners could benefit greatly in the long run if a substantial proportion of the formal learning time available were given over to training students in ways of learning for themselves. Given the opportunities for exposure to English which lie all around them, it would be wise to help learners develop their ability to take advantage of those resources for their own learning purposes.

[Willing, 1987]

From 'Towards task-based language learning'

From what has been said so far, a number of characteristics of communicative language teaching have emerged which impose conditions on task design . . . .

From such conditions we can derive some criteria for what could be termed 'good' language learning tasks . . . .

(11) Should allow for co-evaluation by learner and teacher of the task and of the performance of the task.
(12) Should develop the learners' capacities to estimate consequences and repercussions of the task in question.
(13) Should provide opportunities for metacommunication and metacognition . . . .
(15) Should promote learner-training for problem sensing and problem solving . . . .
(19) Should promote a critical awareness about data and the processes of language learning.

[Candlin, 1987]

1.5 Outlining your rationale for promoting learner autonomy
Refer to arguments in the reading and to those you listed in Task 1.4 to outline the reasons you would use to convince a colleague that it is important to help students learn how to learn and so to become more autonomous.

Conclusion

In this chapter, you examined two learner accounts to determine the characteristics of autonomous language learners and read excerpts from the professional literature for insights on the importance of helping learners learn how to learn. The excerpts focused, to a large extent, on why some learners are more successful than others. In effect, 'successful' or 'expert' or 'intelligent' learners have learned how to learn. They have acquired the learning strategies, the knowledge about learning, and the attitudes that enable them to use these skills and knowledge confidently, flexibly, appropriately and independently of a teacher. Therefore, they are autonomous. The literature also argued, implicitly or explicitly, for the need to provide learner training, especially for those learners who may not be as varied and flexible in their use of learning strategies as their successful classmates. This information, hopefully, has stimulated you to develop your rationale for making learner autonomy a twin objective with linguistic autonomy in your learning plans. In the chapters that follow you will examine and evaluate resources that can be used to develop and implement these plans.

Valuable readings

Teachers who are interested in reading further about the theory and research related to learner strategies and learner autonomy may choose any one of the references from which the excerpts in this chapter were taken.

Chapter 2

Learning strategies

Focus   Think about a particular language learning problem that one or more of your students often have. How do they deal with this problem?

Process   • Characteristics of learning strategies
            • Kinds of learning strategies

Outcome   An inventory of learning strategies

Characteristics of learning strategies

2.1 Identifying Laszlo's strategies

The following is an abbreviated version of Laszlo's learner account presented in longer form in Chapter 1. As you read through the account find the learning strategies he says he used

(a) to help himself learn English before coming to the United States,
(b) to figure out the meaning of words he heard in conversations,
(c) to retain what he had understood,
(d) to practise what he had learned,
(e) to deal with his errors and
(f) to find words or expressions to meet his communication needs.

LEARNER ACCOUNT 2.1 — COGNITIVE STRATEGIES

In Hungary I read and I learned alone . . . I bought a book. It's English, a verb book. Then I went through it . . . four lessons.

When you found something you didn't understand, how did you deal with it?

I looked it up in the dictionary.

   I came here in March . . . so two months I spent in Ohio. I worked, I got a job . . . I was [an] aluminium polisher. After work, I had some friends . . . Americans. Whenever I didn't understand anything, I asked, I inquired and they explained.

What did you do after they explained it to you?

I kept it in my mind. I practised . . . I tried to keep it in my mind.

You tried to remember it?

Yes, [to] memorize and to recollect it more times in a day . . . and to use it to build a sentence by myself and in conversation.

Did you have any other ways to figure out the meaning?

Sure . . . the word is not isolated. It's in the environment of other words. Sometimes I inferred the meaning. Sometimes I didn't ask because I found it out on my own . . . .

   I remember in Hungary three years ago, at the very beginning I used the method where I connect the English word to the object and not to the Hungarian word, so I made an associative relation — the objects and the English word . . . . I think of the idea, the image and not the Hungarian word.

Of course, when I talk, I always have the feeling that I'm making a mistake, so I ask my friends to correct me.

After they corrected you, what did you do?

I try to remember. I think about the meaning.

Sometimes I try to figure out my mistakes myself by connecting the word or phrase to the situation where I learned it.

What about when you don't know how to say something, for example ordering a sandwich in a restaurant? What do you do?

I hear how others ask . . . . I always pay attention to people's speech.

2.2   Identifying Ilse's strategies

In this next abbreviated learner account, Ilse describes the learning strategies she used to help herself learn. Identify those she says she used

(a)   to understand television,

(b)   to figure out the meaning of unknown words in a written passage,

(c)   to retain the new words she read,

(d)   to improve her listening skill,

(e)   to figure out the meaning of new words in spoken English,

(f)   to learn from her teacher's explanations and

(g)   to practise her language skills.

LEARNER ACCOUNT 2.2 — COGNITIVE STRATEGIES

When I first came . . . I only walked and listened to the people speaking . . . . It's very important to get the sound and to keep it and then to transfer everything to thinking . . . .

I watched a little TV too . . . . I tried to understand to get the main idea . . . according to the few words I understood . . . .

Of course, some idioms, those that are very unusual, you can't understand at the beginning. . . . and you ask one day what it is and what it means. . . .

Exercises in class were very useful. When the teacher notices the class didn't understand something, then we repeat it over again and I see if what I thought before was not right and then I compare it. I just don't take it as it comes. I change it in my mind. There's always a movement . . .

When I read, I try to avoid memorizing vocabulary. I try to get it out of the context and to get it by using it. Sometimes I try to find other examples for it — other meanings to explain the word in English. That's what I mean by using. . . .

When I don't understand a passage, I read it more and more and I look up only the words that are really important. Then I try to remember the meaning in English and not to translate everything into German.

I'm also taking Spanish classes. That's a good way to learn because I also have the exercise in English that I told you about — listening to the people and putting the sound in my mind. I do that there too.

> It's difficult [Spanish] but also I compare. Some words are similar in English and Spanish
> . . . . Some words in German and Spanish are similar . . .

Learning strategies are mental steps or operations that learners use to learn a new language and to regulate their efforts to do so. They are one type of learner training content that should be included in plans to promote learner autonomy.

2.3 Examining the characteristics of learning strategies

Refer to Laszlo and Ilse's strategies to answer the following questions.

(a) When or why should learners use learning strategies?
(b) Are they conscious, i.e. is the learner aware of using them? Or are they unconscious, i.e. do they remain below consciousness?
(c) Are they observable? Can they be seen?
(d) Are learning strategies innate or do we acquire them through learning? Can they be changed?

Researchers in second language acquisition have not been able to come to a consensus regarding what a strategy is. This is reflected in the literature where strategies are referred to as 'techniques', 'tactics', 'potentially conscious plans', consciously employed operations', 'learning skills, basic skills, functional skills', 'cognitive abilities', 'problem solving procedures', and 'language learning behaviors'. The following characteristics, illustrated by the strategies Laszlo and Ilse reported using, are based on an analysis of the strategies documented in the learner strategy research reported in Wenden and Rubin (1987).[1] They define what is intended by the term in this chapter and elsewhere in the book.

*   Some *can be observed* — there is an observable behavior that accompanies the mental act as when learners ask a question to clarify something they do not understand. Other strategies *cannot be observed* as when learners infer or compare.
*   Cognitive strategies may be *deployed consciously* in response to a problem a learner has clearly perceived and analyzed. They can also become *automatized*. The decision to use them remains below consciousness — a learned solution to a class of learning needs or problems with which learners are familiar.
*   Strategies, unlike more enduring personality characteristics of a learner, including learning style, are *amenable to change*. They are a part of our cognitive software, acquired in the same way as we acquire language. Ineffective ones can be changed or rejected, new strategies can be learned and well-functioning strategies can be adapted to new situations.
*   Strategies are *problem oriented*. Learners use them in response to different kinds of learning problems or needs.

Kinds of learning strategies

In this chapter we shall look at two main kinds of learning strategies — cognitive strategies and self-management strategies. These are distinguished on the basis of their function in learning.

Cognitive strategies

Cognitive strategies are mental steps or operations that learners use to *process* both linguistic and sociolinguistic content. The strategies you identified in Tasks 2.1 and 2.2 are examples of cognitive strategies.

2.4 Classifying cognitive strategies
In this task you will consider more specifically how cognitive strategies contribute to the learning process. What are their specific functions?

(a) Examine Laszlo and Ilse's strategies for those that appear to have similar purposes and group them.
(b) Determine why they were used and give each group a name.

Information processing theorists analyze the act of human learning as falling into the following four stages or steps: (1) selecting information from incoming data; (2) comprehending it; (3) storing it; and (4) retrieving it for use. Each of these steps, included in the conceptual model shown in Figure 2.1, points to one function of cognitive strategies.[2]

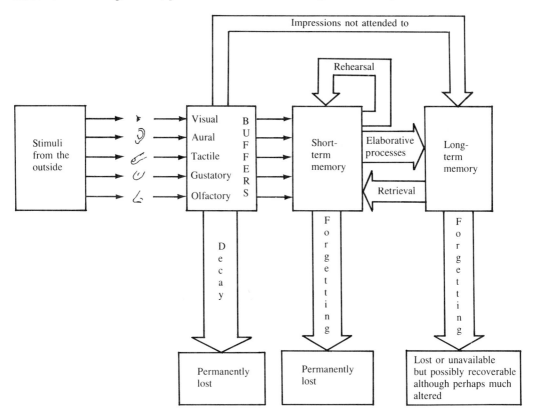

FIGURE 2.1 *Flow chart of the human memory system (Hunt, 1982).*

Selecting information from incoming data

According to information processing scientists, what we know and learn begins as input which impinges upon our sensory organs. What we see, hear, touch, taste and smell is sent to the sensory buffers where it is either selected for further processing or forgotten. More information comes into the buffers than we can attend to and it remains there only a very short time, and so it is important that learners be prepared to select the information they wish to process. Selective attending is a strategy that can help them to do this. When learners use this strategy they decide in advance what aspect of input they will pay attention to. The following indicate Laszlo's and Ilse's use of strategies for selective attending:

Laszlo   attended to native speakers in selected contexts
Ilse   attended to the sound of the language

Comprehending and storing the information

At this stage, the selected information is transferred to short-term memory where it is transformed into a meaningful symbol, such as a sound, a word or a syntactic structure, and then into a more permanent representation, which is stored in long-term memory.

Elaboration is the basic kind of processing necessary for comprehending and storing information. However, in order for elaboration to occur, efforts must be made to keep the information in short-term memory or it will quickly disappear. Rehearsal strategies are used for this purpose. Chamot (Table 2.1) defines rehearsal as 'imitating a language model, including overt practice and silent rehearsal'. That is, rehearsal strategies involve no more than the actual repetition of the data and do not transform the material.

In contrast, elaboration does transform the material. When learners 'elaborate', they use strategies that identify patterns in the data, make associations, identify deeper meanings, elicit knowledge from long-term memory and relate the knowledge to these meanings and classify them. In her taxonomy, Rubin (Table 2.2) refers to inferencing and deductive reasoning — two general types of cognitive strategies which help with elaboration. Other examples of elaboration strategies, such as grouping, recombination and contextualization, are included in Chamot's taxonomy (Table 2.1).[3]

Elaboration strategies used to comprehend the incoming information, at one and the same time, help to classify it in a way that it can be integrated into an existing schema and stored in long-term memory. Mnemonic strategies are another type of strategy that can be used to store processed information. When learners use mnemonic strategies, they choose verbal, spatial and visual clues to work out a storage plan that will aid future retrieval. Examples of mnemonic strategies are included in Rubin's taxonomy (Table 2.2). The strategies that Laszlo and Ilse reported using for comprehension are as follows:

Laszlo   looked up unknown words in a dictionary
              asked friends for an explanation
              inferred the meaning of words from context
              thought about the meaning of corrections
              read a verb book

Ilse   used familiar words to infer the meaning of television news
              found examples to explain a new word

TABLE 2.1
Learning strategy definitions

Learning strategy	Description
Cognitive	
Repetition	Imitating a language model, including overt practice and silent rehearsal
Resourcing	Defining or expanding a definition of a word or concept through use of target language reference materials
Directed physical response	Relating new information to physical actions, as with directives
Translation	Using the first language as a base for understanding and/or producing the second language
Grouping	Reordering or reclassifying and perhaps labeling the material to be learned based on common attributes
Note-taking	Writing down the main idea, important points, outline or summary of information presented orally or in writing
Deduction	Consciously applying rules to produce or understand the second language
Recombination	Constructing a meaningful sentence or larger language sequence by combining known elements in a new way
Imagery	Relating new information to visual concepts in memory via familiar easily retrievable visualizations, phrases or locations
Auditory representation	Retention of the sound or a similar sound for a word, phrase or longer language sequence
Key word	Remembering a new word in the second language by (1) identifying a familiar word in the first language that sounds like or otherwise resembles the new word and (2) generating easily recalled images of some relationship between the new word
Contextualization	Placing a word or phrase in a meaningful language sequence
Elaboration	Relating new information to other concepts in memory
Transfer	Using previously acquired linguistic and/or conceptual knowledge to facilitate a new language learning task
Inferencing	Using available information to guess meanings of new items, predict outcomes or fill in missing information

Source: Chamot, 1987; for a more recent version, see O'Malley and Chamot, 1990

> compared the teacher's correction with her understanding
> figured out meaning from context when reading
> read and reread what she did not understand
> compared English, Spanish and German words

The following strategies were used for storage:

Laszlo   memorized explanations of new words
associated new words with an image

Ilse   memorized meanings in English
memorized whole chunks

Retrieving the information

This is the fourth stage in learning according to the theory outlined by information processing scientists. Information that has been attended to, comprehended and stored must be easily retrieved when needed. Successful communication requires that acquired knowledge about the language be brought to bear upon a communication task. Automatic retrieval of information

TABLE 2.2
Strategies for cognitive learning

Getting process

1. Clarification/verification strategies (attention focus)
    (a) Seek confirmation of their understanding of the grammar or phonology of a language
    (b) Ask for validation of their production of words, phrases or sentences
    (c) Ask for clarification or verification of communication rules
    (d) Define or expand a definition of a word or concept or grammar point through use of target language reference materials
    (e) Ask for repetition paraphrasing, explanation or examples
    (f) Observe teacher or native's mouth for correct pronunciation

2. Guessing/inductive inferencing strategies
    (a) Use own language or second language to infer meaning (prior knowledge)
    (b) Use knowledge about world, culture, communication process to infer meaning or predict outcomes (prior knowledge)
    (c) Relate new information to physical actions
    (d) Use key words to infer rest
    (e) Distinguish relevant from irrelevant clues for determining meaning

3. Deductive reasoning strategies
    (a) Infer grammatical rules or word formation by analogy
    (b) Look for regularities and exceptions in grammar, word formation, phonology style
    (c) Synthesize understanding of language system
    (d) Use schema to grasp overall semantic intention

4. Resourcing strategies
    (a) Use second-language reference materials such as dictionaries, glossaries, textbooks

Storing process

1. Memorization strategies
    (a) Associate or group words or phrases according to some principle (phonetic, semantic, visual, auditory, kinesic, kinesthetic, olfactory or sensory)
    (b) Use key word (using one item to recall a number of others)
    (c) Use a mechanical means to store information (flash cards; make lists of new items, with or without context, with or without definitions; other mechanical devices — put new words in right pocket and move to left when learned, or write out item to be learned several times)
    (d) Put selective attention focusing on specific details
    (e) Put items in special context to facilitate storage
    (f) Use imagery
    (g) Silent rehearsal with delayed production

Retrieval and using process

1. Practice strategies
    (a) Repeat
    (b) Rehearse
    (c) Experiment — use word/phrase in new sentences
    (d) Consciously apply rules
    (e) Imitate
    (f) Answer to self questions asked of others
    (g) Use wider world to enlarge exposure to second language (television, radio, second-language books, or newspapers, movies)
    (h) Talk to self in second language
    (i) Drill self

2. Monitoring strategies
    (a1) Identify problem
    (a2) Determine solution
    (a3) Make a correction

3. Social strategies (less direct since they do not involve transformation of the language)
   (a) Join a group and act as if you understand
   (b) Count on your friends for help
   (c) Create opportunities for practice
       (i) Initiate conversation with native speakers
       (ii) Attend parties or other social events
   (d) Work with peers to obtain feedback, pool information or model a language activity

Source: Rubin, 1989

that is appropriate for a particular communication task is evidence of acquisition — that the item has been fully learned.

Practice strategies are cognitive strategies that can facilitate the development of automatic and appropriate retrieval. Formal practice strategies are used to deliberately recall a specific item strictly for focused practice (see the taxonomy in Table 2.2 for examples). When learners use functional practice strategies they place themselves in a situation where they can use the language to communicate, e.g. listening to the television, speaking to a foreign friend, reading the paper, and in this way develop automaticity or facility in retrieval.

Not all retrieval strategies will be used to develop automaticity. Faerch and Kasper (1983) report on research which identified six retrieval strategies that learners can use when they cannot remember something they have already learned: waiting for the term to appear; appealing to formal similarity; retrieval via semantic fields; searching via other languages; retrieving from learning situations; and sensory procedures.

Retrieval goes on together with the elaboration process, for elaboration involves relating what is new to what is already known. Therefore, to store new information, learners must retrieve from long-term memory information that is related to the new input. Cognitive strategies can also be used to enable students to elicit the relevant prior knowledge.

The formal and functional practice strategies that Laszlo and Ilse reported using to develop facility in retrieval are as follows:

Laszlo recalled new words several times during a day
used new words in sentences in conversation
used new words to make sentences on his own
connected an error to the context in which he learned it to correct himself
went out with his work colleagues

Ilse walked around and went to museums
watched television
listened to people's conversations
took a Spanish class

Developing an inventory of cognitive strategies

An inventory is a list of available resources. In language teaching, materials developers, syllabus planners and classroom teachers usually have inventories of language functions, listening skills, grammar structures and useful vocabulary in their resource files. They refer to these inventories as they develop plans that guide them in the writing of new materials, in the outlining of a syllabus for a particular course and, more broadly, in the development of a whole language curriculum. In the absence of their own formally developed lists, teachers may refer to the table of contents of textbooks or to old lesson plans. In other words, inventories are planning resources with which language teachers are already familiar.[4]

Strategy inventories can serve as a useful reference and guide for classroom teachers, materials developers and curriculum planners in the planning of learning to promote autonomy. The taxonomies of strategies documented by the learner strategy research, which illustrate different ways of grouping and labelling strategies, can be used to develop these inventories.

2.5 Comparing taxonomies of cognitive strategies

In this task, you will look at different approaches to developing taxonomies. Compare the two taxonomies in Tables 2.1 and 2.2 to answer the following questions.

(a) How are they different from one another?
   (i) What criteria has the researcher used to classify the strategies?
   (ii) Which taxonomy appears to be more comprehensive, if any?
   (iii) How do the three taxonomies compare in terms of generality?
(b) Do they overlap with one another? Find examples.
(c) Test the utility of the taxonomies by using them to name Laszlo's and Ilse's strategies.

2.6 Developing an inventory of cognitive strategies

To develop your inventory of cognitive strategies, select from the taxonomies in Tables 2.1 and 2.2 those strategies you would want your students to be able to use. Also refer to the valuable readings for references to other taxonomies to consider in making your choice.

The following are some of the criteria you can take into account in selecting the strategies:

(a) *comprehensiveness* — aim for as comprehensive an inventory as possible;
(b) *a particular language skill* — choose only those strategies that would be useful for a particular language skill you often teach (e.g. listening);
(c) *specialized language use* — choose only those strategies that are necessary for language use in specific settings (e.g. English for academic purposes);
(d) *utility* — look for strategies that learners can use most often in any setting.

2.7 Testing the usefulness of your strategy inventory

Complete the following task if you wish to test the usefulness of your inventory.

(a) Consider your own language learning experience. Focus on a particular

stage (e.g. when you first began; the first few weeks in the target culture) or a particular skill. List the cognitive strategies you used.
(b)   Classify these strategies using your inventory.
(c)   Does your inventory include all the strategies you remember using? If not, you may wish to revise and expand it.

Self-management strategies

Self-management strategies are utilized by learners to *oversee* and *manage* their learning. In the research literature in cognitive psychology, they are referred to as metacognitive strategies or regulatory skills (e.g. Brown *et al.*, 1983) and in the methodological literature they are referred to as the skills of self-directed learning (e.g. Holec, 1981).[5]

2.8   Describing the functions of self-management strategies

The following abbreviated versions of Laszlo's and Ilse's accounts contain three sets of statements each of which implies the use of a different self-management strategy.

(a)   Read the portion of each statement in bold type to determine what the strategy is. That is, what is the learner doing to manage or regulate his learning?
(b)   How do these strategies differ from cognitive strategies? How do they contribute to learning?

LEARNER ACCOUNT 2.3 — SELF-MANAGEMENT STRATEGIES

1

LASZLO

I bought a book . . . a verb book. Then I went through it . . . four lessons . . . but one of my deficiencies was I didn't resolve the exercises. **In a short time I wanted to . . . [acquire] a large quantity of knowledge.**
   I plan to acquire this language perhaps in another ten years.

ILSE

I especially want to take the habits from the people when I'm in this country. **I want to learn everything, all the customs and everything.**

2

LASZLO

   . . . I had problems with my spoken English and the practical way of expressing my thoughts to put the ideas into forms was my problem. I understand by reading much more than speaking. In the first [when he had arrived in the United States], **I couldn't catch [what] other people said . . . .**
   I couldn't speak to anybody . . . my problem [is] I understand a lot of words . . . that is only the passive way of improving my knowledge . . . .

What about when you don't know how to say something, for example ordering a sandwich in a restaurant? What do you do?

I hear how others ask. **Not that I couldn't [ask myself] but it wouldn't sound American. My version wouldn't be the highest level.**

ILSE

I studied eight years in high school — but only one or two lessons a week. **I saw I knew very much grammar [when I came to the United States] but I couldn't speak a word.**

I didn't dare to speak a word . . . **I couldn't express myself in the right way . . . .**
I didn't understand the TV news very well at the beginning . . . a few words but it didn't give me the content.

I watched a little TV too. **I didn't get what they spoke.**

I also listened to people's conversations. **Of course, some idioms, those that are very unusual, you can't understand at the beginning.**

3

LASZLO

But . . . here I have [the] opportunity to speak more to practise the theoretical knowledge I acquired in Hungary . . . . **I had some improvement.**

I bought a book. It's English, a verb book. Then I went through it . . . four lessons. I learned the verbs, the grammar . . . . **I only accumulated a great deal of the words and expressions.**

When you found something you didn't understand, how did you deal with it?

I looked it up in the dictionary. I had a good dictionary though it was English–Hungarian so **I didn't eliminate the Hungarian language.** Here I have an English dictionary . . . Webster's . . . so the explanation of the word is in English; **it's much better. I don't have to think in my native language.**

I came here in March . . . so two months I spent in Ohio. I worked, I got a job . . . I was [an] aluminium polisher. **I didn't have the chance to speak.**

Of course, when I talk, I always have the feeling that I'm making a mistake, so I ask my friends to correct me. It's a good way to learn from those kind of mistakes . . . good because **I learned by that. I became aware of my mistakes.**

ILSE

But here, as far as I'm concerned **after some time I began to think also in English.**

When I first came, I spent most of my time walking. I only walked and listened to the people speaking and went to museums and interesting places. **Little by little I lost the fear of everything foreign and I became accustomed to the sound.**

I watched a little TV too. **Maybe I didn't increase my vocabulary much, but I got used to the sound. Now I understand with the same vocabulary.**

I also listened to people's conversations. Of course, some idioms, those that are very unusual, you can't understand at the beginning. . . . and you ask one day what it is and what it means. **Then you know it and get it into your vocabulary.**

Laszlo's and Ilse's accounts imply the use of the three following self-management strategies.

Planning

Both Laszlo and Ilse refer to particular objectives they had set for themselves at different times in their language learning (Learner Account 2.3, part 1). At the outset of his learning (in Hungary) Laszlo said he wanted to acquire a 'large quantity of knowledge'; later, in the United States, he had decided to give himself ten years to acquire the language. Ilse reported that she wanted to learn everything she could about the culture. These statements refer to a planning strategy that had been deployed at a period previous to the time of the account.

In the performance of a learning task, planning may precede the task. Learners determine what their objectives are and decide on the means by which they will achieve them. This phase of the planning is called *pre-planning*. In their research on high school learners, O'Malley *et al.* (1985) noted two kinds of decisions that learners made in preparing to do an academic language learning task. They decided in advance (1) to attend to a learning task and to ignore irrelevant distractors (directed attention) and (2) to attend to specific aspects of input (selective attending). They also identified two strategies that learners actually implemented as a kind of advance preparation — before actually engaging in the task. Learners would preview the main ideas and concepts of the material to be learned, often by skimming the text for the organizing principle (advance organizer). Then, understanding the conditions that help one learn, they arranged for the presence of these conditions (self-management).

Planning may also go on while the task is being performed. This is *planning-in-action*. Depending on how well learners progress through the task. i.e. how effective their strategies are and how much they learn, objectives may be changed, as will be the means of attaining them. Planning-in-action will depend, in part, on information provided from the implementation of the two other self-management strategies — monitoring and evaluation.[6]

Monitoring

In their second set of statements, both learners refer to the difficulties they experienced in using the language in the United States, especially when they first arrived. The use of a monitoring strategy may be inferred from these statements. Laszlo, for example, said he could not express his ideas or understand what others said: he had not acquired a 'practical' vocabulary. Ilse said she could neither express herself appropriately ('in the right way') nor could she understand, especially television and strange idioms.

When monitoring their attempts to learn, learners tune into or become aware of 'on-line' difficulties in processing. Functioning as participant observers or overseers of their language learning, they ask themselves: 'How am I doing? Am I proceeding through this learning task smoothly? Without obstacles?' Having become aware of a problem, learners assess their knowledge and skills to seek the cause: What do they know and with what degree of certainty? What can they do and with what degree of facility? They refer to their perceived level of proficiency to explain an obstacle to task accomplishment or successful strategy deployment or, sometimes, they may also refer to affective or cognitive factors.

When learners monitor their learning, self-assessment goes on *during the act* of learning as a *part* of the monitoring strategy. Self-assessment can also be done in the *pre-planning stage* of learning when learners need to set their learning objectives. At that time, they draw upon the knowledge gained through monitoring to assess their knowledge and skills. In this situation, self-assessment is used as a planning strategy and is quite separate from monitoring.

Laszlo's and Ilse's second set of statements (Learner Account 2.3) are statements of 'self-assessment' which suggest that monitoring has occurred at a time previous to the interview. When Laszlo says his version 'wouldn't sound American' it may be assumed that he has been monitoring his use of English and his choice of words in particular. The knowledge acquired from such on-line monitoring is the basis of his assessment. Similarly, Ilse's report that at the beginning she did not understand the television news well must be based on knowledge that resulted from her monitoring of herself as she was listening.

The scope of the experience that learners monitor may vary from an attempt to understand a vocabulary item in a reading text, to reading a whole text, to a whole semester's course in writing or reading. Monitoring can involve a narrow focusing in on a single event, such as understanding a vocabulary item or reading a passage of text, or be a broad overview of a series of learning activities, such as a semester course in writing or reading.

Evaluating

In contrast with monitoring, which results in statements of self-assessment about a learner's level of proficiency made *in the course* of learning or communicating, when learners evaluate, they consider the *outcome* of a particular attempt to learn or use a strategy. The focus is on the result and the means by which it was achieved (i.e. the strategy). Table 2.3 illustrates how Laszlo and Ilse evaluated some of their strategies.

Evaluating involves three mental steps: (1) learners examine the outcome of an attempt to learn (e.g. studying in the target language culture, reading a verb book, watching television); (2) they access the criteria they will use to judge it (e.g. opportunity for language use; opportunity for language learning); and (3) they apply it. Laszlo says he improved because he had the opportunity to speak more in the United States; he accumulated many words by

TABLE 2.3
Evaluating: examples from Laszlo's and Ilse's accounts

Strategy	Evaluation
LASZLO	
Here (i.e. studying in the target language culture)	I have (the) opportunity to speak more. I had some improvement
Reading a verb book	I only accumulated a great deal of the words and expressions
Using an English–Hungarian dictionary	I didn't eliminate the Hungarian language
Using Webster's dictionary	It's much better ... I don't have to think in my native language
I worked, I got a job	I didn't have the chance to speak
I ask my friends to correct me	I learned by that. I became aware of my mistakes
ILSE	
Studying in the target language culture	Here, after some time I began to think in English
Listening to people speaking; visiting museums and interesting places	I lost the fear of everything foreign. I became accustomed to the sound
I watched a little TV too	Maybe I didn't increase my vocabulary but I got used to the sound. Now I understand with the same vocabulary
Exercises in class	'Very useful'

reading a verb book. Ilse said watching television enabled her to get used to the sound but that she did not increase her vocabulary. These three mental steps are rarely referred to separately. More frequently they can be inferred in a learner's statement about what they learned ('I only accumulated many words and expressions').

Statements of evaluation often point to learning gains as a sign of a strategy's success (e.g. I began to think in English). They may also evaluate the utility of a particular strategy. Laszlo, for example, said that he did not learn from the verb book because he did not have a good system. Here he evaluates his strategy.

Developing an inventory of self-management strategies

The cognitive literature refers to three main kinds of self-management strategies: planning, monitoring and evaluating. They are named in terms of the function that they serve and are applicable across all kinds of learning tasks. Unlike cognitive strategies, self-management strategies are not task specific and therefore are not differentiated and diversified. Moreover, to date, except for a few pre-planning strategies referred to earlier (p. 27), researchers have not come up with long lists of strategies that learners use to plan, monitor and evaluate, and so it is neither relevant nor possible to develop an inventory of self-management strategies. However, this does not in any way simplify their use in learning, for efficient use of these strategies will depend on the quality and refinement of learners' acquired store of task knowledge as it applies to a particular learning task. Thus, helping learners to use self-management strategies will require helping them to develop the relevant task knowledge. This topic will be discussed in Chapter 3.

> **2.9 Analyzing your language learning for self-management strategies**
> If you wish to further reflect on how self-management strategies are used in learning, you may consider your language learning experience, or one phase of it. Were you actively involved in regulating or managing your language learning?
>
> (a) What were your objectives as you started out? How did they change as you increased in proficiency?
> (b) To what extent did you monitor your use of your second language? Your attempts to learn? What did you learn about yourself as a user and learner of language from this information?
> (c) Did you evaluate the outcome of the strategies you used to help yourself learn? What criteria did you use?

Schema of learning strategies

Learning strategies are one category of learner training content to be included in plans to help learners become more autonomous. In this chapter, three kinds of learning strategies have been defined and illustrated. These strategies are outlined in Table 2.4 together with the functions that they serve in the learning process.

Interest in learners' strategies reflects the radical change in scientific thinking on the nature

TABLE 2.4
Learning strategies

Strategies	Function
Cognitive	1. Select input
	2. Comprehend input
	3. Store input
	4. Retrieve input
Self-management	1. Planning
	2. Monitoring
	3. Evaluating

of the human mind. Wenden and Rubin (1987) outline some of the historical developments which made this change so significant and some of the theoretical concerns in several disciplines which led to it. Here, let me mention briefly the outcomes of the change. First, the learner–environment equation tilted in favor of the learner. Learners were no longer viewed as passive organisms responding to environmental influences but were considered as acting upon the environment and through this action defining it. Second, this changed view opened up new avenues of research, and the 1970s saw an increasing number of studies on learners' strategic action, i.e. on their use of strategies in a variety of academic disciplines, including the learning of foreign and second languages.

Brown *et al.* (1983) summarize the outcome of some of the research as it applies to the deliberate learning of subject matter content in academic settings by younger and older children. An impressive body of knowledge about the development of acquisition strategies of knowledge, such as rehearsal, categorization, elaboration and retrieval, was collected together with information on how learners controlled their use of strategies. Earlier studies focused on memory strategies used by small children (e.g. rehearsal) and later studies investigated how older learners approached the studying of text, writing and scientific reasoning.

This research led to hypotheses as to how strategies were developed. It was suggested that a major obstacle to the development of strategies for academic literacy was learners' preference for attractive but less appropriate strategies. While these strategies could be used in academic situations with success, in fact they were more appropriate for the type of reasoning that is used in everyday situations. Differences between the use of strategies by younger novice learners and older more mature expert learners were also noted. It was reported that a young child's use of a primitive memorization strategy is unreliable. She fails to refine it to conform with changing task demands and often does not know to use it in situations where it would be applicable. In contrast, strategy use in mature users is characterized by its stability — and by its transituational quality. Training studies conducted during this time also showed convincingly that less productive learners could be trained to use strategies with a consequent improvement in their task performance. Finally, it became clear that the use of strategies was the outcome of a variety of factors, especially

- the subjects' background knowledge about subject matter content and about learning,
- the nature of the materials to be learned and
- the product or outcome that the learner or teacher has in mind.

Conclusion

In this chapter you were introduced to the notion of 'strategy' and examined two kinds of learning strategies, which research has shown that active and successful language learners use. For students to use these strategies appropriately and flexibly, it is important that they have some basic knowledge about the nature of language and the language learning process. In Chapter 3, you will be introduced to the notion of 'metacognitive knowledge', which refers to learners' acquired beliefs about these aspects of learning.

Valuable readings

The research on learner strategies in second language learning has been inspired, in part, by trends in the field of cognitive psychology. Brown *et al.* (1983) present an excellent overview on the development of these trends as it applied to the study of cognitive development in children. For an introduction to the concepts and themes from cognitive psychology, the work of Morton Hunt (1982) is both clear and engaging. McLaughlin (1987: chapter VI) presents the main concepts of cognitive theory which underlie the ideas presented in this book, and O'Malley *et al.* (1987) and O'Malley and Chamot (1990) outline some applications of cognitive theory to second language acquisition.

The following publications will provide background on learner strategy research in second language learning. In Chapter 2 of Wenden and Rubin (1987), Rubin provides background on the typology of strategies presented in this chapter and a review of the earlier research on learning strategies. Later chapters include reports of empirical studies of strategies and a review of the literature on memory strategies, primarily outside the field of second language learning. For more recent publications on learner strategy research, which also provide literature reviews and classification schemes of strategies, see O'Malley and Chamot (1990), Cohen (1990) and Oxford (1990).

The section on the regulatory skills or metacognitive strategies in Brown *et al.* (1983) outlines the theoretical and research background on self-management strategies. Holec (1981) gives a detailed analysis of what is involved in the planning, monitoring and evaluating of language learning. Weinstein and Rogers (1985), Rubin (1987) and Casanave (1988) discuss comprehension monitoring — why it is important and what it entails. Oskarsson (1980) describes some approaches to self-assessment (a pre-planning strategy) and the outcome of research on its use. Dickinson (1987) discusses the reasons why learners should engage in self-assessment, to what extent and how successfully, and Leblanc and Painchaud (1985) describe a series of experiments leading to the use of self assessment as a placement instrument.

Notes

1. Learner strategy research in the field of language learning seeks answers to the following questions: (1) What do learners do to help themselves learn? (2) How do they regulate these efforts? (3) What beliefs and/or knowledge do they bring to their language learning process? (4) How can learners be helped to refine and develop the skills of learning referred to in the first three questions? See Wenden and Rubin (1987), O'Malley and Chamot (1990) and Cohen (1990) for reviews and research reports.
2. According to Hunt (1982), his model is a synthesis of various versions that represents the median position on

information processing. For a comprehensive explanation of information theory see, for example, Lachman *et al.* (1979); for a cognitive perspective on learning that advances notions not included in the earlier views on information processing, see the work of Anderson (1981, 1983). For an application of Anderson's theory to second language acquisition see O'Malley and Chamot (1990).

3. Only that part of the Chamot taxonomy pertinent to the discussion of cognitive strategies is displayed. Her complete taxonomy includes a listing of both cognitive and metacognitive strategies.

4. For inventories of language functions, notions, forms, see Van Ek's *Systems Development in Adult Language Learning: The Threshold Level* (1975). For an inventory of listening skills, see Richards (1985).

5. The notion of an executive function in learning is a long-standing tenet of cognitive psychology. Its renewed importance is an offspring of the computer revolution, especially developments in the use of computers to simulate human thought. Theories of artificial intelligence posited an executive or regulatory function responsible for planning, monitoring and generally overseeing the learning. This idea has been adopted by information processing scientists. In the development of their models of human learning, they too included a mechanism that would function as an executive (Brown *et al.*, 1983).

6. The distinction between pre-planning and planning-in-action is introduced by Brown *et al.* (1983).

Chapter 3

Knowledge about language learning

Focus   What might your students say if you asked them 'what is the best way to learn English?' What other beliefs do they hold about language learning?

Process   • Characteristics of metacognitive knowledge
               • Kinds of metacognitive knowledge

Outcome   A resource file of materials about language learning

Characteristics of metacognitive knowledge

3.1 Identifying three kinds of knowledge about language learning

The following sets of statements are taken from Laszlo's and Ilse's accounts of their language learning. As you read the statements, determine which of the following aspects of the language learning process each set refers to: personal, task, or approach to language learning.

LEARNER ACCOUNT 3.1 — KNOWLEDGE ABOUT LANGUAGE LEARNING

1

LASZLO

[Referring to how he approached his learning in Hungary] I was impatient.

That's not a good feeling to know how little I know and how much I have to improve to reach a good level . . . it gave me power, it gave me energy to get over these difficulties and at the same time it was despairing how much I have to learn but usually it gave me an energy and a motivation to work [on] these problems.

I was not ashamed to ask. That was the main point. I tried to overcome this shame . . . this fear and . . . .

ILSE

I was afraid to speak

2

LASZLO

After work, I had some friends . . . Americans . . . it was very good. Whenever I didn't understand anything, I asked, I inquired and they explained . . . . This is the only way to learn to ask always.

When I talk . . . I try to eliminate my native language so the idea and the word are almost simultaneous . . . . It's the best.

ILSE

It's very important to get the sound and to keep it and then to transfer everything to thinking.

Sometimes I try to find other examples for it — other meanings to explain the word in English . . . . It's better for thinking in the language.

When you are forced to speak, it comes at that time. That's the benefit of studying in the country. In school in your country, you can study a long time (and never learn) ... because you have to translate everything into your language.

3

LASZLO

I never imitate without understanding. There is always movement in my mind. My mind is always open to accept information about the language. I always concentrate.

ILSE

I just don't take it as it comes. I change it in my mind. There's always a movement.
  Using is better than memorizing only.

4

LASZLO

The word is not isolated. It's in the environment of other words.
  A language has to reflect the reality and not in another language.

ILSE

Some words don't have the same meaning in different languages. Some have only a meaning in one language. You couldn't translate it 'cause it wouldn't sound very good, so I don't try.
  But they [unusual idioms] are used very often.

5

ILSE

It [watching TV] was very difficult and boring. ... [on TV] the sound was difficult. It was too fast.
  Of course, some idioms, those that are very unusual, you can't understand at the beginning ....
  But some things [i.e. unlike some idioms] are hard to use because the conversation goes so fast.

Metacognitive knowledge about language learning is the second kind of learner training content to be included in learning plans to develop learner autonomy. John Flavell, a cognitive psychologist, describes it (metacognitive knowledge) as '... that segment of your (a child's, an adult's) stored world knowledge that has to do with people as cognitive creatures and with their diverse cognitive tasks, goals, actions and experiences. In other words, in a broad sense, metacognitive knowledge includes all facts learners acquire about their own cognitive processes as they are applied and used to gain knowledge and acquire skills in varied situations' (1979: 906). In the case of language learners, it includes beliefs, insights and concepts that they have acquired about language and the language learning process.

3.2 Examining your acquired knowledge about language learning
In Task 3.1 you looked at Laszlo's and Ilse's 'metacognitive' knowledge, i.e. their beliefs about language learning. In this task you will examine yours.

(a) Do you agree with Laszlo's and Ilse's views? If not, what do you believe?

(b) What are some other beliefs that you hold about language learning? For example, what factors facilitate second language acquisition? How would you define the nature of language?

3.3 Determining the characteristics of metacognitive knowledge

Refer to your beliefs about language learning listed in the previous task as you discuss the following questions.

(a) Have you held these beliefs for a long time?
(b) Are they readily available to awareness?
(c) Have these beliefs changed over time? Have you discarded some as erroneous? Which ones have you had to change?
(d) To what extent have your beliefs influenced your approach to learning your second language? To teaching a second language?

Four ways of characterizing metacognitive knowledge are given below.[1]

- *Stable* The facts that learners acquire about their language learning process are a permanent part of their store of knowledge and not fundamentally different from other knowledge stored in long-term memory, acquired through experience both in formal and informal learning contexts.
- *Statable* Learners can talk about these beliefs. They are available to awareness, activated either as a result of a deliberate search or unintentionally and automatically by retrieval cues in the learning environment. Of course, they may also influence the course of a cognitive enterprise without entering consciousness (Flavell, 1979: 907–8).
- *Fallible* What language learners know about their language process is not always correct. Some of it may represent the 'folk wisdom' about learning acquired from family, friends and teachers or the outcome of a learner's experience. It may appear to make good sense, but it is not always empirically supportable.
- *Interactive* It is one of four factors that interact to influence the outcome of a learning activity (Flavell, 1979, 1981a). In other words, metacognitive knowledge can be used to analyze a learning task or goal (the second factor); it can influence one's choice of strategies (the third factor); it can be used to evaluate whatever transient awareness of learning (the fourth component) that can occur in the course of a learning task, and be changed by this new insight.

Kinds of metacognitive knowledge

In his writings Flavell describes three kinds of metacognitive knowledge: person knowledge, strategic knowledge and task knowledge. Each kind is illustrated in Ilse's and Laszlo's accounts.

Person knowledge

First, person knowledge is general knowledge that learners may have about the 'laws of human learning'. That is, how does learning take place? What facilitates or inhibits human learning? In the case of language learning, second language acquisition research has identified some of the cognitive and affective factors that may inhibit and/or facilitate the acquisition of another language. In their reviews of this recent research Ellis (1986), Brown (1987) and McLaughlin

(1988) include reports on factors which distinguish learners and which, according to Ellis, will influence the rate and ultimate success of second language acquisition. They are briefly defined as follows:

- *Age*: the notion that there is a certain period when language is learned most efficiently; that after this period, it is not possible to learn or to learn well (Ellis, 1986); the differences there may be between children and adults in the rate and ultimate product of language learning (McLoughlin, 1988).
- *Language aptitude*: the abilities of language learners to discriminate the meaningful sounds of a language, to associate sounds with written symbols and to identify the grammatical regularities of the language (Ellis, 1986: 112).
- *Intelligence*: a general academic or reasoning ability; a general factor that underlies our ability to master and use a whole range of academic skills; the underlying ability to learn rather than the actual knowledge measured by intelligence tests (Ellis, 1986).
- *Motivation*: a learner's purpose for or orientation toward learning another language; it may be instrumental or integrative; it may also refer to the interest felt by learners in performing different learning tasks, i.e. task motivation (Ellis, 1986); inner drive, impulse, emotion that moves one to a particular action (Brown, 1987: 114); the fact that this changes over time (McLaughlin, 1988).
- *Personality*: personal traits, e.g. extroversion/introversion; social skills; inhibition (Ellis, 1986); the intrinsic side of affectivity or factors that influence human behavior, e.g. self-esteem, inhibition, risk-taking, anxiety, empathy, extroversion (Brown, 1987).
- *Sociocultural factors*: extrinsic factors that emerge as the second language learner brings two cultures into contact and in some sense must learn a second culture along with a second language, e.g. attitudes towards the culture or language, acculturation, social distance, language and thought (Brown, 1987); the fact that attitudes and social distance change over time (McLaughlin, 1988).
- *Cognitive style*: general characteristics of intellectual functioning that influence how one approaches a learning task (Brown, 1987); the manner in which people perceive, conceptualize, organize and recall information (Ellis, 1986).
- *Learning style*: this notion overlaps with cognitive style, but it is more comprehensive; it includes cognitive, affective and physiological behaviors that indicate learners' characteristic and consistent way of perceiving, interacting with and responding to the learning environment; more concrete than cognitive style (Willing, 1988).

Person knowledge also includes what learners know about themselves as learners. How do the same cognitive and affective factors listed above apply in their experience? For example, do learners consider their age to be an impediment to their learning? How do they assess their language aptitude? Their general intelligence? Do they view themselves to be the type of person who can easily learn a language? What is their personal motivation for learning a language? How do they perceive themselves to be reacting to the culture? How do they feel they learn best? What do they prefer to learn? The knowledge learners have acquired about how these factors relate to their own experience is also a form of person knowledge and may influence the formation of their self-concept as language learners.[2]

In the first set of statements (Learner Account 3.1), Laszlo and Ilse both refer to motivation — one aspect of person knowledge. Laszlo admits being impatient to learn as much as he could as quickly as possible. He has a clear awareness of how he reacted to having his mistakes corrected — it was not a good thing to know how little he knew, but it gave him power and energy to improve himself. Ilse confesses to a fear of speaking out — a fear of speaking most language learners will have experienced. Neither of them, however, refer to any of the cognitive factors listed above.

Developing a resource file about person knowledge

The cognitive and affective factors that research has shown can facilitate or impede second language acquisition have been listed above. A resource file on person knowledge for use in developing learning plans to promote learner autonomy should include materials on each of these factors which can be adapted for classroom use. In Tables 3.1 and 3.2, there are

TABLE 3.1
Explanation of learning style preferences

Students learn in many different ways. The questionnaire you completed and scored showed which ways you prefer to learn English. In many cases, students' learning style preferences show how well students learn material in different situations.

The explanations of major learning style preferences below describe the characteristics of those learners. The descriptions will give you some information about ways in which you learn best.

Visual major learning style preferences
You learn well from *seeing words* in books, on the chalkboard and in workbooks. You remember and understand information and instructions better if you read them. You don't need as much oral explanation as an auditory learner, and you can often learn alone, with a book. You should take notes of lectures and oral directions if you want to remember the information.

Auditory major learning style preference
You learn from *hearing words* spoken and from oral explanations. You may remember information by reading aloud or moving your lips as you read, especially when you are learning new material. You benefit from hearing audio tapes, lectures and class discussison. You benefit from making tapes to listen to, by teaching other students and by conversing with your teacher.

Kinesthetic major learning style preference
You learn best by experience, by being involved physically in classroom experiences. You remember information well when you actively participate in activities, field trips and role-playing in the classroom. A combination of stimuli — for example, an audio tape combined with an activity — will help you understand new material.

Tactile major learning style preference
You learn best when you have the opportunity to do 'hands-on' experiences with materials. That is, working on experiments in a laboratory, handling and building models, and touching and working with materials provide you with the most successful learning situation. Writing notes or instructions can help you remember information, and physical involvement in class-related activities may help you understand new information.

Group major learning style preference
You learn more easily when you study with at least one other student, and you will be more successful completing work well when you work with others. You value group interaction and class work with other students, and you remember information better when you work with two or three classmates. The stimulation you receive from group work helps you learn and understand new information.

Individual major learning style preference
You learn best when you work alone. You think better when you study alone, and you remember information you learn by yourself. You understand new material best when you learn it alone, and you make better progress in learning when you work by yourself.

Minor learning styles
In most cases, minor learning styles indicate areas where you can function well as a learner. Usually a very successful learner can learn in several different ways.

Negligible learning styles
Often, a negligible score indicates that you may have difficulty learning in that way. One solution may be to direct your learning to your stronger learning styles. Another solution might be to try to work on some of the skills to strengthen your learning style in that area.

See Reid 1987 for the questionnaire based on this explanation.

Source: Adapted from the C.I.T.E. Learning Styles Instrument, Murdoch Teacher Center, Wichita, Ks 67208; Reid 1984

TABLE 3.2
Age and language learning: a survey

Read each of the following statements and indicate whether you agree or disagree with each one. Write A if you agree and D if you do not. Be prepared to discuss your opinions.

Adults and children learn in the same way.
Adults can continue to learn all their lives.
The ability to learn does not decrease with age — only the speed at which one learns.
Education and experience, not age, is the best predictor of success in learning at any age.
Learning strategies, not age, are related to success in learning.
Adults appear to have more difficulty learning another language because they already know one or more languages — which they may depend upon.
Adults feel learning another language means giving up their culture.
Adults do not have many opportunities to meet with people who speak their second language.
Adults are afraid that learning a new language will change their personality.
The kind of language that adults use is more complicated than the language children use, so it is more difficult for them to learn a second language.
Adults feel frustrated because they do not have the language to talk about adult topics.

Ideas in the survey are based on Kidd (1976) and Robbins (1981).

illustrations of how materials drawn from the literature on learning style and adult learning have been adapted. In the next set of tasks you will adapt information from the literature on other cognitive and affective factors for your resource file.

3.4 Developing a resource file on person knowledge
Consult the references on person knowledge listed on p. 50 or others included among the description of valuable readings at the end of this chapter.

(a) Select excerpts that contain information that you feel your learners need to know and understand.
(b) Read each excerpt to identify the key ideas and important supporting information.
(c) Decide how you can adapt the material for classroom use and do so (e.g. devise a short oral lecture, a survey to be completed and discussed, a reading, journal writing assignments).

3.5 Analyzing your language learning for person knowledge
Use the list of personal factors (p. 36) as a guide to write about the affective and cognitive factors that have influenced your learning (of another language and/or other subject matter or skills). Which factors influenced your learning and how?

Strategic knowledge

Strategic knowledge is the stored knowledge that learners have about strategies. There are two facets to strategic knowledge, both of which were referred to by Laszlo and Ilse in the second and third set of statements (Learner Account 3.1).

Knowledge regarding strategies that work best

First, strategic knowledge is knowledge that learners have acquired about which strategies can be used effectively in the accomplishment of specific language learning tasks.[3] For example, in the second set of statements (Learner Account 3.1) Laszlo reports on the effectiveness of two strategies — asking about what you do not know and trying to eliminate your native language when you speak in your target language. Ilse spoke of the effectiveness of 'getting the sound and ... transferring everything to thinking', i.e. memorizing whole routines in English; of 'using', which means actively manipulating input to understand it; of the benefit of studying in the TL country. Implicit in these statements is knowledge about the strategies they use and a primitive sense of what strategies are.

Knowledge about how best to approach language learning

This second facet of strategic knowledge refers to general principles about language learning that can guide a learner's choice of strategies. In the third set of statements (Learner Account 3.1) both Laszlo and Ilse refer to one such principle — always being mentally active. Laszlo says he never imitates without understanding; his mind is always open to learn. Ilse reports making a deliberate effort to understand; that is what she means by 'using'.

Developing a resource file on strategic knowledge

An action plan for helping language learners learn how to use strategies is outlined in Chapter 7. One step in the plan requires that learners discuss the significance of the strategy they are learning to use. Another step shows learners ways of evaluating strategy use and so determining its efficiency for a particular task. In this way, knowledge about effective strategies will be acquired as learners learn how to use new strategies. In this section, therefore, the tasks will concentrate on developing a resource file on general principles about language learning.

3.6   Developing a resource file on strategic knowledge
(a)   What would you tell a student who asked you, 'What is the "best way" to learn another language?' How would you advise her?
(b)   Below are excerpts from writings of language educators and researchers which describe the characteristics of successful language learners.
   (i) Determine where these descriptions overlap with each other and with the list you developed in part (a) of this task.
  (ii) Use these descriptions to develop a list of general guidelines for language learning.
 (iii) Decide how you would go about helping your students to understand and use the guidelines.
(c)   If you wish to expand your list further, check the references on strategic knowledge in the list of valuable readings.

EXCERPTS

From 'Language learning on the spot'

It is important for students who live in a country where English is spoken to understand the differences between language learning in school and language learning 'on the spot'. Learning a language 'on the spot' or outside the classroom is quite different. People don't worry about whether you have studied the words they use and the tenses they use. English comes to you from all sides — the people you talk to on the street, from the TV set, the newspapers, movies; from friends you make and from sightseeing tours. In school you may experience very little 'real' language. 'On the spot' you experience more than you can manage.

You must be prepared for this experience and challenge. First you must understand that in language learning on the spot, *you are on your own*. You find yourself wanting to say something — to get angry at a bus driver or to order in a restaurant. But you will not be able to do so. You will feel frustrated. You must learn to deal with such situations. *You must learn to learn on your own or to take language learning into your own hands.* You have to learn to use the people around you as teachers and the situations where you hear, read English as your textbook.

It is also important to *know yourself as a language learner*. There are many different ways to learn a language. Some people absorb themselves in the second language by just quietly observing and getting attuned to the voices. They prefer to sit and listen and let others do the talking. Other language learners, however, do like to talk. They don't worry if their speech is not perfect. Others like to have a dictionary handy and some want everything translated. Others want to use only English and to act like members of the English speaking community. You must find out which way suits you. Probably good language learners will mix the strategies.

Next, you have *to get attuned to the language*. Although you have learned English six, seven or eight years, you will probably have a very hard time understanding English during your first weeks in an English speaking country. You will become embarrassed when you don't understand what people say and want to blame your teachers for not teaching you properly. But remember it takes time to get attuned to the language. Learn to listen for a word or expression that will give you a clue to the meaning. The important thing is not to get upset.

When you have gotten attuned to the language, you must take a chance and *plunge in*. Be prepared to start a conversation. Don't worry about your mistakes. It's more important to get your meaning across. You should also learn *to think about the language*. Carry a small notepad and when you hear something interesting or a word you do not understand, take notes. Later, you can discuss these notes with a friend or teacher.

[Stern, 1980]

From 'Successful language learners: what do we know about them?'

Only a cynic would argue with the statement that most people learn their native language with a fair degree of success. Although some people seem to have more verbal skills than others, almost everyone can acquire his or her first language easily and well. Why is it, then, that the success record for acquiring competence in a second or foreign language in a formal instructional setting is so poor for so many students? What makes some foreign language learners succeed — often in spite of the teacher, the textbook, or the classroom situation — while others fail to acquire certain basic skills, even in the best of circumstances?

Several researchers have been intrigued by these questions in recent years, and have designed studies that attempt to discover what makes the 'good' language learner good. They argue that if we knew more about what successful learners did, we might be able to teach these strategies to poorer learners and thereby increase their chances of success. The studies have typically focused on three aspects of the problem: (1) What personality and cognitive style variables are most frequently associated with good language learners? (2) What specific strategies and techniques do good language learners tend to use in approaching various language learning tasks? (3) Are these techniques teachable? If so, what kinds of remedial activities do they suggest?

Strategies and techniques

The following language learning strategies have been synthesized from interviews, direct observation, empirical investigations, insights from experienced language learners and teachers, and theoretical arguments about the nature of language learning tasks.

1. Successful language learners *have insight into their own language learning styles* and preferences as well as the nature of the task itself. They adopt a personal style or positive learning strategy that fits their needs and preferences. They can adapt to various methodologies and materials and know how to find, sort, analyze, synthesize, classify and retrieve relevant linguistic data. Poor learners, by contrast, lack insight into their own learning difficulties and the nature of the task. They are often frustrated by methods that are not appropriate for them. They cannot organize linguistic input into a coherent system; instead, they regard the incoming data as an untidy assortment of separate items.

2. Successful learners *take an active approach* to the learning task. They select learning objectives for themselves and deliberately involve themselves in the second language. They will seek out opportunities to communicate in the target language, with native speakers whenever possible, and to understand acts of communication in the fullest sense. They are sensitive to connotative and sociocultural meaning. The poor learner, on the other hand, often leans too heavily on the teacher and adopts a passive, detached attitude.

3. The good language learner is *willing to take risks*. These students accept their status as 'linguistic toddlers'. They are willing to appear foolish sometimes in order to communicate, using any means at their disposal to convey meaning. This often involves the use of circumlocution, paraphrase, cognates or gestures, and may sometimes involve the creation of new words by analogy with familiar forms (such as nominalizing a verb).

4. Good language learners are *good guessers*. They use clues effectively and make legitimate inferences. For example, successful reading comprehension strategies that involve guessing include using syntactic and contextual clues to determine meaning and reading 'around' unknown words. Good language learners constantly search for clues to meaning, be they from context, situation, explanation, trial and error, or translation.

5. Good language learners are prepared to *attend to form as well as to content*. They constantly look for patterns, classifying schema, and rule-governed relationships. They monitor their own speech and others', seeking correction from informants.

6. Successful learners actively attempt to *develop the target language into a separate reference system* and try to think in the target language as soon as possible. They purposefully revise their evolving system by testing hypotheses, learning from errors,

and reorganizing the system when preliminary rules do not seem to apply.

7.   Good language learners generally have a *tolerant and outgoing* approach to the target language. They are able to put themselves in another person's place, identifying to some extent with the native speaker.

[Omaggio, 1978]

3.7   Analyzing your language learning for strategic knowledge

Think about your own language learning experience. Choose a particular aspect of the language you worked hard to acquire (e.g. listening, specialized vocabulary, pronunciation).

(a)   Were you guided by the same general principles as those included in your resource materials? If so, which ones?

(b)   Were any of the guidelines that you used not on the list you prepared in Task 3.6? If so, expand your list to include it.

Task knowledge

When teachers ask students to 'do a cloze', 'read and find the main idea', 'look up the classified ads for a job they might be interested in', they are setting tasks which they expect will help students learn and acquire fluency in the use of their new language. Task knowledge refers to what learners need to know about the procedures that constitute these tasks to accomplish them successfully.

Working through tasks, learners must draw upon their store of strategies, and in some cases, as when learners are asked to 'guess the meaning of a word' or 'make sentences with new words' or 'listen for specific information', tasks are, in effect, strategies. When teachers set them, they are referred to as 'tasks', but when students determine them for themselves, they are referred to as strategies. The following are different aspects of task knowledge that learners need to be aware of if they are to navigate these tasks sucessfully.[4]

Knowledge of the purpose of the task

Learners must know why they are being asked to perform a task to appreciate its significance. Breen (1987) suggests two purposes which determine a task's significance — achievement and survival. Learners will seek to relate a particular task to a linguistic need they have (e.g. improving their vocabulary, understanding spoken English) or to how it will help them achieve their survival needs (e.g. getting a job, passing an exam).[5] Learners' appreciation of a task's significance will be achieved, in part, as they come to understand the 'nature of the task' — a second aspect of task knowledge.[6]

Knowledge of the nature of the task

This means knowing how to classify a task. That is, what *kind of learning* is language learning? Language learners need to know that learning a second language is not the same as learning biology; nor is it the same as learning to drive a car, although learning to drive, like language learning, is a form of procedural knowledge. They need to know about the nature of language.

In their guide on how to be a 'more successful' language learner, Rubin and Thompson (1982) list three characteristics of language — creativity, systematicity and similarity. These defining characteristics are examples of the knowledge that language learners should acquire about the 'nature of language'. Learning about the nature of language also means learning about the nature of communication, including what is particular to the spoken language and the written language.

Some of Laszlo's and Ilse's stored knowledge about the nature of language is illustrated in Learner Account 3.1, part 4. Their accounts refer to the fact that the meanings of words can be derived from the verbal context (Laszlo); some words cannot be directly translated from one language to another (Laszlo); certain types of words recur in conversation (Ilse). Laszlo also says that a language clearly reflects a culture.

Task knowledge about the nature of language and communication is general. It represents knowledge that language learners acquire over time from teachers, fellow students and from their own experiences and provides the basis for the next two aspects of task knowledge which are task specific.

Knowledge of when deliberate learning is required

Language learners must know when a particular task will require conscious effort. With regard to self-management strategies, it has been suggested that learners are most aware of 'managing their learning' in the following kinds of situation (Lefebvre Pinard, 1983):

1. when they are learning something new — the behavior is being acquired;
2. with behaviors that are automatized but performed inefficiently;
3. when they are doing tasks that involve novel unexpected elements.

In his writings John Flavell (1979) describes when metacognitive knowledge is more likely to come to consciousness. Some of these situations are similar to those that Lefebvre Pinard has outlined for self-management strategies. They are as follows:

1. when the nature of the task requires conscious thinking;
2. when one is learning/behaving in a new or unaccustomed way;
3. when it is important that the outcome be accurate and the knowledge is seen as relevant to that success;
4. when one encounters a difficulty.

In summary, Lefebvre Pinard's and Flavell's analyses suggest *four kinds of tasks* that can require conscious thinking:

1. a new task — learners have never done it before;
2. the nature of the task is such that it requires conscious thinking, e.g. writing;
3. the task requires accuracy, e.g. doing a math problem, writing;
4. the task has not been learned correctly/efficiently.

The other situation — when one encounters a difficulty — could apply to any task and does not suggest a special classification.

Knowledge of task demands

This aspect of task knowledge refers to what is entailed in completing a task. More specifically, what resources are necessary to complete the task? How does one go about doing the task? Will it be hard or easy?

Knowing what resources are necessary to complete the task

Learners need to ask themselves what kind of knowledge is necessary to complete a task. Will they need only knowledge about language or world knowledge? What specific aspects of their general knowledge about language will they need? Learners who wish to speak as fluently as a native speaker, for example, will need to draw upon their store of knowledge about the nature of the spoken language. Achieving this goal will also require some cultural knowledge. Students who are asked to do a cloze exercise should have some knowledge about the nature of the written language; they should be able to identify different discourse patterns; they should know the general organization of the various patterns. They will need knowledge about the topic that the passage is about.

Knowing how to go about doing the task

First, learners need to know how the general task can be broken down into smaller parts — the steps or sub-objectives. The language learner who wishes to be fluent 'as a native speaker' will need to know that he has to work on intonation and pronunciation; he will have to learn vocabulary and general verbal routines appropriate to the topics he wishes to discuss and to the settings in which these discussions take place. He must know that each of these constitutes one separate step that must be achieved in order to complete the task successfully. The learners who are asked to complete a cloze would need to know that they must figure out (1) what the topic is, (2) what they know about it, (3) what kind of discourse pattern is being used and (4) what tense the writer used.

Learners will also have to know which strategies they need to use to acquire the knowledge or skills they are seeking. Language learners who want to work on intonation, for example, could decide that they need to attend selectively to native speaker speech or devise some formal practice exercises — taping their statements and playing back to listen. As noted earlier (p. 21) Ilse, for example, found it very useful to walk around and listen to the sound and try to transfer it to memory as one 'chunk' without analyzing it. To complete a cloze, learners will need to elicit background knowledge; inferencing will be another key strategy; applying the grammar rules they have learned about sentence structure, i.e. deduction, is a third strategy.

To be able to make these strategy selections, learners need to select from their store of acquired strategies (i.e. their strategic knowledge) those that would be most appropriate for the task at hand.[7] Neither Laszlo nor Ilse referred to this facet of task knowledge in their accounts.

Knowing whether the task is hard or easy

Brown *et al.* (1982: 55) say that a task is easy or hard to the extent that it maps onto the pre-existing knowledge base and preferences of learners. In the case of language learners, level of difficulty is not only a measure of what they have learned about the language but also a measure of how well they use it. For Ilse, listening to television and to conversations by native speakers is difficult because of the speed at which people speak — evidence of her lack of facility in understanding the spoken language. She also knows that unusual idioms will not be understood at first — a measure of her limited pre-existing knowledge. Moreover, level of difficulty will depend on whether or not learners know how to go about doing the task. Do they know what steps to follow? Do they know what strategies to use?

Developing a resource file on task knowledge

Of the four aspects of task knowledge described above, three are task specific — knowledge of task purpose, task demands and of the need for deliberate learning. What language learners need to know about these three facets of task knowledge will vary depending on the language skill or function they are trying to aquire. In fact, this is knowledge that is usually determined by teachers as they plan a lesson. That is, in a lesson plan, teachers determine

1. what they are going to teach about a particular language skill;
2. in what order;
3. which activities students will be asked to do;
4. how difficult this will be for the students.

This is an outline of that task's demands (see above). Then, in thinking about how to motivate students to do a particular task, teachers will also list why it is important for students to do the task — they determine the task purpose (cf. p. 42).

At the same time, as noted earlier, this task-specific knowledge is based on more general knowledge about the nature of language and communication. Therefore, in order to help learners learn how to plan their own learning, it is necessary that they first acquire some of these basic general concepts, and so the resource file on task knowledge that we shall develop in this chapter will focus on concepts related to the nature of language, communication and the language skills.

3.8   Developing a resource file on the nature of communication

An excerpt on the nature of communication from the Rubin and Thompson guide *How To Be a More Successful Language Learner* is given below.

(a)   Read the excerpt to identify key ideas about the nature of communication that you feel it is important for students to understand.
(b)   Note related supporting information that should also be included.
(c)   Decide how you can adapt the materials for classroom use and do so.
(d)   If you wish to develop a resource file on the nature of language, refer to Chapter 1 in the Rubin and Thompson manual for source materials. Follow the procedures outlined above to develop your materials.

EXCERPT

From *How To Be a More Successful Language Learner*

The communication process

About communication

As you think about your goals in studying a foreign language, many possible answers will come to mind: to learn the grammar or pronunciation, to have a good vocabulary, or to be able to speak correctly. While all of these are useful goals, we want to emphasize that for most people, the main goal of studying a foreign language is to be able to communicate. The essence of communication is sending and receiving messages effectively and negotiating meaning. If you want to learn another language quickly and efficiently, you should keep this main goal in mind, for the others will follow naturally.

We all learn our first language quite naturally by focusing on this need to communicate. We learn how to send and receive messages in an effective way in order to accomplish our social goals.

All native speakers communicate without thinking about the process. However, in order to speed up learning another language, it is helpful to become more aware of the knowledge and skills we bring to the process. By identifying and recognizing what we already know, we can more effectively guide our learning. We may be able to take shortcuts or recognize where we have gone wrong in expressing ourselves or in interpreting others' messages.

Two kinds of messages
Many people mistakenly think that language learning entails learning to translate word for word from the native to the new language. Those who hold this basic misunderstanding of the communication process will find language learning next to impossible!

Behind this belief is the idea that sending messages is just a matter of supplying information about something the speaker knows or wants. This type of learner thinks that the task is to find the exact words that express this knowledge or desire in another language.

The fact is that we can say the same thing in many different ways. For example, if we wanted a window closed, we could say so directly by giving a command: 'Close the window!' Or, we could do so less strongly by asking, 'Would you please close the window?' However, under other circumstances, we might choose to be quite indirect by saying, 'I feel cold', or 'It's cold in here'. The way we choose to make this request would depend on whom we are talking to, how important the request may be, and how we feel that day. The point is that at the same time that we share information about our knowledge or desires we also send vital social messages. The two occur together inseparably in a language. It is next to impossible to send the one kind of message without the other.

There are very few situations in which referential meaning is paramount and little variation is tolerated. An exceptional example of this is the exchange that takes place between an air traffic controller and a pilot. In this case, variation is not possible and basic information exchange is of the essence. On the other hand, sometimes we use language only for social purposes with little exchange of information. For example, when English speakers ask 'How are you?' they don't really want to know the answer in detail. Most of the time, we send both referential and social messages at one and the same time, with the social side being somewhat more important.

There is much more to language differences than mere differences in pronunciation, grammar, vocabulary, and expression. Communication is governed by rules that specify such things as who can participate, what the social relationships are, what subjects can be discussed, who initiates the conversation, how turns are taken, who chooses the form of address, and so forth.

Here is an example of how word-for-word translation might mislead us and how focusing only on referential meaning might cause us to miss the real message of a communication. In many parts of the world it is not polite to accept an offer of more food the first time it is offered. Americans may be surprised or annoyed that their polite 'no, thank you' brings yet another offer of food. When native English speakers say no to offers of food, they really mean no. However, when translated into another language in another social setting, saying no to an offer of food may be interpreted as a polite refusal with anticipation that the real refusal will be made after the second or third offer. In fact, in many parts of the world, people are reluctant to appear too greedy or childlike by accepting food or drink the first or second time it is offered. On the other hand, foreign visitors to the United States may be disappointed when their polite 'no, thank you' does *not* bring a second or third offer of food. The point is that although a form may permit translation, its social meaning (positive or negative) depends on customary use and on the associated social values within a particular social context.

Finding the *appropriate* expression to use and paying attention to the *way* something is expressed are important because they are part of the messages people send and receive. Through the *form* we use, we express our feelings about a person or situation. For example, consider the distinction many languages make between the formal and familiar forms for 'you' and 'thou'. With just a change of pronoun form, you can express contempt or respect, friendship or indifference. Further, knowing when to switch from 'you' to 'thou', and who may initiate the switch, is essential. Premature use of 'thou' can nip a budding friendship or, if intentionally employed, be a deadly insult. On the other hand, failure to shift from formal to familiar at the right moment can be read as indifference or stuffiness.

It is usually more important to find the *appropriate* way of expressing yourself than to be grammatically *correct* or to pronounce a foreign language like a native because appropriateness in expression is linked to basic attitudes about how people should interact with one another and their social values.

Sending messages not only involves sharing information; it also, *at the same time*, involves trying to accomplish one of several social functions. Among these are:

1. *Establishing or maintaining one's social status.* A British person may use phrases such as 'to have one's bath' (not 'to take a bath') or 'false teeth' (not 'dentures') to establish that he or she is a member of the upper class. Similarly, an American who never uses colloquial expressions such as 'ain't' or 'gosh' or uses Latin expressions such as *non sequitur* or *ad hominem* may be working to maintain the impression that he or she is a member of an educated class.

2. *Establishing or maintaining social group membership.* A person may deliberately speak like a jazz musician to indicate membership in a jazz group (jazz musicians have many expressions that they uniquely use). Also, in most countries it is essential for academics to speak and write in a particular way to show that they belong to the academic subculture. A third well-known example is the language of teenagers. If young people don't use the popular expressions of their generation, they are not accepted by their peers.

3. *Showing respect or deference.* In French, use of the pronoun *vous* (formal 'you') indicates greater respect than use of *tu* (familiar 'you'). In Chinese, people are addressed by their occupational titles to show respect, hence 'Manager Wong' or 'Engineer Li'.

4. *Showing intimacy.* In Russian, use of diminutives indicates intimacy. Thus, friends normally use nicknames with diminutive suffixes, such as *Ninochka* (Nina) or *Boren'ka* (Boris). The greater the intimacy and affection, the greater the proliferation of such

diminutive forms. Pronouns are also used to signal intimacy versus distance. In French, use of the pronoun *tu* shows greater intimacy than use of the pronoun *vous*, and the same is true of such languages as Spanish, German, and Russian.

5. *Setting yourself apart from the group.* If you are normally a member of a jazz group but refuse to use their special expressions and phrases, you may be trying to show that you are no longer a member of the group. When American blacks refuse ever to use Black English, choosing instead the English used by middle class whites, they may also be setting themselves apart deliberately from other blacks.

[Rubin and Thompson, 1982: ch. 4]

3.9   Developing a resource file on listening, writing, reading, speaking
To complete this task, refer to the references on task knowledge described in the section on valuable readings.

(a)   Identify information on one of the four communication skills that it would be important for learners to think about and understand.
(b)   Follow the steps outlined in Task 3.8 to adapt the excerpts for classroom use.

If you would like practice in analyzing the demands of tasks that you often ask your students to do, you may do Task 3.10.

3.10   Identifying task demands in your lesson plans
Think of one of your favorite lesson plans and/or a unit or lesson from a textbook you often use.

(a)   How is the content that is to be presented divided within a lesson? Within a series of lessons on the same topic?
(b)   What tasks are students assigned to understand and practise the skill?
(c)   What prior knowledge and/or skills do you expect your students to bring to the task?
(d)   Do you view the task (or aspects of it) as difficult? For all students? Why? Why not?

Schema of metacognitive knowledge

Metacognitive knowledge about language learning is a second category of learner training content to be included in plans to help students become more autonomous. In this chapter, three main kinds of metacognitive knowledge have been defined and illustrated. They are outlined in Table 3.3 together with their defining aspects.

The different kinds of metacognitive knowledge outlined in the schema have been illustrated with examples from Laszlo's and Ilse's accounts. However, classroom experience testifies to the fact that all language learners have acquired such a body of knowledge about learning. This knowledge is implicit in the resistance that teachers experience when they decide to try a new method or in learners' requests for particular content (we need grammar), and

TABLE 3.3
Knowledge about language learning

Kind	Defining aspects
Person	Cognitive factors that facilitate learning
	Affective factors that facilitate learning
Strategic	Effective strategies for particular tasks
	General principles to determine strategy choice
Task	Task purpose or significance
	Nature of language and communication
	Need for deliberate effort
	Task demands
	• knowledge required to do the task
	• how to complete a task: steps and strategies
	• level of difficulty

explicit in what students say if teachers listen carefully to their questions and the reasons for their requests and preferences. To be more in control of their learning, they need to be made aware of the knowledge they have already acquired and be given opportunities to reflect upon it in order to revise or reject what is inappropriate and to acquire new insights.

The research and theory on self-directed learning in the field of adult education argues for the importance of such reflective activities (e.g. Chene, 1983; Brookfield, 1985). Critical of the exclusive emphasis on the teaching of skills of self-directed learning, theorists in the field have advocated that training in the techniques of learning be wed with a reflective approach. For without an internal change in consciousness to accompany expertise in the use of self-instructional techniques, true autonomy is not achieved. Learners will use their strategies somewhat mechanically and not become aware of when and why they need to adapt or change them.

Conclusion

In this chapter you have been introduced to the concept of 'metacognitive knowledge' and have looked at examples of three different kinds of metacognitive knowledge that learners can acquire about language learning. You also began to develop a resource file of materials which can be used to help learners examine, change and expand this knowledge. Whether or not they will act on these new insights, however, will depend on how they evaluate their role and capability as learners — two learner attitudes towards autonomy that will be discussed in Chapter 4.

Valuable readings

Learner beliefs or knowledge about the language learning process is referred to as metacognitive knowledge. Flavell's work on metacognitive knowledge has had a strong influence on the field. The notion of metacognition and its role in the monitoring of cognitive activities is outlined in his first article (1979). He also describes three types of metacognitive knowledge that form the basis of Chapter 2. A second article (Flavell, 1981b) should be of special interest to language teachers and researchers in its application of metacognition to social cognitive enterprises.

Yussen (1985)'s critical analysis of the concept of metacognition suggests how it may be strengthened. Of special interest to language teachers and researchers are the sections dealing with the differences between metacognitive development in children and adults and with the need to move metacognitive research out of the 'puzzle-solving framework' to tasks that might be more relevant to the use of metacognition in adult life.

In the field of second-language learning and teaching, Bialystok and Ryan (1985) use the notions of metacognitive knowledge and metacognitive strategies to offer an explanation of the nature and development of language proficiency, specifically in the area of conversation, literacy and metalinguistic tasks. Wenden's review article (1987) illustrates and describes metacognitive knowledge and skills with references to some of the related second-language learning research. Breen's article (1987) on learner contributions to task design analyzes various facets of task knowledge from the perspective of language learners. Rivers (1979) is a good example of how diaries can be a rich source of information on all three kinds of metacognitive knowledge discussed in this chapter.

Special references on person knowledge

Brown (1987) and Ellis (1986) both provide background on the cognitive and affective factors that constitute person knowledge.

Willing's report (1988) of a research project on the learning styles of adult immigrants in Australia includes a comprehensive review of the literature on learning styles and cognitive styles. Omaggio (1981) defines different types of learning styles and provides an inventory of learner problems that relate to cognitive styles.

Kidd (1976) discusses issues related to how adults learn in general. Burling (1981) describes the social factors which make it difficult for adults to learn another language.

Costa (1985) includes a chapter on the behaviors of intelligence illustrating how the research can be translated into terms comprehensible to grade school children. In *Learning 88* (November–December), there is a special 16-page section which applies recent learning theory to how children learn. It includes very readable articles on learning styles, intelligence, and learning theories.

Special references on strategic and task knowledge

Manuals written for language learners

Brown, D.H., 1989, *A Practical Guide to Language Learning*, New York: McGraw Hill.
Pimsleur, P., 1980, *How to Learn a Foreign Language*, Boston, MA: Heinle & Heinle.
Rubin, J., and Thompson, I., 1982, *How To Be a More Successful Language Learner*, Boston, MA: Heinle & Heinle.
For references to other manuals see Wenden (1983a) and Toney (1983).

Textbooks and articles on methodology

The introductory sections of textbooks written especially 'for the student' as well as explanatory sections within the body of the texts are examples of task knowledge as are some methodology articles on the four skills. Here are some examples:

Bode, S., and Moulding Lee, S., 1987, *Overheard and Understood*, Belmont, CA: Wadsworth.

Ferrer, J. and Whalley, E., 1985, 'Learning to listen and listening to learn', in *Mosaic I: A Listening/Speaking Skills Book*, New York: McGraw-Hill.

Gairns, R., and Redman, S., 1986, *Working with Words: A guide to teaching and learning vocabulary*, New York: Cambridge University Press.

McKay, S. (ed.), 1984, *Composing in a Second Language*, New York: Newbury House.

Richards, J., 1985, 'Listening comprehension: approach, design and procedure', in *The Context of Language Teaching*, New York: Cambridge University Press.

Robinson, T.H., and Modrey, L., 1986, *Active Writing*, New York: Macmillan.

Wiley, T.G., and Wrigley, H.S., 1987, *Communicating in the Real World: Developing communication skills for business and the professions*, Englewood Cliffs, NJ: Prentice Hall.

Notes

1. These four characteristics are drawn from Brown *et al.* (1983) and Flavell (1979). According to Yussen (1985), the work and ideas of these two researchers has had the greatest collective impact on defining and classifying the two main areas of metacognition: metacognitive knowledge (Flavell) and metacognitive strategies (Brown). For some of the research on language learners' metacognitive knowledge, see Wenden (1986, 1987).

2. There are two other aspects of person knowledge that have not been included in the explanation provided in this chapter. One is revealed when learners make statements of self-assessment indicating what they know or do not know and/or what they can and can not do, as when Laszlo said that he had had difficulty expressing his ideas. Such statements can be taken as evidence both of monitoring and of the 'person' knowledge that resulted from the use of that strategy. In this book, these statements have been included as evidence of monitoring (see Chapter 2, pp. 27–28) and so have not been brought into the discussion of person knowledge in this chapter. In Chapter 4, a second aspect of person knowledge which relates to a learner's self-concept as learner will be discussed, i.e. learners' beliefs about their role in learning and their capability as learners.

3. Just as monitoring can lead to person knowledge, evaluating can be the source of strategic knowledge. That is, knowledge about the effectiveness of a strategy acquired by evaluating its usefulness in a specific situation can become a part of a learner's body of strategic knowledge.

4. The defining aspects of task knowledge presented here are derived from Flavell's definition, which is based to a large extent on memory research of content learning (Flavell and Wellman, 1977). The definition has been adapted for the purpose of language learning.

5. The importance of 'survival' purposes appears to be supported by the research on motivation that has shown the relationship between instrumental motivation and acquired proficiency (Gardner, 1985).

6. One way of having students acquire this knowledge is incorporated in the action plan for strategy training (Chapter 7). Negotiated approaches to curriculum development, as suggested by Nunan (1988), would also help the learner make the link between task and need.

7. This aspect of task knowledge overlaps with the first dimension of strategic knowledge described earlier (cf. pp. 39).

Chapter 4
Attitudes towards learner autonomy

Focus   What would your students say if you asked them whether or not they need a teacher to learn? Do they consider themselves good language learners?

Process   • Defining learner attitudes towards autonomy
               • Factors influencing learner attitudes towards autonomy

Outcome   An understanding of two attitudes necessary for autonomy

Defining learner attitudes towards autonomy

Defining the term 'attitude'

In the literature on attitude change, attitudes have been referred to as 'learned motivations', 'valued beliefs', 'evaluations', 'what one believes is acceptable' or 'responses oriented towards approaching or avoiding'. Implied in these various definitions, are three characteristics of attitudes:

1. attitudes always have an object;
2. they are evaluative;
3. they predispose to certain actions.

In other words, attitudes have a cognitive component — beliefs, perceptions, information about the object of the attitude. In language learning, this could be what learners believe about their role in the learning process or about their capability as language learners. Attitudes have an evaluative component — the attitude object may evoke like or dislike, agreement or disagreement, approval or disapproval. Some language learners may agree with the notion that they should be more responsible for their learning, while for others an independent role is something they may prefer to avoid. Finally, attitudes have a behavioral component — they predispose people to act in certain ways. Learners whose evaluation towards autonomy is positive will try to become more responsible in their learning and those whose evaluation is negative will not.[1]

Two learner attitudes towards autonomy

4.1 Identifying learner attitudes towards autonomy
Reread Laszlo's and Ilse's accounts of their language learning (pp. 8−11) to determine answers to the following questions.

(a) How do they view their role in the language learning process? Do they appear willing to take on the responsibility for their learning? Do you expect them to be teacher dependent?

(b) Do they have confidence in themselves as learners? Do they appear to believe that they can learn English? Do they trust in their own attempts to learn?

4.2   Considering the influence of attitudes on learning
How do these attitudes appear to influence their approach to learning?

Learner attitude towards autonomy is the third kind of learner training content to be included in plans to promote autonomy. Learners need to probe beyond their definition of what it means to learn a language (Chapter 3) and how to do so (Chapter 2) to determine whether they feel they should take on responsibility for their learning and are capable of doing so. These two questions point to two attitudes that are crucial to learner autonomy: attitudes that learners hold about their *role* in the language learning process and their *capability* as learners.

Willingness to take on responsibility

Autonomous learners are willing to take on the responsibility for their learning — they see themselves as having a crucial role in their language learning. Laszlo and Ilse are examples. Laszlo completed the first phase of his language learning in a 'private way' in Hungary, without a teacher. He had studied a verb book on his own and had assessed the outcome of this effort and the utility of the strategies he used. Once in the United States, he continued to be actively involved — taking advantages of resources in his social environment — and, as noted in the excerpt, always kept his mind 'open' for information on the language.

Ilse had already realized the limitations of classroom learning in her own country. Feeling it would be easier to 'study the language' where she could 'watch the culture and background', she came to the United States. She had a clear objective with an explicit rationale and acted upon it. Once in the United States, she not only took formal classes but also spent a great deal of time on her own just getting accustomed to hearing the sound of the language and to the culture in general. She chose strategies that were consistent with her objective and understanding of the nature of language learning.

Confidence in their ability as learners

Autonomous learners are self-confident learners — they believe in their ability to learn and to self-direct or manage their learning. Laszlo reports asking his friends to correct his mistakes and says that he did not give in to despair when they did so although the corrections made him realize there was so much that he did not, yet, know. Instead he derived energy and motivation from knowledge of his errors and continued to work even harder. Nor was he completely dependent on outside resources to get the information he needed about the language, for he was confident in strategies he used — strategies that utilized his own acquired knowledge (e.g. his strategy for self-correction and for inferring the meaning of words).

When Ilse arrived, she realized she could not speak, but although she was afraid to open her mouth she placed herself in situations where she would be forced to. She trusted in her ability to be able to speak. When reading, she avoided looking up unknown words. She had confidence in her own strategies to understand.

4.3   Identifying attitudes towards language learning that may influence learner attitudes towards autonomy

The literature in second-language acquisition and language teaching methodology points to other attitudes that may hinder or facilitate the learning and acquisition of second or foreign languages.

(a)   What are some of these attitudes?
(b)   To what extent might they also influence learners' attitudes towards their role and capability as learners?

Learner attitudes and metacognitive knowledge

The beliefs that are central to language learners' attitudes about autonomy — their beliefs about their role and capability as learners — are a form of metacognitive knowledge. However, this knowledge differs from person, strategic and task knowledge (described in Chapter 3) in some basic ways.

First, learner beliefs about their role and capability as learners will be shaped and maintained, in part, by other beliefs they hold about themselves as learners. For example, when on the basis of their understanding of language aptitude (person knowledge) learners decide they have no ability to learn a language, this will contribute to a general belief that they cannot learn a language successfully and, certainly, never without a teacher. Or if learners believe that certain personality types cannot successfully learn a language and if they believe they are that type of person, again, this will influence their attitudes towards their role and capability as language learners. Though influenced by such aspects of person knowledge, learner beliefs about their role and capability as learners are more encompassing. They go beyond acknowledgments about affective or cognitive factors (e.g. I have to read it to understand) to a sweeping attribution, which determines a learner's total self-concept as a language learner (e.g. I can't learn on my own).

Second, evaluations of acceptability and unacceptability are intrinsic to the beliefs learners hold about their role and capability as learners. Moreover, these evaluations predispose learners to be willing or unwilling to take on responsibility for their learning. However, evaluations are not necessarily intrinsic to task and strategic knowledge, nor will this knowledge necessarily predispose to action until and unless experience demonstrates its significance.

For example, language learners who have heard from their teachers that 'practice is important for language learning' may decide to spend more time practising. Then, if they develop skill in their second language as a result, they may become more convinced of the importance of practice and continue to learn in this way — they will have formed a valued belief. Sometimes, however, if the action implied by task and strategic knowledge is not clear, learners just do not act upon it, and in other cases, even when it is, knowledge does not lead to action. As a result, the knowledge will acquire no value for the learner; it is not transformed into an evaluation. This is one of the key differences between the knowledge central to learner attitudes towards autonomy and their strategic and task knowledge. At the heart of a learner attitude towards autonomy is a *valued* belief, and this is not always the case for other aspects of metacognitive knowledge.

Finally, learners will usually be strongly invested in the valued beliefs that are central to their attitudes towards their role and capability as language learners. Of course, when beliefs related to strategic or task knowledge do acquire significance and value in students' eyes, they will not give them up or change them (the beliefs) or the behavior they imply very easily. Resistance to new language teaching methodology is evidence of the strength of such beliefs. Still, it may be assumed that students will react even more strongly when beliefs about their responsibilitites and capabilities as learners are opposed. Because these beliefs are integral to their self-concept, students will cling to them much more tenaciously and, it may be assumed, they will be harder to change.

These differences have important implications for the learning plans to help learners become more autonomous. Unless these plans take into account learner attitudes about role and capability, attempts to induce strategy use will be limited in success. Nor will efforts to expand and/or change learners' task and strategic knowledge have much influence on their approach to language learning.

Factors influencing learner attitudes towards autonomy

4.4   Identifying other factors that influence the formation of learner attitudes towards autonomy
Your experience will have suggested other factors which play a key role in determining learner attitudes towards autonomy. Refer to this experience as you discuss the following questions.

(a)   Why would some learners take more initiative in their language learning while others are teacher dependent?
(b)   What experiences contribute to the formation of a negative self-image on the part of language learners?

Not all learners will respond as Laszlo and Ilse did to the task of being responsible for their language learning. Some will not be willing to take initiative and will be more teacher-dependent, nor will they approach language learning with the same sense of self-confidence. Others will feel that they are not capable of taking on the challenge of autonomy. The formation of such attitudes is a complex matter, and so the following examples from selected research in adult learning, cognitive psychology and second-language acquisition can only be suggestive of some factors which influence the development of learner attitudes towards autonomy in learning.

Socialization processes

Mezirow's (1985) research in adult learning has shown that in some cases socialization processes lead to the acquisition of beliefs that encourage dependence rather than independence on the part of the adult. In matters related to learning, Knowles (1976) suggests that this attitude may be acquired in grade school where, gradually, students find that responsibility for their learning is taken on by formal institutions and the teacher. Consequently, as young children, students begin to believe that to be a learner is to be dependent, and when they enter into an educational activity as adults they expect to be treated like children. This attitude persists despite their resentment at learning under conditions that are incongruent with their self-concept as autonomous individuals. In fact, this expectation, based on early socialization, is so strong that they often put pressure on their teachers to behave towards them in this way.

Research done at the University of Nancy (Holec, 1987) confirms this view. It has illustrated how such socialization influences the expectations of adult language learners as regards their role and the role of the teacher in language learning. The students in the study saw themselves as consumers of learning while teachers were perceived as the source of knowledge and the ultimate decision makers about success or failure in examinations. As consumers, the students expected to learn in exchange for the money they paid for language courses, textbooks and teacher hours. If they did not, teachers were held responsible.

Conflicting role demands

Earlier socialization regarding roles in learning is not the only reason why learners may refuse to take on a more active role in learning. For adult learners, acquiring competence in their new language is often a means to achieving some other goal. For the immigrant learner the second language is a tool for daily survival, while for the international student, the second language is a necessary requisite for a degree. Clearly, many needs and concerns compete for the adult learner's time and energy, and so learning the second language is not necessarily given top priority. It is the final goal — the purpose for which they have enrolled in the language course — which preoccupies learners. Learning the language is seen as a necessary hurdle, one which should take as little time and effort as possible. As a result, adults are not willing to take on a responsible role in their learning simply because they do not have the time. Even if they agree that learning the language is important, the demands of an adult learner's role as language learner may conflict with the demands of other roles.

Complexity of roles

In his discussion of factors which influence role formation and maintenance, Wright (1987) distinguishes interpersonal factors from task-related factors, both of which can influence the role that learners assume in the classroom and the expectations they hold regarding the teacher's role and that of their classmates. Interpersonal factors he cites include status and position, attitudes and beliefs about teaching and learning, personality and motivation while task-related factors may be the task goal, the task itself and the topics or subject matter of the task. Role changes, therefore, will entail changing learner perceptions about these interrelated factors and helping them acquire behaviors that are appropriate to their new perceptions. This is not a simple matter. Learner resistance to taking on more responsibility for their language learning or an apparent lack of self-confidence in their ability to do so may also be a reflection of role complexity.

Lack of metacognitive knowledge

Ignorance about their mental processes is another reason which may contribute to learners' apparent lack of willingness and self-confidence when it comes to taking on responsibility for their learning. Referring to college freshmen he worked with, Schoenfield (1982) noted that many enter the classroom completely unaware that they can observe, evaluate and change their own cognitive behavior. It is, he says, as if their mind was an independent entity and they passive spectators of its activities. It has not occurred to them that they might be able to be actively involved in their own learning. They are not aware of, and therefore cannot believe in, their intellectual potential. These freshmen were native English speakers, but the same attitude can also typify language learners.

Learned helplessness

Learners' beliefs about their capability as learners may be the outcome of what the metacognitive literature refers to as 'learned helplessness'. Research on this topic has shown that failure in learning leads some learners to engage in nonproductive thoughts about their lack of ability. The resulting inaccurate attributional patterns and expectancies, it has been noted, can lead to a deterioration in cognitive performance and so further confirm a learner's view of him/herself as incapable of learning (Diener and Dweck, 1978, 1980). Knowles (1975) has also noted how such beliefs, acquired in childhood, have become a part of the adult's self-concept, and so adults who have been leading successsful lives in a number of roles (e.g. professional, parent) will find themselves influenced by these earlier views when they return to the classroom. As a result, many regress to a state of 'learned helplessness', believing themselves incapable of learning without a teacher.

Self-esteem

Self-esteem is a factor that is related to but not necessarily identical with 'learned helplessness'. The second-language acquisition literature includes 'self-esteem', i.e. the evaluation a person makes and holds with regard to himself or herself, as a factor to consider in understanding how the process of second-language acquisition differs among individuals. Brown (1987) distinguishes three types of self-esteem. General self-esteem is thought to be relatively stable in a mature adult. Situational self-esteem is a second level of self-esteem related to how we appraise ourselves in specific situations, such as work or school, or as regards specific abilities, such as communicative ability, athletic ability .... Task self-esteem refers to particular tasks within specific situations. An example of task self-esteem in second-language acquisition could be how one rates oneself in a particular skill, such as writing, reading .... Specific self-esteem and, by implication, task self-esteem will vary depending upon situation or task. Brown also cites research which shows that self-esteem appears to be an important variable in second-language acqusition (Gardner and Lambert, 1972; Brodkey and Shore, 1976; Heyde, 1979). Heyde found that all three levels of self-esteem correlated with performance on an oral production measure, with the highest correlation occurring between task self-esteem and performance on oral production measures. While Brown is concerned with the relationship between self-esteem and acquired language proficiency, it is also possible that a lack of self-esteem would contribute to the formation of learners' negative attitudes towards their capability to learn autonomously.

Self-image

Self-image is the outcome of the evaluations that persons make with regard to themselves (i.e. of their self-esteem). Bailey's research (1983) on competitiveness among language learners led to some interesting insights regarding how self-image can influence language learning. She proposes that when learners see themselves as successful *vis-à-vis* other learners their learning is enhanced, but if they perceive themselves as unsuccessful, i.e. as not being able to learn, anxiety results. In some learners, Bailey notes, the anxiety is facilitating, and the learner will try harder to improve. For others, however, the anxiety can be debilitating, and the learner will avoid contact with the second language — the source of his failure.

Bailey's analysis was based on self-image generated as a result of competitiveness with other language learners. However, other factors in a language learning experience can also contribute to the formation of a negative self-image and the consequent experience of anxiety. Laszlo, for example, became very anxious when his mistakes were corrected because he realized how little he knew. In his case, such anxiety was facilitating and gave him energy to work even harder, but, as Bailey's analysis suggests, not all language learners can react so positively in the face of difficulty or failure. The result, a negative self-image, can therefore not only influence their language learning outcomes (as Bailey suggests) but also shape their attitudes towards learning autonomously.

Schema of learner attitudes towards autonomy

The questions discussed in this chapter that define learner attitudes about their role and capability as learners are outlined in Table 4.1. These two attitudes constitute the third category of learner training content to be included in plans to help learners become more autonomous.

TABLE 4.1
Learner attitudes towards autonomy

Attitude toward role	Attitude toward capability
Should I learn independently?	Can I learn?
Should I take initiative?	Can I learn autonomously?
Should I assume responsibility?	

Earlier literature on autonomy in language learning, which stresses the need for 'psychological preparation' for autonomy, also notes the importance of the two basic attitudes outlined in Table 4.1. According to this literature, psychological preparation means helping learners become *willing* to take responsibility for their learning. We are told that learners must be helped to *accept* this mode of learning (Allwright, 1981) or to *try* self-instruction (Dickinson, 1987); that false and long-held assumptions and prejudices which underlie their attitudes towards their *role* in learning must be changed (Dickinson, 1987). According to Holec, a learner needs to go through a 'deconditioning process' which will cause him to:

> break away . . . from a priori judgments and prejudices of all kinds that encumber his ideas about learning languages and the role he can play in it — to free himself from the notion that there is one ideal method, that teachers

possess that method, that his knowledge of his mother tongue is of no use to him for learning a second language, that his experience as a learner of other subjects, other know-how cannot be transferred even partially, that he is incapable of making a valid assessment of his performance and so on.

[Holec, 1981: 22]

Finally, psychological preparation means that learners need to build *self-confidence in their capability to work independently* of the teacher (Sinclair and Ellis, 1985; Dickinson, 1987) — a notion that is also alluded to by Holec (above).

The need for psychological preparation underscores insights from the research described in the preceding section and supports what many of us know from experience — that learners have often formed nonproductive attitudes with regard to learning autonomously. Still, other insights from the theory and research in adult learning and language learning provide opposing evidence, which should encourage us to develop learning activities that will seek to re-orient these negative attitudes.

Theorists in adult learning agree that autonomy is one of the main goals of adult striving and activity throughout the life cycle — adults desire to be autonomous. In fact, according to Brookfield (1984) research in adult self-directed learning (in areas other than language learning), the 'chief growth area in the field of adult education research in the last decade', has demonstrated the propensity and capacity of adults to engage in purposeful learning outside formal institutions. In the field of language learning, the research on good language learners also testifies to the capacity of language learners to engage autonomously and effectively in their language learning (cf. Wenden and Rubin (1987) for some of the earlier research). Finally, recent research on the process of attitude change in adults has also concluded that adults wish to hold the 'right' attitude (Petty and Cacioppo, 1986). Of course, standards used to judge what is right will vary, but basically it is expected that people will engage in behaviors to ascertain that the attitudes they hold are correct.

Conclusion

In this chapter, you have examined two attitudes that are necessary to encourage and support learner autonomy — willingness to take responsibility for one's learning and confidence in one's ability as a learner. You have also considered some of the factors that may militate against the formation of such attitudes. In the following chapters you will learn skills for applying the knowledge you have acquired about attitudes (in this chapter) and about strategies and metacognitive knowledge (in earlier chapters) to the devising and implementing of learning plans to help learners become more autonomous.

Valuable readings

Mezirow (1985)'s description of the three kinds of learning that adults engage in, i.e. technical learning, dialogic learning and self-learning, is the basis in adult learning theory for the three kinds of learner training content outlined in Chapters 2–4. His discussion on self-learning suggested the definition of attitudes towards autonomy presented in this chapter.

Curran (1976) deals explicitly with learner confidence in language learning. Wright (1987) analyzes the concept of role, the factors that influence role and the roles of teachers and learners in language learning.

Gardner's publication on the role of attitudes and motivation in second-language learning (1985) provides research evidence that supports the assumption that attitudes influence behavior, one of the propositions underlying this chapter. His report also highlights the complexity of attitudes.

Note

1. There is no strong consensus on what the term 'attitude' means and though the synthesis suggested by social psychology books includes three dimensions — cognitive, conative and evaluative — often the term 'attitudes' is used interchangeably with 'evaluations'.

Chapter 5

Planning learning to promote learner autonomy

Focus   Think of a language learning task you often ask your students to do. What learning strategies would they need to do the task? What should learners know about the language learning process to complete the task successfully? How will their attitudes towards autonomy influence their approach?

Process   • A content schema for learner training
    • Guidelines for selecting learner training content

Outcome   A planning guide

A content schema for learner training

In earlier chapters, we defined three categories of content to be included in learning plans to help language learners become more autonomous (or 'to promote learner autonomy'). They are presented schematically in Table 5.1.

Based on documented research on language learners' attempts to learn and to use another language, each category in the schema is grounded in the experience of language learners. [1] In the following set of tasks, you will consider how content from the schema is selected for individual lessons and course syllabi that incorporate learner training with language training.

> **5.1   Analyzing learner training content in a notetaking course**
> The following course in notetaking is for a group of ESL students at a high intermediate level enrolled in regular college classes. They needed to develop facility in understanding academic lectures and, more generally, to expand their passive knowledge of academic English. As you read through the procedures try to find answers to the following.
>
> (a)   Which learning strategies are learners taught to use?
> (b)   What aspects of metacognitive knowledge are included?
> (c)   How are attitudes towards autonomy dealt with?

A COURSE IN NOTETAKING

> ### Introductory lesson
> #### *Procedures*
> 1. Students complete the following listening survey.
>
> #### *A listening survey*
> (i)   List three different places where you have an opportunity to listen to English. Think about each place to decide whether you have problems understanding English there. If you do, describe each problem in a short sentence.

TABLE 5.1
A content schema for learner training

Strategies	Kind	Function
	Cognitive	Select input
		Comprehend input
		Store input
		Retrieve input
	Self-management	Planning
		Monitor
		Evaluate
Knowledge about learning	**Kind**	**Aspect**
	Person	Affective factors
		Cognitive factors
	Strategic	Effective strategies
		Principles of learning
	Task	Purpose of the task
		Nature of language
		Need for conscious effort
		Task demands
Attitudes	**Kind**	**Aspect**
	Personal responsibility	Should I take initiative?
		What is my role?
	Personal capability	Can I learn?
		Can I learn
		autonomously?

(ii)   Some language learners have special techniques they use to help themselves overcome their problems understanding spoken English. What are your special techniques? Why do you use them?
   (a)   Think of what you do when you are speaking with Americans.
   (b)   Think of what you do in a college classroom when you are listening to a lecture.
(iii)   Is listening to a lecture in a college classroom the same as listening to a television program? As talking with Americans outside class? Why?
(iv)   What do you expect to do in a listening class?
(v)   If a friend who is having difficulty understanding college lectures asks you what he can do to improve his listening skills, what would you tell him? Why?
(vi)   Would you rather listen to a lecture or read a book about the same topic? Why?
(vii)   Is it more important to you to learn how to listen and take notes than to learn how to write good essays? Why?
(viii)   What do you expect to be able to do when you finish this course? How well?
(ix)   Can you improve your listening and notetaking skills without a teacher? If yes, how? If not, why not?

(x) Do you agree that it is easier to learn to understand English and take notes if you are younger? Why? Why not?

2. Students break up into groups of three or four to discuss their answers and come up with a report on points of agreement and disagreement.
3. The teacher records points of disagreement on the blackboard.
4. A class discussion is held about the varying viewpoints.
    (a) Students indicate why they hold one opinion and whether their opinion always holds true.
    (b) Students consider the reasoning behind those opinions with which they disagree.
5. Students reconsider their answers to the survey and indicate which ones they would answer differently or somewhat differently after the discussion and how.
6. The surveys are handed in to the teacher. They are analyzed for learners' knowledge regarding (1) the nature of listening, what is involved and how difficult it may be; (2) how best to approach the task of listening; (3) personal factors and attitudes towards listening. Concepts that the teacher feels need to be considered more deeply and refined or expanded are noted and become topics for focused journal writing assignments assigned on a weekly basis. These journals are collected regularly and form the basis for an ongoing dialogue between the teacher and the student.

Lesson 2

Theme   Learning to speak someone else's language[2]

Procedures
1. Students are given the title of the lecture.
    (a) They tell what they already know about that topic.
    (b) They predict what the lecture will be about.
2. Technical vocabulary and key words students may not know are presented.
3. Students are prepared for the introspective procedure that follows. They are told the following.
    (a) During the lecture you want to find out what they think as they listen.
    (b) You will lecture one idea/sentence and then stop.
    (c) At the pause they should write down what they are thinking.
    (d) They should not take notes at this time — just write what they think.
4. The lecture is begun, and the procedure is illustrated by having students respond orally for the first few pauses or as long as it takes for them to be comfortable with the procedure.[3]
5. When they are comfortable, have them write their responses. These responses should be numbered sequentially, with each number corresponding to the idea in the lecture used to elicit these thought processes. (See Table 5.2 for excerpts of student reports and the lecture ideas that elicited them.)
6. When a sufficient number of responses have been recorded, student responses to two of these ideas are written on the blackboard together with the ideas that elicited them.
7. Students are told that these responses, the 'thoughts' that come to mind as they listen, are called strategies and that the purpose of the lessons is to learn to use notetaking, a strategy that can help them understand academic lectures.
8. Students compare the different responses to determine the different strategies they used (e.g. self-questioning, association).

TABLE 5.2
Introspective responses during a short lecture

Student 1	Student 2	Student 3
STATEMENT 1 'Our lecture is going to be about language'		
I'm thinking how to listen (to) the lecture . . .	. . . language is the way that make people to come in touch . . .	. . . how can I improve my English? . . .
STATEMENT 2 'Here are two questions we're going to consider. How do we learn a language? How does learning a language influence us?		
I didn't understand the second question . . .	—	What I have to do with language? . . .
STATEMENT 3 'There are two theories about how we learn'		
—	What are the theories?	I'd like to know the theories . . .
STATEMENT 4 'The oldest theory is by imitation and association'		
That's one of the ways I learned English	It's the only way to have better results . . .	What are the imitation and association? . . .
STATEMENT 5 'For example, if a baby touches a hot pot, he cries. The mother may say something like "no, no, hot, hot . . .". The baby will imitate and associate hot with the hot pot'		
—	. . . a child does as the elders do . . .	. . . how do the word and theory relate? . . .
STATEMENT 6 'The second theory was proposed by Noam Chomsky. He said the ability to learn a language is innate'		
. . . what is innate?	. . . my opinion is that Mr Chomsky is right. Our ability to learn is innate . . .	. . . what is the history of Mr Chomsky? What is innate mean? . . .
STATEMENT 7 'Though some words and sentences may be learned by imitation, he felt that many of the things we say are unique, creative. We have not already learned them'		
Interesting . . .	Human being is the only being (that) have the ability to learn creatively . . .	I don't understand innate . . .

9. The introspective reports are collected and used by the teacher as a source of information on the listening strategies the students use.
10. The lecture is now given from beginning to end with students taking notes.

Lesson 3

Theme   Learning to listen and listening to learn

Procedures

Pre-lecture activities

1. Students go through a handout of four sets of student notes on the first lecture 'Learning to speak someone else's language' to identify sections that are 'notes' and sections that are more like 'dictation'.

2. Students compare these two ways of recording information to come up with the difference between notetaking and taking dictation.
3. Students go through the four sets of notes to find examples of 'good notes' and state why they are considered 'good'.
4. These examples are discussed and criteria underlying the students' choice of good notes are written on the blackboard.
5. Use the pre-existing procedures (1 and 2) described in Lesson 2.
6. Students are asked to list (a) the difference between listening and reading and (b) what a good listener does during a lecture.
7. They are told that the lecture is going to be about the differences listed in 6.
8. They are given the technical term for the information they have just provided in 5 and 6, i.e. 'background knowledge'.
9. The teacher gives the lecture.
10. The students go through their notes to find areas that they are unclear about. They ask questions for clarification and these are recorded on the board.
11. The teacher lectures a second time and the students listen for answers to their questions.

Post-lecture activities
12. Answers to the questions students asked in 10 are determined.
13. The students compare the criteria for good notes given in the lecture with those they had already developed, refining and adding to the original.
14. The students reread their notes and find examples of (a) how they followed two of the criteria and (b) how they violated two (if, in fact, they did).

Lesson 4

Theme Family networks and the elderly in the United States

Procedures

Pre-lecture
1. Use the pre-listening procedures (1 and 2) listed in Lesson 2.
2. After students have listed what they know about family and the elderly in the United States, ask them what the term for that kind of knowledge is (give it to them if they do not remember, i.e. background knowledge).
3. Students are asked what they have to do in order (a) to know what information to take down in their notes and (b) to record it.
4. List their answers on the blackboard and tell them that these answers also describe 'strategies' they use.
5. Students arc told that they will be practising two of these strategies: identifying key words, and paraphrasing. (Of course, if thesc two were not listed, clues can be given that will enable students to guess them, and if all else fails they can be given the names of the strategies.)

The lecture
6. Two or three of the students who already seem to have acquired some facility with notetaking do the following task at the blackboard.
   (a) Lecture short short (but meaningful) phrases of thought — pause and have students say what the key words are.
   (b) Repeat the same phrase and have the students restate the idea orally in a simpler and shorter version (paraphrase).

(c) Students write down what they have paraphrased orally.
7. The class evaluates the notes on the blackboard. At this point emphasize only the
    following criteria.
    • notes are not dictation;
    • use of short short sentences or short phrases;
    • use of only necessary function words;
    • appropriate use of abbreviation and symbols.
8. Repeat procedures 6 and 7 until about half the lecture has been given. Then the
    students continue doing these strategies on their own at their desks as the lecture
    is completed.

Post-lecture activities
9. When the lecture is over, students each compare their notes with those of a classmate
    and together they come up with areas they wish to have clarified.
10. The teacher or students answer their questions.

Lesson 5

Theme   The cardiac muscle

Procedures

Pre-lecture activities
1. Students examine teacher-prepared model notes of the previous lecture on 'family'
    to determine the following:
    • Which are specific facts? Which are related generalizations?
    • How are notes written to show this?

Pre-listening
2. Students are given the title of the lecture and asked (a) what they know about it
    and (b) what they think the lecture will be about.

The lecture
3. Two or three students work at the board; others work at their desks.
4. Follow procedures 6 and 7 of Lesson 4.
5. Repeat until one main/general point and related subpoints have been lectured.
6. The class evaluates the notes, referring to the relationship between general/specific,
    criteria from Lesson 4 and other criteria from the general list developed in Lesson 3.
7. Continue with procedures 6 and 7 of Lesson 4 for about half the lecture, sending
    different students to the board.
8. Then finish the lecture with students working on their own.

Post-lecture activities
9. Follow steps 9 and 10 of Lesson 4.

Lesson 6

Theme   The niche penguins have in a polar ecosystem

Procedures

Pre-lecture activities
1. Students examine a handout of teacher-prepared model notes of the previous lecture
    and explain how these notes follow the criteria they have been discussing (Lessons

3, 4 and 5). This may be done as a class or in groups. They may also compare these notes with their own to see how accurately and completely they have grasped the content of the lecture and whether they are following the criteria for good notes.

Pre-lecture
2. The title is announced and pre-listening procedures used in previous lessons are followed.

The lecture
3. Follow the procedures used in Lesson 5.

Post-lecture activities
4. Follow procedures used in Lesson 5.

Lesson 7

Theme   Dead people are peaceful

Procedures

Pre-lecture activities
1. Students compare model notes of the previous lecture with their notes to determine how theirs are different and how they are the same. That is, which criteria did they follow? Some of the time? All of the time? Which did they not follow? Some of the time? All the time? How accurate are their notes? How complete?
2. Ask students what two questions they have been answering before starting each lecture (i.e. what do I know about this topic? What will the speaker say about it?).
3. Students give these mental activities a name, i.e. eliciting background knowledge (what do you know about this topic) and predicting (what's the speaker going to say about this topic), with help from the teacher.
4. They are told these are two pre-listening strategies and asked to discuss why they are important.

The lecture
5. This time students are told to listen for key words and to paraphrase and record on their own. That is, there will be no questions or evaluation of notes after each main point as has been done in the previous lectures. Nor will students be sent to the blackboard.

Post-lecture activities
6. The same procedures as in previous lessons.

Lesson 8

Theme   Choices

Procedures

Pre-listening activities
1. Students are asked what strategies they should use before listening to a lecture.
2. The teacher gives them the topic of the lecture and has them apply the strategies in groups of two.

Lecture
3. The procedures used in the previous lesson are followed.

Post-listening activities
4. Students are given model notes on the lecture and asked to compare them with theirs. They use criteria they have been developing to analyze differences.

Lesson 9

Theme   Group dynamics

Procedures
1. The procedures are the same as they were for Lesson 8 except that, when the lecture is completed, students use an evaluation guide, based on the criteria that they have been learning, to evaluate their notes (Table 5.3).
2. Students are asked to list all the occasions in a typical week when they have an opportunity to listen to English — where will they be and who will they be talking to and about what.
3. Students discuss which of these occasions would be appropriate for practising the strategies they have been learning to use and which ones.

TABLE 5.3
An evaluation guide for notetaking

_____
(name)

_____   DATE _____
(title of lecture)

  I You may check your skills as a listener by evaluating the CONTENT of your notes.

  1. Were your notes complete? _____Y; _____No, I missed _____ main points

  2. Were your notes accurate? _____Y; _____No, I misunderstood _____ points

 II You may check your skills as a notetaker by evaluating HOW you take notes.

  3. Used full sentences
       _____most of the time _____often _____a few times _____not at all
  4. Used short sentences
       _____most of the time _____often _____a few times _____not at all
  5. Used short phrases (parts of sentences)
       _____most of the time _____often _____a few times _____not at all
  6. Used symbols and abbreviations
       _____only for key words _____for all kinds of words _____not at all
  7. Meaning of symbols and abbreviations was clear
       _____yes _____no
       Explain your answer.
  8. Showed relationship between ideas _____yes _____no
       If yes, how?
  9. Showed difference between main points and supporting facts
       _____most of the time _____often _____a few times _____not at all
       If yes, how?
 10. Took down unnecessary ideas
 11. Add any other comment you wish to make about your notes here.

---

4. They choose one or more of these situations to practise and write up an evaluation of their efforts in their learning journal.

Lesson 10

1. The procedures are the same as they were for Lesson 9 except that, when the lecture is completed, students use the evaluation guide to assess their notes.
2. Students discuss their attempts to listen outside of the class and evaluate their strategies — how effective were they?
3. They decide upon a situation when they can practise their strategies in the subsequent week.

The last class

The last class can be set aside to re-administer the listening survey. Students and teachers compare answers to the beginning-of-term survey. Reasons for different answers are discussed. Students set up a plan to continue using their new strategies after the course. How do they want to improve their listening? Which strategies will they practise to do so? Where? When?

Guidelines for selecting content for learner training

The notetaking course illustrates two guidelines that must be taken into account in selecting content for learner training: Is the content integrated? Is it task based?

Integrated

In the implementation of a task, learning strategies, metacognitive knowledge and attitudes all come into play. Therefore, in selecting learner training content for autonomy, all three categories must be included.

Task based

Three characteristics of the language learning task will determine the choice of the particular strategies and specific aspects of metacognitive knowledge to be taught. These are as follows.

1. *The kind of language skill* — whether it deals with a receptive or production skill.
2. *The language medium* — whether it deals with the written or spoken language.
3. *The setting* — whether it prepares students for language use in formal or informal contexts.

Learner training content for a course in notetaking

The starred items in Figure 5.1, which identify the main learner training content in the course, were explicitly presented, discussed and/or practised over a series of lessons. The unstarred items were mentioned and briefly discussed (i.e. person and strategic knowledge) *or* applied only a few times but not practised or discussed at all (planning, monitoring).

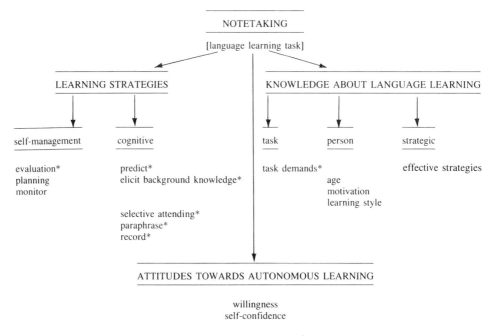

FIGURE 5.1   *Learner training content for a course in notetaking.*

Cognitive strategies

The notetaking course focuses on cognitive strategies that are used in the pre-listening phase of a listening task, i.e. predicting and eliciting background knowledge, and others that make up three of the procedures necessary for notetaking, i.e. selective attending, paraphrasing and translation.

Predicting and eliciting background knowledge

Predicting alerts learners to what they should attend to as they listen, and eliciting background knowledge helps them summon previously learned knowledge that will facilitate understanding. In the notetaking series, students are told to use the strategies in Lessons 2−6. In Lesson 7 the strategies are named and their significance is discussed. From then on, the students are given time to apply them before the beginning of a lecture.

Selective attending, paraphrasing, translation

In the notetaking course, 'selective attending' means listening for key words that recur and point to important concepts. 'Paraphrasing' means restating briefly in one's own words key ideas expressed through the key words, and 'translation' means recording these ideas clearly and briefly. In Lesson 4, students are explicitly introduced to the idea of selective attending and paraphrasing. Teacher-directed practice in the use of these two strategies provided in Lessons 4−6 also gives students the opportunity to experiment and receive feedback on ways of recording this information. After Lesson 6, students are reminded to use the strategies just before the lecture.

Self-management strategies

The notetaking course gives students explicit and systematic teaching in the use of evaluation and some practice in planning; it does not provide any training in monitoring.

Evaluation

Class activities help learners learn and apply criteria for evaluating the format of their notes (are they clear and concise?) and the content (are the notes complete and accurate?)

These activities begin in Lesson 3, when students are asked to outline criteria for good notes on the basis of the sample notes they have been given. The lecture in that lesson offers them more information on evaluation criteria. In Lessons 4−6, students are sent to the blackboard to take notes and the whole class evaluates the format of the notes. In Lesson 6, they evaluate a handout of model notes against the criteria they have been developing and compare their notes with the model notes to come up with the criteria they utilize or violate. They also begin to focus on the accuracy and completeness of the notes they have taken. This activity is continued through to Lesson 9, when an evaluation guide, which emphasizes notetaking format and the comprehensiveness and accuracy of the notes, is introduced and used until the end of the course.

Planning

Planning includes the setting of objectives and the selection of resources necessary to achieve these objectives. The survey administered in Lesson 1 (cf. item (viii)) should make learners begin to think of what they expect to be able to do at the end of the course. Then, during the last class, learners are asked to set objectives to guide their ongoing independent practice in listening and to determine how the objectives will be achieved.

Monitoring

When learners monitor, they become aware of the fact that they are having difficulty with a task and determine the cause. After each lecture, students are asked to note what points need clarification after the completion of each lecture so that they can identify areas of difficulty they had during the lecture. However, they are not asked to reflect on the nature of monitoring, nor are they given opportunities specifically to develop facility in its use.

Metacognitive knowledge about language learning

Aspects of task knowledge and strategic knowledge are explicitly taught in this series of lessons. Some class activities are also intended to raise awareness about person knowledge.

Task knowledge

Only task demands — one aspect of task knowledge — is explicitly and systematically taught. Task demands refer to (1) what learners need to know about the task to complete it, (2) how they must go about doing the task and (3) whether it will be hard or easy. The notetaking course addresses the first two questions.

In Lesson 3 learners analyze a set of notes to determine the difference between dictation and notetaking; then they listen to a lecture which discusses the differences between listening and reading and describes the value of notetaking. In Lessons 4−6, they are made aware of the steps to be followed in notetaking through the directed practice of three strategies: selective attending, paraphrasing and translation. The model notes and evaluation forms, used to help students develop criteria for evaluating their notes, is also a means of developing knowledge about the task demands of notetaking.

Strategic knowledge

Knowing what a strategy is and whether a strategy works efficiently in the performance of a particular task is one aspect of strategic knowledge included in the notetaking lessons.

The notion 'strategy' is introduced in Lesson 2 and is again referred to in Lesson 4. While no time is set aside for discussion of the effectiveness of the three notetaking strategies being practised, the evaluation process, which is carried on from Lesson 4 to the end of the course, should help students determine this for themselves. As they notice that their notes are becoming more comprehensive and accurate, they should also realize that these strategies are effective.

Person knowledge

The listening survey (Lesson 1) is intended to make students aware of their views about their preferred medium of learning (item (vi)), their motivation (item (vii)) and age (item (x)) (all aspects of person knowledge). The discussion that follows the administration of the survey and the ongoing dialogue facilitated through the listening journal should help them continue to examine and refine these views.

Attitudes

While the selection of appropriate learning strategies and metacognitive knowledge is task based, the selection of learner attitudes towards autonomy is not, for these attitudes are extrinsic to the task and often are already formed before the learner approaches a particular task (see Chapter 4 for possible reasons). Attitudes may be specific to a particular kind of task, or they may apply to language learning in general. Therefore, in planning a course, it is essential that activities be planned to determine learners' pre-existing attitudes and to revise them if necessary.

In the course outline presented here, question (ix) of the survey is explicitly intended to elicit these attitudes for discussion, but it is also possible that what learners feel about themselves as independent and capable learners will emerge during the discussion of other questions in the survey (e.g. (i), (ii), (iv), (v)). Then, the discussion of these views initiated during this first class is continued through the use of the listening journals.

The following set of tasks will give you practice in using the guidelines to select learner training content appropriate for the learning of other language skills.

5.2   Selecting learner training content for listening in an informal setting

Consider which strategies and which kinds of metacognitive knowledge would be appropriate for a course preparing students to improve their understanding of conversational English (e.g. an immigrant who needs to survive in his new culture or a tourist who will be visiting for a brief period).

(a)   Would the cognitive strategies selected for the notetaking course be appropriate? If not, which ones would be? Should communication strategies be included in the course content?

(b)   Would the same type of advance planning appropriate for listening to a lecture be necessary for a listening task in an informal situation? If not, what kind of advance planning would be necessary?

(c)   How is the outcome of an attempt to listen and understand in an informal conversation to be evaluated? Is this different from how comprehension of a lecture or class discussion would be evaluated? If so, how is it different?

5.3   Selecting learner training content for reading and writing

Consider the following language learning tasks to determine how the skill, medium and setting of the task will dictate learner training content:

(a)   a writing course for college bound students;
(b)   a reading course for new immigrants who wish to learn to read a newspaper.

5.4   Analyzing your planning procedures for selecting learner training content

How did you go about choosing learner training content for the language learning tasks listed in task 5.3?

(a)   Reflect upon your process to identify procedures you followed and list them.

(b)   Did you use the same procedures for each task? The same order? If not, note the differences.

(c)   What difficulties did you encounter?

A planning guide

In the preceding section we examined two guidelines to use in selecting learner training content. In this section you will examine and evaluate a planning guide which you can use to apply

TABLE 5.4
A planning guide

Learning strategies

1. Which cognitive strategies should be included in this learning plan?
2. How can learners be helped to become aware of their language learning problems? To determine the cause of the problems they encounter?
3. What criteria should learners learn to use to evaluate the outcome of their learning?
4. How can they be helped to determine the specific objectives (or outcomes) they will strive to achieve?

Knowledge about language learning

6. What specific concepts about the nature of language and communication need to be taught in this plan?
7. What specific steps should be followed to perform the language learning task that is the main objective of this plan?
8. What guidelines about second-language learning need to be taught?
9. What knowledge about affective and cognitive factors that affect learning do learners need to be made aware of?

Attitudes towards autonomy

10. How can learners be helped to appraise their views on their role in learning and on their capability as learners as it pertains to this task?

The reference point for each question is the language learning task that is the main objective of their learning plan and the language skills that constitute this task.

these guidelines (Table 5.4). The guide translates the content schema for learner training (Table 5.1) into a set of questions. It assumes that the learners' communicative and linguistic needs have already been determined and that the *language* learning task that will help them cope with these needs has been selected.

The guide is not intended to be prescriptive but to help teachers with the selection of learner training content that is appropriate to the language learning objectives or tasks they set for their students in the development of single lessons, a series of lessons or a course syllabus. What distinguishes the guide from other planning outlines is that it deals exclusively with learning. In the past, teachers may not have felt the need to share their 'learning' expertise with learners. This guide suggests that they should do so.

The planning guide can also be used as a kind of troubleshooter to help find out why students have difficulty doing some of the language tasks they are asked to do. For example, why did they not understand the content of a particular task? Why did they resist doing it? Why did they misunderstand the directions? The guide will help to isolate those reasons related to the students' learning processes. Students who consistently write simple undeveloped and poorly organized compositions, for example, may not know what strategies to use to get ideas or what steps are involved in writing an expository essay; they may not have any knowledge about the nature of the discourse structure specific to the writing task or about the criteria to use to evaluate their writing. Using the planning guide to identify these problems can provide information for use in devising subsequent learning plans.

5.5   Using the planning guide to select learner training content
Consider a lesson you often teach and a course outline you have already implemented.

(a)   What language learning task forms the main focus of each?

(b) Use the planning guide to select the learning strategies and the knowledge about language learning that you could incorporate into each one (the lesson and the course outline).

5.6 Using the planning guide for troubleshooting
In this task you will reflect upon some of the problems you have encountered in the implementation of your lesson plans to see whether the planning guide can help you determine the cause.

(a) Make a list of tasks that went wrong (e.g. a particular lesson, a class activity, an examination, an out-of-class assignment).
(b) Use the planning guide to determine the learner training content necessary to complete the task.
(c) Were your students prepared to do the task? That is, did they have the strategies and knowledge outlined in (b)? Did your analysis yield insight on their attitudes towards the task?

5.7 Evaluating the planning guide
In Task 5.5 you were asked to use the planning guide to select learner training content to go with a particular language learning task. Compare the planning and selection process you used in Task 5.5 with the one used in Task 5.3.

(a) What were some of the differences?
(b) What problems did you encounter in each case?
(c) Did the use of the planning guide for Task 5.5 account for some of the differences?
(d) Would the planning guide help you to resolve problems encountered in doing Task 5.3?
(f) Which approach did you find more usable? Why?
(g) Use insights from your analysis to revise either the planning guide or the procedures you used for Task 5.3.

Conclusion

In this chapter you were presented with a content schema for learner training based on the three kinds of content discussed in earlier chapters. You have examined two guidelines to use in selecting content from the schema and experimented with a guide that applies the guidelines in the planning process. The guide assumes that you have determined your learners' linguistic and communicative needs; it also requires that you obtain information on your students' learning processes. That is, what learning strategies do they already use? What knowledge have they acquired about language learning? Will they be willing and sufficiently confident to undertake autonomous learning? In Chapter 6, you will look at ways of collecting such information.

Valuable readings

In this chapter it is suggested that the selection of learner training content for promoting autonomy be based on the language learning task suggested by learners' communicative and linguistic needs. For a discussion of the issues related to task-based language learning see Candlin and Murphy (1987), specifically the articles by Candlin (Towards task based language learning) and Breen (Learner contributions to task design). For examples of task-based learner training projects which integrate strategies with relevant metacognitive knowledge see Acton (1984), Casanave (1988) and Carrell (1985).

Notes

1. See Chapter 2, note 1, for the learner strategy research in second-language learning upon which the content schema is based.
2. With the exception of one ('Dead people are peaceful' (Stanford, 1976)), the lectures referred to in this series of lessons are taken from *Mosaic I: A listening/speaking book* (Ferrer and Whalley, 1985). The special materials devised to go with the lesson (e.g. model notes and evaluation guide) were prepared by the author.
3. At first students may find it strange to 'say or write what they are thinking'. They may not exactly know what is expected of them. Therefore, encourage them to say *whatever* they are thinking. Also assure them that if they are not thinking anything, it is perfectly acceptable to say so. Another alternative is for the teacher to demonstrate what they are expected to do.

Chapter 6

Getting information on students' learning processes

Focus   Suppose you asked your students to read a short passage and 'figure out' the main idea. How could you determine what they actually do to complete this task?

Process   • Getting information on students' learning processes
            • Using self-reports

Outcome   Procedures for analyzing, recording and planning with information from self-reports

Three ways of getting information on students' language learning processes

6.1 Examining three ways of getting information on students' learning processes

The following are examples of three different ways of getting information on students' language learning processes. Read each example to determine answers to the following questions.

(a) Does the information in the example relate to one task and/or setting or to several?

(b) How close is the information provided in the example to the actual time when the task was done?

(c) How generalized is the information (Examples 2 and 3 only)?

(d) What kind of information about the students' learning processes is provided in each example?

(e) How factual is the information?

Observation

In this example, an ESL student was writing a composition at a word processor. The teacher sat next to her as she wrote and noted down all the student's nonverbal behaviors (e.g. staring into space, gestures) and her unsolicited verbal behaviors (e.g. she asked the teacher a question; she reread her writing aloud). The observation lasted about two hours. A total of eight students were observed in this way.[1]

Self-report 1

This next example is an excerpt of the transcript of one of the eight students referred to in the first example who was writing a composition on whether or not illegal aliens should be made to return to their native countries. Whenever she stopped writing, the teacher asked her to tell what she had just been thinking before the pause or what she was actually thinking at the time of the pause.

LEARNER ACCOUNT 6.1 — EXCERPT FROM AN INTROSPECTIVE REPORT

I was thinking of the way — I told you — how to write and everything . . . I decided it's a big problem and my idea is that they don't have to go back to their native countries. But I'm going to give first why is the problem and then I'm going . . . uh . . . you know the against — the plus and against . . . . But my opinion I will try to put my opinion that they don't have to go back to their countries.

. . . Now I'm just trying to put it in the way that I am thinking . . . to give first a general idea . . . to put everything that I want and maybe I'm going to change.

[*Writes the next sentence and rereads it aloud.*]

. . . I like the ideas but I don't like the place. I'm going to change the place and the grammar. But now I want to put down my ideas in the right order.

[*Starts the third sentence and halfway through rereads aloud . . . .*]

I don't like — you know — the way that I put . . . . I have the idea in my mind but I can't express what I want to say. I don't like the way that I wrote. I want to put it out [and she deletes it]. It's not a fact.

Self-report 2

This third example is an excerpt from a semi-structured interview. The interviewer (the student's teacher) asked general questions about those settings in which the learner had said he used English in a typical week, and, once the general question was asked, interrupted only to keep him on topic or to move him to another topic once a particular one had been exhausted. In the first part of the excerpt he reports on how his writing improved and why; in the next, he evaluates his writing course.

LEARNER ACCOUNT 6.2 — EXCERPTS FROM A RETROSPECTIVE REPORT

1

S: Now I don't have to think first. The words and the sentence come fluently. It's like speaking my own language. And I am very happy of that to overcome that big wall between Spanish and English which is thinking in Spanish and speaking in English.

I: How was this wall overcome?

S: Maybe because, uh, you know that Spanish is different from English and second because the way of writing and the way of thinking is different. It's not the same thing 'I love you' or 'you are my friend', you know. It's completely different. You have a different way of saying things and you say something and maybe you are not saying what are you thinking. Or maybe . . .

I: You realized that?

S: Yeah. I realized that if you think in Spanish, in English it is not the same thing.

I: When did you start realizing that? How did you start realizing that?

S: Well, by experience or by studying or by talking to persons.

I: Can you give me an example?

S: Yeah, for example, when I started writing I was doing this and this and this but you say it in that way. You are more precise and more conscious. In Spanish we are very romantic. We use several words in one sentence to explain what are you trying to speak of. But in English you say a word and it means all the things and if you say the same word and then you use a synonym, then another word that means the same thing and the person who is listening to you will say well she's saying the same thing all the time.

I: So you noticed this . . .

S: Yeah, while I was taking an English course.

I: You noticed about this redundancy while taking your course?

S: Yeah and then I had to change.

I: You changed?

S: Yes. It was very hard because when I tried to, you know, when I had a composition for example, about population or whatever, you know what are your mistakes in that type of composition, but if you have another type of composition which is completely different in the meaning, word, sentences, it is difficult . . . .

2

I: What else did you find useful in the course?

S: Writing . . . the professor points out your mistakes. It makes you change. Still when you try to be better, you make more mistakes than when you don't pay attention to it. When you notice you make more mistakes, you feel bad for the teacher who is giving part of her life for this. So I put more effort into my compositions but the more you think in your own language the more errors you make.

I: What did you do with the errors?

S: I read them and tried to understand the correction. I changed the sentence but until you really understand the error, in a new composition the error appears again because it is a new topic. For me speaking is easier than writing.

Differences between observation and two kinds of self-reports

To collect information on how students approach a learning task, a teacher may observe them as they perform a task or have them describe what they do. This second way is called self-report. Self-reports may be tied to a task, i.e. students report on what they do *while* they perform a particular task or just after, or about one language learning task or several that took place quite some time before the interview. Each of these approaches may be distinguished from the other in four ways.

1. Recency: How closely linked in time is the report to the event that is being reported on? Is it reported while the event is going on? Just after? Or some time after?
2. Specificity: Is the learner reporting on a particular learning or communication task

(e.g. learning vocabulary; listening to a speech) or what is happening in a particular setting (in a restaurant or classroom) or on several events of the same nature? Is the report an unedited 'play-by-play' description of the event or is it more analyzed and edited?

3. Content: What kind of information does it reveal on a learner-as-learner? Does the report focus primarily on strategies? Metacognitive knowledge? Attitudes towards autonomy?

4. Accuracy: To what extent is what the learner saying factual or assumed?[2]

Observation

Some limited information on students' learning processes may be gained by observing them in the classroom as they perform a range of language learning or communication tasks. Teachers may assign a task to a whole class and observe the students as they complete it. Learners can be observed *while* one is teaching them — in a less systematic manner or by video-taping the lesson and analyzing it. In the first example, individual students were observed as they completed a writing task at the word processor.

The kinds of behaviors noted during the eight sessions were as follows.

- *Nonverbal behaviors*
  Reread silently what had been written
  Looked up
  Reread the assigned composition topics
  Paused
  Used gestures
  Referred to dictionary
  Used quotes to emphasize an idea
  Deleted words/sentences
  Changed/added/substituted what had been written

- *Verbal behaviors*
  Asked researcher for information
  Asked researcher for verification
  Reread aloud what had been written
  Read aloud while writing

Students were observed rereading and revising what they wrote; they referred to the dictionary for information, or they asked the teacher either to clarify the task or to verify that what they had done was correct. In other words, observable behavior can be both nonverbal and verbal. Interviews and conferences with language learners can often provide information on the latter kind.[3]

Observed behaviors are tied to one task, which is performed in a classroom setting or in a conference setting with a teacher. There is no separation in time between what is observed and the performance of the task. Ordinarily, these behaviors will represent strategies that a learner is actually using at the time, but for the greater part the strategies are limited to those that are accompanied by a specific overt behavior, such as asking a question, looking up a word in a dictionary, underlining a word.

Of course, what learners intend by what they are seen doing is not clear. When writers reread a sentence they have just written, are they evaluating it? When they take out a dictionary, are they looking for a word? For example, the writer in Learner Account 6.1 was not only evaluating when she reread her sentence: she indicated in the self-report that she was also having trouble expressing her ideas — she was monitoring. Moreover, though she took out her dictionary, she never really used it. Then, how is one to interpret a pause, looking up, gestures — all behaviors used by the writers observed in example 1. Clearly in such cases a learner's intent must be assumed, and the assumption may not always be accurate.

Introspective self-reports

A second way of getting information on students' learning processes is to assign a task and have them tell you what they are thinking as they are completing the task. That is, students can be asked to *think aloud* or *introspect*, orally reporting to a listener or into a tape recorder or writing down what they are thinking while doing a task. At the outset, many students may be uncomfortable with the idea of thinking aloud, but researchers and teachers who have used this technique maintain that they learn quickly.

Very simply, training procedures require that, first, students be told what they are going to be doing and why. It may be necessary to illustrate what kind of response is appropriate. For example, students may be asked to solve some sort of mental problems and as they are solving the problem they may be stopped and asked to repeat exactly what they were thinking when interrupted.[4] Teachers may model think aloud for the students and then allow them to practise. Feedback during the practice time should help students distinguish between thoughts they have had before (retrospective information) and what they are thinking 'at the moment' (introspective information).

Introspective self-reports are often collected with one student at a time. In the second example, the student was writing a composition at the word processor. It is also possible to collect introspective data by working with whole classes at one time. In the listening class described in Chapter 5, for example, it is suggested that the teacher lecture and at certain points in the lecture stop and ask students to write down what they are thinking at that moment. Some researchers (e.g. Raimes, 1985) have had whole classes think aloud while writing. The whole group was given an assignment and asked to complete the task in a language laboratory where they could write and speak into a tape recorder at the same time. In this type of situation (i.e. the writing), the teacher remains free to guide those students who may need help with 'thinking aloud'.

Introspective reporting is tied to the specific learning task or event that the student is talking about. It is a report on one learning or communication task that takes place in a particular setting. As students complete the task, they verbalize their thought processes, so there is no separation in time between the report and the task.

The extent to which an introspective report may be edited and/or analyzed varies. In some cases, thinking aloud is like assuming the role of sportscaster and player in a soccer game at one and the same time. One plays (learns/does a task) and provides a description of what is happening, making it impossible to edit or analyze. In such cases, the self-report is a verbalization of one's stream of consciousness. In other cases, thinking aloud can be more like being a player and a participant observer of one's own play. At one and the same time one plays (learns/does a task) and observes the play (learning) by standing back to note what is happening and to describe it. These think aloud reports will be somewhat edited and analyzed. The second example (Learner Account 6.1) is an example of this second type of introspective report.[5]

Introspective reports provide information primarily on the strategies that learners are actually using to perform a particular task at the time they are reporting. The following is an analysis of the introspective self-report presented earlier (Learner Account 6.1).

PLANNING: she decides what her view is on the topic and how she is going to present it (i.e. on rhetorical structure)
I was thinking of the way — I told you — how to write and everything . . . . I decided it's a big problem and my idea is that they don't have to go back to their native countries. But I'm going to give first why is the problem and then I'm going . . . uh . . . you know the against — the plus and against. . . . But my opinion I will try to put my opinion that they don't have to go back to their countries. . . .

MONITORING: she is trying to find words to express her ideas
Now I'm just trying to put it in the way that I am thinking . . .

PLANNING: she announces her choice of production strategy
. . . to give first a general idea . . . to put everything that I want and maybe I'm going to change. . . .

EVALUATION: she evaluates what she's written
[*Writes the next sentence and rereads it aloud.*] I like the ideas but I don't like the place.

PLANNING: she announces her decision to revise
I'm going to change the place and the grammar.

PLANNING: she announces a revised production strategy
But now I want to put down my ideas in the right order.

EVALUATING: she evaluates how she has expressed her idea
[*Starts the third sentence and halfway through rereads aloud*] . . . I don't like — you know — the way that I put . . . .

MONITORING: she is experiencing difficulty because of her limited linguistic repertoire
I have the idea in my mind but I can't express what I want to say.

EVALUATING: she is looking either at what she wrote and/or how she wrote it
. . . I don't like the way that I wrote. . . . It's not a fact.

PLANNING: she decides to revise and does so
. . . I want to put it out [and she deletes it].

In this brief excerpt, the learner's main emphasis is on self-management strategies. Her statements suggest that she is planning, monitoring and evaluating. She announces several decisions: what she plans to write about; how she is going to organize her ideas; that she plans to revise; which production strategy she will use. These are all evidences of planning. She further indicates that she is having difficulty expressing her ideas (monitoring) and checks her writing for content and mode of expression (evaluating).

When students introspect, since they report what they are doing *while* completing the task, it is assumed that the report is fairly accurate. Of course, for language learners who have to use their second language to report on a task they are doing in that same language, this may be especially difficult. The concentration put on thinking aloud might detract from their ability to do the task efficiently. Second, the report may not always be so precise or exact since it is not done in their native language. Finally, if what students report is fairly accurate, it should not always be interpreted as being comprehensive. They might use more strategies if they did not have to think aloud, for the very act of thinking aloud may slow down the actual processing of information and so reduce the number of strategies they might otherwise use. Besides, at another time, they could use other strategies.

Retrospective self-reports

Language learners can also be asked to think back or retrospect on their language learning and to write about it. Retrospective self-reports vary in the extent to which they limit what a student may say.

Open-ended reports

Some retrospective self-reports can be quite open ended. For example, students can be asked to complete fairly open-ended statements:

1. 'When I listen to . . . . in my second language, I sometimes have difficulty getting the meaning.' Why? What do you do?
2. 'Listening to . . . . in my second language is quite hard for me.' Tell why. What do you do?

As students write or respond orally to such statements, they are allowed to follow their own train of thought with no limit put on what they say. Teachers simply provide a question or statement that points to the topic in a very general way and students are allowed to respond as they wish. Of course, questions can be asked to help students clarify and expand their ideas, but in each case the focus remains on what the student was saying. Diaries (e.g. Rivers, 1979) are another example of an open-ended approach.

Semi-structured interviews

Retrospective reporting can be more focused, as in a semi-structured interview. The interview may focus on a specific skill or on one or several social settings in which students typically use English with the questions based on general areas the interviewer wishes to find out about. For example, questions can focus on (1) students' feelings towards the particular skill/setting, (2) the learning or language problems encountered, (3) techniques used to cope with these problems, (4) views on how best to approach the skill/learning task under discussion and (5) the utility of the task as a means of improving/learning the language. These oral semi-structured interviews can be conducted with one student at a time or with small groups. Learner Account 6.2 is an example of a semi-structured interview.

Retrospective reports, which are focused in a manner similar to the semi-structured interview, can also be written. A survey questionnaire, like the one used in the listening course (Chapter 5), is an example. This questionnaire seeks information on a variety of topics but it is also possible to focus the retrospection on a particular task. For example, students may be asked to listen to a short lecture or do a reading and, immediately afterwards, to write answers to questions such as those listed in the preceding paragraph. Of course, in such a situation, it is not possible to probe or clarify.

Unlike the open-ended interview which allows for free reporting, in a more focused or 'semi-structured' interview the questions outline the areas within which students are free to report, and the teacher/interviewer must keep the students on the topic, probing to help students clarify their ideas and/or to ascertain what they mean. Then, when it is felt that the area covered by one of the questions is exhausted, the interviewer leads the learner on to the next one.

Structured questionnaires

The most restrictive type of retrospective self-report is the structured questionnaire. Techniques devised to collect information on students' learning processes in this way are explicit and specific about the kind of information they seek, and students are asked (1) to agree or disagree, (2) to write true or false and (3) to answer yes or no to a series of statements or questions. Sometimes they may be asked to represent the strength of their views by choosing a number from 1 to 5. The good language learner questionnaire (Table 8.3) is an example.

Retrospective reports may be collected on a series of similar tasks that have been done in a variety of settings quite some time after they have taken place. The student in the third example, for instance, was not talking about a specific writing task but about a number of writing tasks he had done at different times over a period of several years. Retrospective reports are analyzed and edited — the learner generalizes from his experience to make a particular point about it and leaves out many other details.

Unlike introspective reporting which provides information on strategies that students use while doing a task, think back or retrospective reporting is primarily a source of insight on what learners know about their language learning, i.e. their metacognitive knowledge. Some statements in retrospective reports can also point to the use of self-management strategies. An analysis of the third example (Learner Account 6.2) is given below.

1

TASK KNOWLEDGE: writing no longer requires deliberate effort
Now I don't have to think first. . . .

SELF-ASSESSMENT: he refers to the facility with which he is now able to write
The words and the sentence come fluently. It's like speaking my own language. . . .

PERSON KNOWLEDGE: he refers to his feelings
And I am very happy of that to overcome that big wall between Spanish and English which is thinking in Spanish and speaking in English.
[*How was this wall overcome?*]

TASK KNOWLEDGE: he refers to his knowledge of the nature of language (i.e. Spanish and English)
Maybe because, uh, you know that Spanish is different from English and second because the way of writing and the way of thinking is different. It's not the same thing 'I love you' or 'you are my friend', you know. It's completely different. You have a different way of saying things and you say something and maybe you are not saying what you are thinking. Or maybe . . .

[*You realized that?*]

TASK KNOWLEDGE: nature of language
I realized that if you think in Spanish, in English it is not the same thing.

[*When did you start realizing that? How did you start realizing that?*]

Well, by experience or by studying or by talking to persons.

[*Can you give me an example?*]

Yeah, for example, when I started writing I was doing this and this and this but you say it in that way. You are more precise and more conscious. In Spanish we are very romantic. We use several words in one sentence to explain what are you trying to speak of. But in English you say a word and it means all the things and if you say the same word and then you use a synonym, then another word that means the same thing and the person who is listening to you will say well she's saying the same thing all the time.

[*You noticed about this redundancy while taking your course?*]

PLANNING: he decided to change his way of writing
Yeah and then I had to change.

[*You changed?*]

TASK KNOWLEDGE: he refers to how new topics can be difficult and why
Yes. . . . It was very hard because when I tried to, you know, when I had a composition for example, about population or whatever, you know what are your mistakes in that type of composition, but if you have another type of composition which is completely different in the meaning, word, sentences, it is difficult. . . .

2
[*What else did you find useful in the course?*]

EVALUATING: he specifies why writing was useful and also notes the outcome of trying to monitor his writing more carefully
Writing . . . the professor points out your mistakes. It makes you change. Still when you try to be better, you make more mistakes than when you don't pay attention to it. . . .

PERSON KNOWLEDGE: he refers to the feelings evoked by his errors
When you notice you make more mistakes, you feel bad for the teacher who is giving part of her life for this. . . .

TASK KNOWLEDGE: he realizes there is a need for more conscious control — a more deliberate approach
So I put more effort into my compositions. . . .

EVALUATING: he tells what happened when he tried to monitor his writing
. . . but the more you think in your own language the more errors you make. . . .

STRATEGIC KNOWLEDGE: he reports on strategies he used to deal with his errors

[*What did you do with the errors?*]

I read them and tried to understand the correction. I changed the sentence. . . .

TASK KNOWLEDGE: he acknowledges the special difficulty of a new task
. . . but until you really understand the error, in a new composition the error appears again because it is a new topic. . . .

TASK KNOWLEDGE: he refers to the level of difficulty of two different types of task
For me speaking is easier than writing.

In this report, the learner refers to all three types of metacognitive knowledge described in Chapter 3. He refers to feelings evoked by his progress and by the difficulties he faced (person knowledge). He recognizes (1) when deliberate learning is necessary, (2) when a task may be hard and (3) differences between Spanish and English (task knowledge). Finally, he refers to strategies he used (strategic knowledge). Some of his statements also reveal the use of self-management strategies. In part 1 he assesses the facility with which he is now able to write (self-assessment) and refers to a decision to change his way of writing (planning). In part 2, he refers to the utility of writing as a strategy for improving his English and on two occasions to the outcome of trying to monitor his writing more closely (evaluating).[6]

Retrospective reports can also be a source of insight on a learner's attitudes towards autonomous learning. Often it is necessary to infer this information as learners will not explicitly refer to their feelings about learning independently. Learner Account 6.2 suggests that the writer was self-confident and willing to take an active role in his learning. He appears to have persisted in trying to improve his writing despite difficulty; he recognized the need to be more personally involved, i.e. 'make a greater effort'; and he had clearly spent time trying to figure out the cause of his difficulty with writing (see his analysis of the differences between Spanish and English).

As a source of information on strategies learners actually use in a *particular situation*, retrospective reports may not always be exactly accurate. Sometimes learners will have forgotten what they actually do and so will tell us what they think they did or what they think they should have done. However, these reports are a useful source of information on learners' metacognitive knowledge, including the strategies they generally use.

Table 6.1 summarizes the differences between observation and the two kinds of self-report discussed above.

TABLE 6.1
Differences between observation and self-report

	Observation	Introspection	Retrospection
Recency			
During task	×	×	
Just after task			×
Some time after			×
Number of events and settings			
One	×	×	
More than one			×
Level of generalization	not relevant		
Unedited/unanalyzed		×	
Some editing/analysis		×	
Edited and analyzed			×
Primary kind of content			
Strategies	×	×	
Metacognitive knowledge			×
Attitudes			×

6.2   Using observation and self-respect to collect information on a reading task

In this set of tasks, you will practise using observation and self-report to get information on how language learners approach a reading task.

(a)   Think about a student you are presently teaching.
   (i)   Do you consider the student a good reader?
   (ii)   List the reasons why you do.
   (iii)   List the reasons why you do not.
   (iv)   What problems does the student appear to have with reading?
(b)   Interview this same student about her/his general approach to reading. Use the following questions as a guide, probing and asking questions to clarify in order to make the report as complete as possible. The interview should be recorded.
   (i)   Do you like reading in your second language? Why?
   (ii)   What particular difficulties do you encounter?
   (iii)   How do you deal with them?
   (iv)   What advice would you give a language learner about reading in a second language? How should they do it? Why?
   (v)   Do you find reading in a second language a useful way to improve your English? Why?
(c)   Give this student an in-class silent reading assignment and list the behaviors you observe during the first 15 minutes of the task.
(d)   Have the same student continue with the reading and ask him/her to think aloud as he/she reads, as the student in the second example did (Learner Account 6.1). Tape record her comments.

6.3   Comparing observation and self-report of a reading task

Listen to the information obtained from the think aloud report and the interview. Examine your observation notes.

(a)   How many events and/or settings does the learner refer to in each report?
(b)   Compare the level of generalization used in each type of report.
(c)   What kind of information does each type of report provide on your student's learning processes? What kind of information did the observation provide?
(d)   How accurate do you consider the information from each source to be, i.e. the think aloud, the interview and the observation?
(e)   Which method of getting information do you prefer? Why?

6.4   Using observation and self-report to get information on how students learn

In the previous task, you considered the differences between observation and self-report. In this task you will determine how these two forms of getting information can work together. Can observation be used as a means of generating hypotheses about students' approach to learning? Can self-report techniques be used to get information to confirm or disconfirm these guesses?

(a) Devise a language learning task that will require your students to interact in small groups.
(b) Observe one of the groups, noting all behaviors both verbal and nonverbal.
(c) Note down what you have learned about particular students from this task.
(d) Use this information to generate a few questions you would like answered about the learning processes of one student.
(e) Use both self-report techniques to collect information that will provide insight into this problem.
(f) Assess the information you have received from the self-report.
    (i) Did it answer the question(s) you had raised?
    (ii) If yes, was the answer adequate?
    (iii) Were other questions raised?

6.5   Using two forms of retrospective reporting to get information on students' writing processes

In this task, you will see how information from a semi-structured survey and from a structured questionnaire can work together.

(a) Devise and administer a writing survey which makes your students retrospect on various aspects of the writing process.
(b) Analyze the responses to each question on the survey to determine the points that most students hold in common and those for which there is a range of opinion.
(c) Use the findings from the survey to construct a structured questionnaire about your students' approach to writing.
    (i) Use those opinions from the survey that students agreed and disagreed about to make statements and questions.
    (ii) Decide how many responses students may choose from: a dichotomous pair (e.g. true or false; agree or disagree); a graduated range of opinion (e.g. always true, sometimes true, rarely true, never true).
(d) Administer the questionnaire.
(e) Analyze the answers obtained from the structured questionnaire and compare your findings with the findings from the semi-structured written survey.
(f) What do the above tasks reveal about the relationship between these two ways of collecting information on students' learning processes?

Using self-reports

6.6 Assessing the utility of observation and self-report

(a) Compare the information you obtained on your students' reading processes (Task 6.2, (b)−(d)) with what you listed in your initial assessment (Task 6.2(a)).

(b) List insights obtained and/or confirmed by the information.

(c) How can you use information obtained through observation and self-report?

Ways of using self-reports

Self-reports can be diagnostic

At the outset of any language class teachers try to determine what level of language proficiency students bring to the class by administering a language diagnostic test (e.g. a grammar test, a writing task, general class discussion). It is also important that they try to determine how their students learn, specifically how they approach the particular language learning task that will be the objective of the course. What strategies do they use? What knowledge have they acquired about it? What are their attitudes towards this task? Self-reports can be used to collect this information.

For example, in the listening course outlined in Chapter 5, students are asked to think aloud during the first lecture. While the purpose of this task is to introduce students to the concept 'strategy', such reports can also be used to determine what kind of strategies the students are already using. Similarly, the survey questionnaire given at the outset of the listening course can be used to get information on students' metacognitive knowledge and the attitudes they hold towards autonomous learning as it applies to listening. Information about students' learning processes acquired in this way can then be used, together with the planning guide presented in Chapter 5, to select content for learning plans.

Self-reports can also provide insight into the problems of unsuccessful language learners

Often students who are not making progress in learning their second language are unsuccessful because of the way they learn. They may be 'inactive' learners — not using strategies and hoping to assimilate everything without effort, or limited in the range of strategies they use. Some may use inappropriate strategies because they do not monitor or evaluate their use of these strategies and so do not realize that the strategies are not 'working'. Moreover, the knowledge that they have acquired about the learning process can unconsciously influence their choice of strategy, as can their attitudes towards autonomous learning. This lack of success may be limited to one skill or it may extend to all four skills.

Both retrospective and introspective self-reports can be a useful source of information on the cause of these problems. Retrospective reports can provide information about students' attitudes and beliefs while introspective reports can serve as a means of pinpointing the strategies they use. Is it a case of their acquired knowledge? Of their attitudes? Or is it a case of their strategies? Insights gained from both reports should enable a teacher to make more informed hypotheses or diagnosis about a particular learner's difficulty and lead to more effective plans for intervention.

Self-reports can be a means of raising awareness

One of the objectives of learner training is to help learners become aware of how they learn, for without awareness they will remain trapped in their old patterns of beliefs and behaviors and never be fully autonomous. Retrospective reporting, especially the open-ended and semi-structured techniques, serve this purpose. Questioning students and then allowing them to reflect on various facets of their learning — with probes that facilitate the reflection — makes it possible for students to get to know themselves better as learners. Moreover, once the information collected in this way is analyzed and recorded, it can be used as the basis for discussion with students during conferences or suggest topics to write about in a learning journal.

Observation and self-report can provide ongoing information on students' learning processes

Besides helping provide information that can be used to select the learner training content of a particular course or to devise intervention strategies for students with particular problems, self-reports together with observation can help to build up a file of information on the learning processes of each learner. Diagnostic tasks given to aid course planning will need to be supplemented since all these ways of collecting information are limited in the information they can provide at any one sitting. It is also necessary to keep in touch with the changes in the students' learning processes that, hopefully, will result from the learner training that is provided.

Both observation and self-reports can be used for this purpose. Informal observation of students can lead to questions and hypotheses that can be tested more specifically and systematically with self-reports. Information obtained from the initial or 'diagnostic' self-reports can also serve to indicate what kinds of questions to include in the next self-report, administered either to the class as a group or to individual students.

Once this information is analyzed and recorded, teachers can use it to build up a 'learning process file' on each student. Over time, information gathered in the file should give the teacher a picture of a student's overall approach to language learning. Together with the planning guide, this learning process file is another planning tool that teachers can use in selecting the content of learning plans to promote learner autonomy.

Analyzing self-report data

In order to use the information on students' learning processes obtained through self-report, it will first be necessary to analyze it. Table 6.2 lists a set of questions, based on the content schema for learner training, which can be used to guide the analysis of self-reports.

TABLE 6.2
A question outline to guide analysis of self-reports

STRATEGIES

Cognitive strategies
1. What cognitive strategies does the learner report using?
2. What is the function of each strategy?
3. What is the name of the strategy? (refer to inventory or taxonomies)

Self-management strategies
4. Does the learner refer to his objectives? Prioritize them in anyway? Or determine in which order they will be done?
5. How does the learner assess his knowledge and skills in the language?
6. What aspects of his language learning does he evaluate? What criteria does he use?

METACOGNITIVE KNOWLEDGE

Person
7. What statements refer to affective factors? To cognitive factors?
8. Are these statements personal? Or do they refer to the learning process in general?

Strategic
9. Does the learner refer to 'best strategies'? Which are they?
10. What general guidelines for language learning does the learner report following (e.g. the best way is . . .; it is better to . . .?

Task
11. What does the learner perceive to be the purpose of the language learning tasks or objectives described in the self-report?
12. What knowledge has the learner acquired about the nature of language? Communication? Learning? About particular language learning tasks he undertakes?
13. Which aspects of his language learning does the learner find difficult?

ATTITUDES

14. Does the report show the learner taking initiative in his learning?
15. Does the report reveal the learner to be confident in his ability to learn and to self-direct his learning?

6.7 Analyzing information from self-reports

In Task 6.3 you were asked to do an informal analysis of the reading self-reports. In this set of tasks you will be given practice analyzing the data more closely and more systematically by using the questions outlined in Table 6.2.

(a) Use the questions (Table 6.2) to analyze both the think aloud report and the interview of the reading task.

(b) Look at the responses to the writing survey you administered (Task 6.5) and analyze the answers.

(c) See Table 5.2 for excerpts of the responses of three students to an introspective task administered as part of the course on notetaking (Chapter 5). Use the questions to analyze these reports.

(d) Reflect on your use of the questions (Table 6.2) to determine whether they need to be revised and, if so, how. Or perhaps you may wish to consider another use of self-reports.

Recording information from self-reports

Once the data are analyzed, it is necessary to record them in an organized fashion so that they may be examined for insights necessary to any of the purposes outlined earlier (i.e. planning, conferencing, developing learner process files, sorting out special learning problems). Table 6.3 is an example of a process grid used to record Laszlo's use of strategies.

Process grids can be organized to highlight different kinds of information. Table 6.3 focuses on the three different types of strategies that Laszlo used and the particular language skill that is the focus of each strategy. (Evaluation is the exception as the focus of this strategy

TABLE 6.3
A process grid for strategies

Strategies	Language skills
Cognitive	
Attending	
Read a verb book	Grammar
Attends to NS in context of need	Vocabulary
Comprehend	
Refers to dictionary	Vocabulary
Asks friends to explain	Vocabulary
Infers meaning	Vocabulary
Thinks about meaning	Vocabulary
Store	
Associates meaning/object	Vocabulary
Practise (retrieve)	
Recalls word during the day	Vocabulary
Uses new words in conversation	Vocabulary
Makes sentences with words	Vocabulary
Connects error to context	Errors
Goes out with friends	Oral fluency
Changes job	Oral fluency
Self-management	
Planning	
To learn a lot in a short time	General
To acquire English in ten years	General
Monitor/self-assessment	
Can't express ideas in a practical (authentic) way	Oral expression
Couldn't catch what others say	Aural comprehension
Understand a lot of words	Aural comprehension
Evaluation	
Outcome	*Strategy*
Speak more/make improvement	Living in the United States
Learned only words/expressions	Reading a verb book
Continued to think in natural language	Using a target language/natural language dictionary
Can avoid thinking in natural language	Using a Webster's dictionary
No opportunity to speak	First job

was not a language skill but a cognitive strategy.) However, the information can be recorded to highlight the strategies, knowledge and attitudes specific to the learner's performance of one particular language skill or a learner's metacognitive knowledge as it applies to all aspects of his language learning. Once the material is organized on the grid, it can be added to the information that makes up the teacher's learning process file on that particular learner, form the basis for a student conference and lead to an intervention plan designed by both student and teacher.

6.8   Recording information from self-reports

In the following tasks you will devise your own process grids for recording information collected through self-reports.

(a)   Refer to your analysis of your student's reading reports (Task 6.7) and devise a form that would be appropriate to record the information on the strategies, knowledge and attitudes revealed by that analysis.

(b)   Use the same form to record the analysis of Ilse's strategies, metacognitive knowledge and attitudes (Chapters 2—4). Make any revisions to your grid suggested by this application.

(c)   Laszlo's acquired knowledge about the language learning process is analyzed in Chapter 3. Devise a form that can be used to record this kind of information.

Planning with information from self-reports

Table 6.4 outlines questions you can use to interpret self-reports. Based on the outline for analysis (Table 6.2), these questions look for relationships between various aspects of the learning process revealed by the analysis and between the learning process and the learner's communicative and linguistic needs. In the following set of tasks you will practise using the outline to interpret self-reports and then plan interventions based on your interpretation.

6.9   Examining the information from Laszlo's process grid

Use the interpretation outline to determine what the information on Laszlo's process grid (Table 6.3) reveals to you about his approach to language learning.

6.10   Planning with the information from Laszlo's process grid

Although Laszlo had been in the United States two years at the time of the interview, he still had difficulty expressing his ideas in conversation — he was not fluent. Of course, he communicated a good deal of information during the interview, but it took him quite some time to express his ideas. There were long pauses, hesitations and false starts not reflected in the account.

(a)   What insights does the process grid provide regarding the reasons for this problem?

TABLE 6.4
Question outline for interpreting self-reports

This outline is based on the outline for analysis, the main difference being that, to interpret, you will look for relationships between the questions and between the questions and the learner's linguistic and communicative needs.

Learning strategies

Metacognitive
1. Objectives
   Does she have any? Are they global? Specific? Relevant? Realistic?
   Are they related to her self-assessment (of her language/learning problems)?
   Are they related to her teacher's asessment of her proficiency?

2. Self-assessment
   Is the learner capable of assessing her proficiency?
   If so, what does she perceive her strengths and weaknesses to be?
   Does her assessment correspond with your view? Her teacher's?
   Is it related to her communicative needs?
   Does she monitor her performance/learning — while using/learning the language?
   What does she notice when she does? Is this awareness related to her self-assessment?

3. Evaluating
   Does she evaluate her use of strategies? By what criteria? Is it related to her self assessment? To her objectives?
   Her teacher's assessment of her proficiency? Her communicative needs?

Cognitive strategies
For which skills does she deploy the most strategies? Are they appropriate to their purpose? Are they evaluated?
Are they related to her stated objectives? Her self-assessment? Her teacher's assessment?

Knowledge/beliefs

Consider the knowledge she has acquired about herself (person), language learning task(s) (task) and how to approach language learning or a particular task (strategic) to see whether these beliefs shed light on (1) her choice and use of strategies and (2) the way she regulates/manages her learning (planning, monitor/self-assess, evaluate). Does her acquired knowledge need to be changed? Expanded? Revised?

Attitudes

Did the analysis reveal her attitudes towards her capability and role in language learning? If so, do these attitudes appear to influence her beliefs? Her use of strategies? If so how? Do they need to be changed?

(b) Plan a conference you would have with Laszlo using the grid. What would be the objective of this conference? What further information would you seek from him?

(c) Devise an intervention plan that you would use to help Laszlo deal with his main problem. Refer to information from the grid as you plan.

6.11 Examining information from two reading self-reports
In this task use the interpretation outline (Table 6.4) to interpret your record of your student's reading self-reports, both the think aloud and the interview.

6.12 Planning with information from two reading self-reports
What insights does the process grid provide regarding the reasons for the student's problem(s)?

(a) Plan a conference you would have with the student using the grid. What would be the objective of this conference? What further information would you seek?

(b) Devise an intervention plan that you would use to help the student deal with his reading problems and/or further expand and refine his skills as a reader. Refer to information from the grid as you plan.

Conclusion

In this chapter, you have looked at ways of collecting, analyzing and recording information on your students' learning processes. This information can be used at the outset of a course to select learner training content appropriate to the needs of your class. Collected over the length of a course, it can provide insight on the problems and approach to learning of individual students. The last tasks in the chapter have suggested that you use this information to devise intervention plans to help students deal with these problems. In the next two chapters, you will look at guidelines for developing such plans — for individual students and for whole classes.

Valuable readings

Cohen (1987)'s article describes three different kinds of self-report data and a rationale for using this approach to collecting information on students' learning processes. Cohen and Hosenfeld's article (1981) on some uses of mentalistic data outlines some of the thinking that led to Cohen's (1987) article. Both articles are written from a researcher's point of view.

The following publications are more practical.

Hosenfeld (1976) illustrates guidelines to be used in getting students to think aloud. Wenden (1985) shows how the semi-structured interview can be used to collect information on student's learning processes during a teacher conference. Chamot (1987) describes an observation guide and a semi-structured interview guide used to collect information specifically on the strategies of high school students.

Horowitz (1987) describes how to go about collecting learner beliefs on any aspect of language learning and how to use this information to generate a survey questionnaire. Willings' report on the learning style research of immigrant adults in Australia (1988) includes an example of a semi-structured interview and structured questionnaire. He also shows how the information from the interviews led to a structured questionnaire.

For other examples of structured questionnaires to collect data on students' strategies see the *Strategy Inventory for Language Learning* (SILL) developed by Oxford (1990) and *The Learning and Study Strategies Inventory* (LASSI) developed by Weinstein (1987). Oxford's version has been developed for learners of other languages and focuses on learning strategies. Weinstein's is designed for college students and measures students' use of learning and study strategies as well as attitudinal factors such as motivation and anxiety.

See Wenden (1983b) for background readings outside the field of language learning pertinent to procedures for collecting learner accounts, and Kahn and Connell (1957) for a discussion of the dynamics of and approach to interviewing.

Notes

1. These eight writers were high intermediate students of English as a second language. The composition they wrote was typical of what they would be expected to write in order to complete the prerequisite necessary to enter the Freshmen English sequence. Besides their ESL course in writing, they were also enrolled in credit-bearing college courses.

2. Some of the ideas in my analysis of verbal report are based on ideas in Cohen (1987). In that article, he distinguishes verbal report data according to the number of participants, contexts, recency, mode, formality and degree of external intervention.

3. See Abraham and Vann (1987) for examples of the kinds of strategies that can be observed during an extended interview.

4. Table 7.1 provides examples of mental problems that can be used to get students to attend to and understand what is meant when they are asked to report what they are thinking.

5. Cohen (1987) describes three types of verbal report data: self-report, self-observation and self-revelation. I have referred to only two of these in this chapter. Self-report, as defined in Cohen (1987), refers to what I have described as think back or retrospective reporting. What I have referred to as think aloud or introspective reporting is viewed as self-observation by Cohen.

6. This self-report illustrates the relationship and overlap between self-management strategies and metacognitive knowledge already mentioned in Chapter 3 (notes 2 and 3). In the excerpts included here, the learner's statement of self-assessment ('the words and the sentence come fluently . . .') can also be considered as acquired person knowledge about his proficiency. The statements of evaluation that refer to the outcome of monitoring his writing more carefully ('Still when you try to be better, you make more mistakes than when you don't pay attention to it . . .') are also evidence of strategic knowledge.

strongood featuring the motin of the Neva River; later bringing the finest European architects to create an elegant ensemble of palatial buildings. Built on a hundred islands and criss-crossed by canals and innumerable bridges it is a city of infinite charm. Nevsky Prospekt, the city's main boulevard, is lined with churches and palaces, restaurants and bars, shops and arcades. Nearby can be found the fine collection of Russian Art at the Russian Museum in Mikhailovskiy Palace. Though still cold in March and April the sites are relatively crowd-free and the exquisite architecture takes on a special appeal in the clear winter air and later as spring starts to take hold.

THE HERMITAGE

Visit the baroque splendour of the Winter Palace and Hermitage of which the highlight is its magnificent collection of European art, founded by Catherine the Great.

THE PALACES

In the Russian countryside at Pushkin, lies the great blue and gold rococo Catherine Palace, reflecting the contrasting styles of the Italian Rastrelli and the Scot Cameron. The nearby avlovsk Imperial Palace is a Palladian ansion in a landscaped park and also signed by Cameron.

ITINERARY – 3 nights

ray 1 Fly from London Gatwick to t. Petersburg and transfer to your bosen hotel.
ray 2 Optional full day city tour includ-ng visits to the Peter and Paul Fortress nd Cathedral and to the Hermitage.

Day 2 Optional ½ day city tour including Peter and Paul Fortress. Optional folkloric show with dinner at Nikolaevsky Palace.
Day 3 Optional morning guided visit to the Hermitage. In the afternoon remain in the Hermitage or explore independently.
Day 4 Optional day excursion visiting Catherine Palace and Pavlovsk Palace.
Day 5 Depart from the hotel after breakfast for a visit to Nevskiy Prospekt. Transfer to airport for return flight to Gatwick.

ITINERARY – 7 nights

Follow the 3-night itinerary (Fridays) or the 4-night itinerary (Mondays) with subsequent days free for independent exploration. The Nevskiy Prospekt visit and airport transfer will be on Day 8.

HOTEL ST. PETERSBURG

Built in 1970, the 3-star hotel St. Petersburg represents simple, good value accommodation with restaurants, bars, shops, sauna and 410 rooms with private facilities and satellite TV – some with river view. Upgrading of hotels since the end of the Soviet era has of necessity been slow but some rooms have been improved and are now classified as renovated. The hotel affords fine views across the river to central St Petersburg. 30 minutes walk along the waterside.

HOTEL PULKOVSKAYA

A 4-star hotel on Victory Square. Opposite the Monument to the Heroic Defenders of the siege of Leningrad, it is located on the city outskirts with direct metro connection to the centre. 840 rooms with private facilities, hairdryer, fridge and satellite TV. Restaurants, cafés, shops and sauna with plunge pool.

DATES & PRICES

per person in a twin room at St Petersburg Hotel

2003 Fridays – 3 nights

Mar 7, 14	£295	Apr 18	£375
Mar 21, 28	£295	Apr 25	£325
Apr 4	£315	May 2	£345
Apr 11	£325	May 9	£345

2003 Mondays – 4 nights

Mar 10, 17	£325	Apr 14	£345
Mar 24, 31	£325	Apr 21, 28	£345
Apr 7	£325	May 5	£375

2003 Mondays – 7 nights

Mar 10, 17	£395	Apr 14	£445
Mar 24, 31	£395	Apr 21, 28	£445
Apr 7	£425	May 5	£495

2003 Fridays – 7 nights

Mar 7, 14	£395	Apr 11, 18	£445
Mar 21, 28	£395	Apr 25	£445
Apr 4	£425	May 5	£495

SUPPLEMENTS

per person
St. Petersburg Hotel
Single room:
£12 per night (May £20 per night)
Renovated twin room :
3 nights £36; 4 nights £48; 7 nights £84
Renovated single room:
£25 per night
Renovated room with river view (twin only):
3 nights £45; 4 nights £60; 7 nights £105
Pulkovskaya Hotel
Twin room:
3 nights £30; 4 nights £40; 7 nights £70
Single room:
£25 per night (May £32 per night)

Optional excursions

City tour with St Peter & Paul fortress and Hermitage (3 night itinerary) £27
City tour with St Peter & Paul fortress (4 night itinerary) £17
Hermitage ½ day (4 night itinerary) £20
Catherine Palace and Pavlovsk Palace £35
Folkloric evening with dinner £25

Price includes: Air travel and taxes, transfers, breakfast daily, itinerary as described, services of local guides, guidebook. Not included: Travel insurance, optional excursions, visa procurement fee, gratuities, any government taxes or compulsory charges introduced after publication. Our current Conditions of Booking (available on request) shall apply to all reservations.

Chapter 7

An action plan for strategies

Focus Imagine a language learner who pulls out his dictionary each time he encounters a new word while reading. What other strategy could he use to figure out the meaning of new words? How can you help him learn to use the strategy?

Process
- An action plan for strategies
- Guidelines for strategy training
- Evaluating the guidelines

Outcome Guidelines for teaching strategies

An action plan for strategies

7.1 Determining the objectives of an action plan for teaching strategies

The purpose of the following action plan is to train students to use 'inferencing', a cognitive strategy. As you read the plan, determine the objective of each session.[1]

INFERENCING: AN ACTION PLAN
_____

Session 1

Resources
Handout: 'Which questions can you answer without thinking?' (Table 7.1).

Procedures
(a) Students read the questions and check those they can answer immediately.
(b) Students figure out the answers to those they have to 'think about'.
(c) Their answers are written on the blackboard.
(d) Students are given the general term for 'what they do when they think', i.e. they use 'strategies'.
(e) They discuss whether and how strategies can help them learn another language.

Special notes
In the discussion teachers should refer to the differences in mental activity involved in answering questions immediately and answering questions after trying to figure out the answer, i.e. the automatic as opposed to the deliberate or conscious use of strategies. In the first instance, mental processing takes place below consciousness because the answer is something they know very well, and in the second the processing becomes conscious because the problem is unfamiliar.

Session 2

Resources
A video recording in which people are interacting in everyday situations. The recording should be in the language the students are learning.

TABLE 7.1
Introducing strategies

READ THE FOLLOWING QUESTIONS.
CIRCLE THE ONES YOU CAN ANSWER 'WITHOUT THINKING'.

1. Does the front door of your home open at the left side or the right?
2. What's George Washington's phone number?
3. How do you get from the bus stop nearest your home to your front door?
4. What's a seven-letter word ending in 'y' that means 'a group of interacting individuals living in the same region and sharing the same culture'?
5. How would you say 'what's the time' in your second language?
6. How would you say 'nuclear disarmament' in your second language?
7. ACORN is to OAK as INFANT is to ....
8. Which word in the following group doesn't belong?

    rose, lily, potato, tulip

9. What's the answer to the following addition?

    $1 + 2 + 3 + 4 + 5 + 6 + 7 + 8 + 9 + 10 =$

10. Memorize the following list of words

    bowl   log   painting   chair
    cup   sock   TV set   cigarette

WHICH OF THE ABOVE PROBLEMS COULD YOU ANSWER RIGHT AWAY 'WITHOUT THINKING'?

Go back to the questions you could not answer 'without thinking', i.e. questions you need to spend more time on.

(1) FIGURE OUT THE ANSWER.
(2) NEXT TO THE ANSWER TELL WHAT YOU DID TO GET IT.

On the other side of the page make a list of what you and your classmates do when you can't figure out an answer to a problem right away, i.e. when you have to consciously think about the answer. These special techniques we will call STRATEGIES.

Source: Adapted from Hunt, 1982

Procedures

(a) Play a five-minute segment of the video recording.
     (i) Students 'think back' and write down the problems they had in understanding during the five-minute segment.
     (ii) They write what they did to help themselves understand.
     (iii) Repeat this procedure two to three times.
(b) Then, continue with the showing of the video, using the following procedures:
     (i) stop every 30 seconds;
     (ii) students write down what they are thinking at that moment.
(c) Collect both types of reports and analyze for strategies that students reported using to help themselves understand.

Special notes

Students will probably not be familiar with what is expected of them when asked to 'write down what you're thinking', and so it will be necessary to show them what to do. After the first few pauses, students can be asked to *tell* what they wrote. The teacher can also demonstrate by thinking aloud and/or writing down her 'thoughts' on the blackboard.

For more hints as to how to prepare learners to introspect refer to Chapter 6, where introspective self-reporting is presented and described.

When doing (b), students should be asked to number their reports, and the place in the recording that corresponds to the number on the students' reports should also be noted.

These reports can also be diagnostic, revealing which strategies students need to learn to use. The action plan assumes that 'inferencing' was one of the strategies and so the remainder of the procedures focus on helping learners to use it.

Session 3

Resources
A videotape in which the nonverbal features of communication are clearly highlighted. Since it will be played without sound, it can be in any language. Tapes of mimes are especially well suited.

Procedures
(a) Play a short segment of the video without sound.
(b) Pause and ask students to tell you what is happening.
(c) Ask how they know.
(d) List the clues the students use on the blackboard.
(e) Repeat (a)–(d) until the various forms of nonverbal communication that serve to communicate meaning in the interaction they are viewing have been listed (e.g. gesture, facial expression). Students should also be helped to become aware of other clues to understanding such as setting, world knowledge and cultural knowledge.
(f) Ask someone to describe the strategy they are using, i.e. what are they doing to figure out what is happening.
(g) Help them to generalize their explanations and write the definition of the strategy on the blackboard.
(h) Ask them whether they can give the strategy a name.
(i) Play another segment of videotape and demonstrate how the strategy works, i.e. the teacher thinks aloud referring to the clues listed on the blackboard to come up with a possible meaning of what has been played.
(j) Students listen and list the clues she refers to.
(k) Other students think aloud to come up with the meaning of other segments with the rest of the class taking down the clues the student has used.
(l) Students may also be encouraged to point out other clues not elicited by the video but which could also be used to infer meaning in an oral/aural context.
(m) The class (or students working in groups) organize the clues listed in the previous procedures into one list.

Special notes
Longman's *Speakeasy* is an example of an excellent mime that can be used for eliciting the list of clues that can be used for inferencing in an aural/oral situation.

If videotapes are not accessible, use pictures that tell a story, making sure that there are no verbal captions under the pictures.

Session 4

Resources

Story line pictures and videotapes of the target language being used in everyday situations.

Procedures

Set A exercises
(a)   The class is divided into groups of three.
(b)   Each group is given the same set of pictures.
(c)   Groups figure out what is happening; they may even be asked to write the dialogue they feel is appropriate.
(d)   They also write down the clues they used to figure out what is happening.
(e)   Groups read their dialogue or tell their story to the class, making explicit the clues upon which their dialogues/stories are based.
 (f)   The teacher may also go over the pictures, thinking aloud as she does so to demonstrate how she would infer meaning.
(g)   Students observe and compare both their classmates' and their teacher's use of clues with their own.

Set B exercises
(a)   The same procedures (a)–(g) can be repeated with each group assigned to work on a different set of stories.

Set C exercises
(a)   The class is divided into groups of three.
(b)   Play a segment of the target language video without sound.
(c)   Students infer what is happening.
(d)   They report their inferences and the clues upon which they are based; these are summarized on the board.
(e)   The video is played with sound and students determine the accuracy of their inferences.

Session 5

Resources

Short videotape segments of people interacting in everyday situations in the language the students are learning. An audiotape of the videotaped conversation.

Procedures

Set A exercises
(a)   Play a segment of the audiotape recording.
(b)   In their groups, students write what they understand and list questions about what they do not understand.
(c)   Write students' reponses to (b) on the blackboard.
(d)   Play the same segment from the videotape, i.e. incorporating sound and picture.
(e)   Using the clues provided by the picture, students determine whether they understood correctly and how completely they understood; they try to answer the questions they had.
 (f)   Students also list what information (other than the answers to their questions) about the theme of the interaction is provided by use of the clues in the picture.

(g) Repeat procedures (a)–(f) with other segments of the recording until the relationship between inferencing and understanding the spoken language becomes clear.
(h) Ask students to discuss why they should use this strategy. How can it help them?

Set B exercises
(a) Student groups list all the places where they hear English during a typical day or week.
(b) Use these lists to compile a general list of social settings where students will hear English.
(c) Discuss the problems they may have in understanding English in these settings.
(d) List the problems on the blackboard.
(e) Students determine which of these problems would be helped by their using the new strategy.

Session 6

Resources
1. A list of television programs to which students have access — list, if possible, news broadcasts, children's programs, soap operas and comedies. These may be programs in the students' target language or in their native language.
2. The list of contexts and listening activities compiled in Session 5.

Procedures

Set A exercises
(a) Ask students to choose one from each type of television program listed and to watch it at home for five minutes with the sound turned off.
(b) Tell them to use inferencing to guess what the program is about and then to turn on the sound to verify their guesses.
(c) Ask them to write up their experience in their learning journal, indicating difficulties they had using the strategy and whether the strategy helped or not and why.

Set B exercises
(a) Ask the students to choose one of the settings or listening activities from the list they compiled (in Session 5) and to use inferencing to help them understand the interaction when it is appropriate.
(b) Ask them to write up their experience in their learning journal, indicating what they could not understand, whether the strategy helped or not and why.

Special notes
These tasks can be repeated over a period of one week, giving students an opportunity to use the strategy in different contexts and with different television programs.

Session 7

Resources
Entries from students' language learning journals based on the tasks assigned in Session 6.

Procedures
(a) Each day, after students' out of class practice, set aside time in class to have them compare journal notes with a classmate or with the class as a group.

(b) Students are asked (1) to determine whether inferencing helped or not and to explain why and (2) to indicate what difficulties they had using the strategy and why.

Special notes

As students discuss their use of the strategy, it is important that they make explicit the clues that they used so that they can be helped to see when and why they were either using inappropriate clues or drawing incorrect conclusions (if that is the case).

They should also be guided in determining appropriate criteria for evaluating the strategy's utility.

(a) Does it help them understand? Understand more? More easily? More accurately?
(b) Does it give them a sense of control over their language learning, specifically their listening problems?
(c) Does it increase their self-confidence?

These discussions should also help students explore the limits of the strategy. When and where should they use it? For example, inferencing may not be as useful for understanding the evening news as it might be in understanding language spoken in

TABLE 7.2
Dear Diary

The following letters are based on authentic student accounts of their language learning. (1) Identify the writer's problem(s) and (2) suggest a solution.

1
Dear Diary,
  These first few days have been terrible. I studied English for eight years . . . just think, eight years, but I only learned a lot of grammar. I can't speak a word. I don't dare. I can't express myself in the right way, so I am afraid to speak.
  The other day I started watching TV, so I could get accustomed to the sound. I don't understand TV news very well . . . only a few words. I can't get the main point. In school it's easy to understand, but I can't understand the people in the stores.
  What can I do?
                    Yours truly,
                    Impatient

2
Dear Diary,
  I've made a few good American friends. We talk about a lot of things. With friends I don't care if I make mistakes. But some people, they talk and talk and talk. So I have to listen. I can't interrupt to speak my opinion. It's very difficult.
  It's even worse when I talk to a professor. I always talk very ridiculously. When I notice that I am speaking ridiculously, I can't talk.
  I need advice!!
                    Yours truly,
                    A silent listener

3
Dear Diary,
  When I first came to the United States, I decided to speak very simply. I try to use short sentences and easy words. But now I think my English is not so good. I can't speak very well. I use only simple words in conversation. I feel my vocabulary is poor. The teacher gives us vocabulary lists, but I don't have time to review them. Really, I feel I'm losing my English.
  Please help me!!
                    Yours truly,
                    An anxious learner

4

Dear Diary,

Well, I finally decided to start using English. I'm going out shopping and eating out in restaurants all by myself. There's no one there to speak English for me. I try, but people don't understand me.

The other day I had to buy a tie. So I thought about what I would say. I prepared everything. I asked the salesgirl for a tie. Then she asked me a question. I couldn't understand her. It was something about the color, I think. We learned a lot of vocabulary in school, but it doesn't help.

What can I do?

        Yours truly,
        Frustrated

5

Dear Diary,

When I came to New York, I was still translating everything from Spanish. I took an English course and I had to write compositions. I found out the way of saying things in English is different from Spanish. I could not say what I was really thinking by translating. It's hard to think in English. The American way of thinking is very different from the Spanish way. How can I suddenly change? How can I learn a new language, a new way of thinking and speaking? I'm trying, but it's really hard. Lately, I seem to be making more and more mistakes.

Can you help me?

        Yours truly,
        Hopeless

6

Dear Diary,

I read the *New York Times* every day. Every day I learn many new expressions — a lot of vocabulary. But I can't use this vocabulary in conversation. The same thing happens with what I learn at school. I can't use it when I want to talk to Americans or even with my own Spanish friends.

I need some help.

        Yours truly,
        Confused

---

everyday contexts while watching movies. Not all strategies can be used efficiently in all contexts. Moreover, sometimes 'inferencing' may help them understand a specific word or expression and in other cases it will help them get the gist of a conversation but not all the details.

Session 8

Resources
1. 'Dear Diary' letters from learners describing their language learning problems, including those related to understanding the spoken language in informal situations (Table 7.2).
2. More videotapes or story line pictures.

Procedures

Set A exercises
Have students read the Dear Diary letters to identify each learner's problem and then to suggest a strategic solution, applying their new strategy where appropriate as well as others they have acquired.

Set B exercises
(a) Play segments from a videotape illustrating different settings and have the students determine what they do not understand.

(b) Replay the video and have them use their new strategy and other strategies that they have learned to use to determine what they are not able to understand in a particular utterance.

(c) Let them know if their final hypothesis is appropriate.

(d) Students evaluate their use of the strategy. Did it work and why/why not? Was it inadequately applied? Was it not as applicable to the listening problem?

Set C exercises

(a) Students may describe difficulties they have in learning or using their new language to a small group of classmates, who will be expected to suggest strategic solutions. Alternatively, they may be asked to write their own Dear Diary letters. These letters can be reproduced and distributed among the class for diagnosis and solution. In suggesting a strategy to use, students are told to choose their *new* strategy, if appropriate, as well as others they have learned to use.

(b) Students try the solutions and write up the results in their learning journal, which is handed in to their teacher for feedback.

Special notes

The Dear Diary letters or other student accounts that teachers may decide to use for review and practice should contain multiple problems. Moreover, these problems should require the use of different types of strategies. In this way, as students' strategic repertoire grows and they have more solutions to match to the analyzed problems, the review tasks will be more challenging.

The learning journal is intended as a means of facilitating a more personal and ongoing dialogue between the student-learner and the counsellor-teacher. The teacher's feedback should raise questions, provide clues, help clarify questions and resolve difficulties.

The purpose of this particular action plan is to train students in the use of 'inferencing', a cognitive strategy. The objectives of each session are as follows:

1. Introduce the concept 'strategy'.
2. Determine the strategies learners use.
3. Demonstrate and name the strategy.
4. Provide in-class practice.
5. Explore the significance of the strategy.
6. Practise in authentic settings.
7. Evaluate the outcome of practice sessions.
8. Provide cyclical review.

Sessions 1 and 2 of the action plan should be done before any formal strategy training takes place. The objective of Session 1 is to introduce students to the concept 'strategy'. The objective of Session 2 is to determine which strategies students already use to comprehend spoken English, and which ones they use inappropriately. This information will then guide the development of a strategy 'syllabus', which can be implemented through the training procedures outlined in Sessions 3–8.

In Session 3 the strategy that is the focus of the training is presented. The tasks are intended to make students observe 'how the strategy works', define it and give it a name. Session

4 provides more practice in using the strategy in class so that students can further clarify the steps involved in using it. Then, in Session 5, students discuss the strategy's significance — considering the relationship between their improved understanding and their use of the strategy. They also determine when or how they can use it to deal with some of their listening problems outside the class. The purpose of Session 6 is to give students the opportunity to use the strategy outside the class in a real life context, and the purpose of Session 7 is to evaluate the outcome of its use. This should lead to a further understanding of how the strategy works. In Session 8 students are given more practice in selecting the type of situation in which it is appropriate to use the strategy so that they can learn to choose it spontaneously and appropriately themselves outside the training situation.

Guidelines for strategy training

Each objective in the action plan is based on one or more of the following principles derived from strategy training research in non-ESL settings.

- *Informed*   Strategy training should be informed. The purpose of the training should be made explicit and its value brought to the students' attention.
- *Self-regulation*   Students should be trained how to regulate or oversee the use of the strategy, i.e. when it is appropriate to use it; the difficulties they have implementing it; and its effectiveness.
- *Contextualized*   Strategies should be contextualized. Training should be in the context of the subject matter content and/or skill for which it is appropriate. It should be directed to specific language learning problems related to the learners' experience.
- *Interactive*   Strategy training should be interactive. According to this mode of training, learners are not told what to do and then left on their own to practise. Rather, until they evidence some ability to regulate their use of the strategy, teachers are expected to continue to work with them.
- *Diagnosis*   The content of the training should be based on the actual proficiency of the learners. Therefore, at the outset of any strategy training, information on which strategies students use and how well they use them should be collected.

7.2   Interpreting the guidelines for strategy training
In this task, you will be able to think about what these guidelines mean.

(a)   How does the action plan for inferencing illustrate each one?
(b)   Why should these principles be considered important for strategy training?

Strategy training should be informed. Informed training is explicit about its purpose and about the value or significance of the expected results. Research has shown that giving students information about the value of a strategy, i.e. about where and how often it may be used, greatly enhances the positive outcomes of training studies (e.g. Paris *et al.*, 1982). Brown and Baker (1984) consider that informed training is, in effect, training for lateral transfer. When students are given information about where a strategy can be used, it will be more likely that they will use it not only in the training context but in a variety of other appropriate settings.

In contrast with informed training, learners may simply be told what to do in order to accomplish a particular task. Such training, which does not inform students about the nature of the activity they are expected to do nor when it is appropriate to use it, is referred to as blind training. When students are induced to use a strategy in this way, they will perform a particular task more efficiently, but even if given numerous practice tasks they will not usually continue to use the strategy on their own. Nor will they initiate its use spontaneously in situations different from the training context.

In the action plan you have just analyzed, strategy training was informed. What students are going to learn is made explicit at the outset. Session 1 introduces learners to the concept 'strategy', and in Session 3 learners are led to describe and name the strategy they are going to learn to use.

The value or significance of the strategy is also discussed in Sessions 1 and 5. In Session 1, learners consider how strategies in general may be helpful in language learning, and in Session 5 the significance of the particular strategy that students are learning to use is illustrated and discussed. Set A exercises demonstrate how nonverbal clues and world knowledge help learners to deal with some of the comprehension problems that they may encounter when completing a classroom exercise. In Set B exercises learners determine how inferencing can help them to deal with some of the listening problems they face in real life contexts.

Strategy training should include training in self-regulation. Self-regulation is a term which refers to how learners manage their learning, i.e. *plan* or decide what they are going to learn and by what means; *monitor* their attempts to learn for difficulties and *check the outcome* of their learning. Research reports on strategy training in non-ESL contexts have demonstrated that learners who were trained to monitor and evaluate their use of strategies were also more likely to continue using them and to initiate their use in a variety of contexts (Brown and Palinscar, 1982). As for planning, the importance of helping learners develop expertise in choosing appropriate strategies to deal with their learning problems is supported by transfer theory. According to this theory, students will transfer learned skills to other contexts only if the tasks share identical elements (e.g. Thorndike and Woodworth, 1901; Gagne, 1967) and, it may be inferred, if students recognize these elements. These views have been confirmed by a study of expert and novice problem solvers (Brown *et al.*, 1983) which has shown that expert problem solvers are distinguished by their ability to move beyond surface features of problems to identify conceptual similarities. Novice problem solvers, on the other hand, tended to focus on surface structure features, such as key words (Brown *et al.*, 1983). Of course, if a problem is not correctly classified, students will use the wrong strategy or no strategy at all and transfer will not occur.

Therefore, providing students with training in self-regulation (also referred to as self-control training) increases the likelihood of strategy maintenance and transfer — commonly acknowledged measures of the success of any kind of skill training. In the absence of this type of self-control training, learners will not become autonomous in their use of strategies and will remain dependent on their teachers even though they may be taught to use strategies and improve their performance on specific tasks.

The action plan also takes into account the importance of self-regulation. Activities that require learners to evaluate and monitor are included in Session 6 where students are asked to keep an account of their attempts to use the strategy in real life contexts: the problems encountered in using it and the final outcome. In Session 7, these accounts are, then, shared with other learners and discussed with a view to helping students further in identifying the reasons for difficulties they may encounter using the strategy, e.g. inappropriate use, inadequate knowledge base, and to develop criteria they must consider in evaluating the outcome of using the strategy, i.e. improved task performance, increase in autonomy and confidence.

In Session 5 (Set B) and Session 8, learners practise matching the strategy with the types of problem it is intended to resolve outside the training context, thus developing their ability to choose strategies appropriately — one dimension of the planning strategy.

Strategy training should be contextualized. A strategy should be trained in the context of a language skill and related to a problem that a student may have in using that skill. Thus, a pre-reading strategy should be taught together with a text that students are expected to read and a pre-listening strategy together with a lecture that the students are going to attend. The strategy should be presented as a response to a problem students may encounter in reading the text or listening to the lecture. When training is contextualized in this way, the relevance of the strategy is emphasized.

In their discussion of recent instructional research, Brown and Baker (1984) criticize earlier studies which taught the strategy in isolation from a context where it was to be used. Transfer in such cases, they maintain, is unlikely, while the more recent research, which contextualizes training, has had more successful outcomes.

In this action plan, inferencing is taught as a strategy that can be used to help understand the spoken language. The demonstration (Session 3) and in-class practice tasks (Sessions 4, 5, 6 and 8) use videotapes of a variety of everyday contexts in which students are likely to find themselves. Students are also given an opportunity to use the strategy to deal with listening difficulties they actually have (Sessions 5 and 8).

Strategy training should be interactive. According to this mode of training, learners are not told what to do and then left on their own to practise. Rather, until learners evidence some ability to regulate their use of the strategy under training, teachers are expected to continue to work with them, giving them ample opportunity to observe the use of the strategy, to imitate what they observe and to receive feedback on their attempts to use it. This interaction allows teachers to remain in touch with the learners' changing cognitive state and so enables them to determine what kind of feedback they should provide and when training is no longer necessary (Brown and Baker, 1984).

This guideline is, in part, a reaction to training studies done in a laboratory, where students were given a task and left alone to complete it. The guideline is also the outcome of training studies that have been influenced by two of Vygotsky's ideas regarding psychological processes: the social nature of learning and the learner's zone of proximal development. According to Vygotsky, learning is an internalization of what was originally a social activity. Moreover, there is a great difference between what a learner actually knows and can do in a particular area and what his learning potential is. Vygotsky maintains that a learner can realize this potential interactively — through the guidance of supportive other persons such as parents, teachers, and peers.

Research with mother—child dyads and teacher—pupil interactions has shown that there is a systematic regularity in how this guidance works out. First the adult (trainer) controls and guides the learner's activity. Gradually, however, the trainer and learner share the problem solving functions, with the learner taking initiative and the trainer correcting and guiding when the learner has difficulty. Finally, the trainer cedes control and functions primarily as a supportive and sympathetic audience (cf. Brown *et al.*, 1983). While it is true that some mature adult learners who have learned how to learn are capable of providing themselves with the guidance and feedback they need, others will need the guidance, control and feedback of a teacher at the outset.

The action plan also takes into account the need for interactive learning. In Sessions 3 and 4 learners observe the teacher and their classmates using the strategy. In-class discussions to evaluate the use of the strategy in authentic contexts (Session 7) will allow learners to explore together the limits of a particular strategy and to reinforce their understanding of the procedures necessary to implement it.

Efficient training should be based on a diagnosis of learners' entering proficiency. There are two reasons for determining which strategies learners already use and how well they use them. First, there are an infinite number of learning skills or strategies necessary for effective learning. Brown and Baker (1984) refer to a study that has listed at least a hundred basic skills. Quite clearly it will be impossible to provide training in all these skills, nor will it be necessary to do so. Diagnosis enables the trainer to exclude what is not necessary and to focus on the need of the student-learner.

A second reason for preceding strategy training with a diagnosis of learners' skills is justified by interventions that ignored the difference between good and poor learners. Raphael and Mckinney (1983) noted that in these situations interventions proved useful for less experienced learners but were disruptive when used with more mature learners, who either were already familiar with the skills or had developed others that were equally effective. The point is not that more mature learners would not benefit from further training but that the intervention should match the need. In the action plan, Session 2 is explicitly intended for the purpose of diagnosis.

Evaluating the guidelines

We have looked at an action plan for training strategies developed on the basis of five guidelines that intervention research in the cognitive developmental literature has shown to be effective. In this section we shall evaluate the guidelines. How do they compare with other approaches to strategy training? How useful are they?

Alternative views on strategy training

The following set of guidelines for developing strategy instruction are taken from *Strategic Teaching and Learning* (Jones *et al.*, 1987). They provide another analysis of how to teach students to use strategies.

EXCERPT 1

From 'Strategic thinking: a cognitive focus'

Developing effective strategy instruction

Just as we have suggested that one cannot be prescriptive with regard to what strategies are appropriate during the phases of learning, the same is true of the instructional processes the teacher uses. There are, however, general guidelines suggested by instructional research, which we will discuss at this point.

Assessing strategy use

Generally, a good first step is to determine if the students are currently using a strategy in the learning situation and what that strategy is. We know that efficient learners do, in fact, use strategies (cf. Bereiter and Bird, 1985), while less successful learners may choose an inefficient strategy or may be unaware of the need to use a strategy. For example, poor readers often report that the way to prepare for a test is to 'read and reread' (Brown and Lawton). The mere repetition of reading is unlikely to produce increments in comprehension and retention if what is read is not understood.

How does one get students to divulge the activity they engage in while learning? One successful means is to have the students think aloud the process they are using. For example, Bird (Bereiter and Bird, 1985) had students think aloud as they processed pieces of text, while Scardamalia and Bereiter (1984) had students think aloud while they planned a composition. Sometimes students, particularly older students, are reluctant to engage in 'think alouds'. In this case a more successful approach might be to interview the students, asking them what advice they would give to a younger student engaged in a similar activity. For a more systematic assessment. Weinstein and her colleagues have developed a test to assess the use of specific learning strategies (see Weinstein and Underwood, 1985).

Explaining the strategy

After evaluating the learning strategy the students are currently using, the teacher is ready to present the proposed strategy. The work of Duffy and Roehler and their colleagues (1986) suggests that what teachers do at this time has tremendous bearing on what students learn. In their experimental work, these authors found that when teachers explicitly informed their students about (1) what strategy they were learning (declarative information), (2) how they should employ the strategy (procedural information), and (3) in what context they should employ the strategy (conditional information), the students indicated greater awareness of what they were learning and why. In addition, these students performed better on achievement measures than did students whose teachers did not fully inform them regarding these aspects of strategy use.

Having provided this information regarding the targeted strategy(ies), the teacher is ready to provide instruction about strategy use (i.e. procedural knowledge). Interestingly, this is a step at which teachers are frequently not as helpful as they might be. For example, it is not uncommon to urge students to summarize, outline the most important ideas, and underline the topic sentences, but to provide no information regarding how one goes about determining what is important, what constitutes a topic sentence, and so forth.

To guard against this possibility, it is helpful for the teacher to reflect on the processes and skills necessary to implement the strategy(ies) successfully and to provide relevant instruction. For example, in the process of teaching summarization as a strategy, teachers can call students' attention to such procedures as those investigated by Day and Brown (1981):

1. determine if there is a topic sentence that represents the gist of the material,
2. invent a topic sentence if one is not present,
3. name lists or steps (identify a superordinate),
4. delete what is trivial, and
5. delete what is redundant.

After these steps or processes have been taught, they can be integrated, demonstrated, and practiced as a strategy and in the appropriate context.

Modeling the strategy

Typically, the teacher demonstrates or models the use of the strategy. For example, a mathematics teacher may choose to demonstrate the solution of a division problem by placing the problem on the board and thinking aloud while working through its solution, making remarks such as: 'What type of problem is this? This sign indicates to me that this is a division problem. Now that I recognize this is a division problem, what is the first step I should take?' Once again, the focus is on modeling the thinking processes.

Scaffolding the instruction

While the explanation, instruction, and modeling that have been described thus far are critical to the success of cognitive strategy instruction, they actually represent only the initial steps in such instruction. If students are expected to be able to apply these strategies independently, they must be given the opportunity to practice and demonstrate their use of the strategies.

The role of the teacher in this phase of instruction has been compared to that of a scaffold. Scaffolding has been described as a 'process that enables a child or novice to solve a problem, carry out a task, or achieve a goal which would be beyond his unassisted efforts' (Wood *et al.*, 1976: 90). The teacher scaffolds during strategy instruction by *supporting* the students' attempts to use the strategy, providing additional instruction and modeling as the need indicates. The support the teacher provides is *adjusted* according to the learning characteristics, nature of the material, and nature of the criterial tasks. For example, some students may require little more than prompting in the use of the strategy, whereas other students might require further modeling. Regardless of how the support is adjusted, it is regarded as *temporary*. The teacher proceeds to remove the support as the student shows increased competence.

There are several ways support is provided. One is by structuring the task so that the demands increase gradually. Another is to keep the level of difficulty constant and begin with a substantial amount of support, which is later faded. (For a discussion of this issue, see Collins *et al.*, in press.) Still another means of support is to help students articulate the conditions under which the strategy is most useful (Bransford *et al.*, 1986; Schoenfeld, 1985). While we generally think of support provided verbally, students can also be provided with visual prompts to aid them through the task: for example, cards picturing or listing the steps of a strategy (Bereiter and Scardamalia, 1984), or a graphic representation of text (Holley and Dansereau, 1984). Regardless of the nature of the support, the aim is to remove the support gradually. This gradual ceding of responsibility for employing the strategy promotes the likelihood that the student will internalize and independently apply the strategy. Whether students actually internalize this responsibility, however, depends on their attitudes and beliefs as much as it does on the instructional strategy. Thus, motivation is a central concern of strategic teachers.

Relating cognitive strategy instruction to motivation

In our discussion of self-regulated learning, we have placed an emphasis on helping students identify and manage the cognitive processes essential to success with learning. However, another dimension of self-regulation cannot be overlooked: the role of motivation. Paris and Oka (1986) described this as the 'skill and will' to learn, which increasingly is being considered a part of metacognition in the research literature (e.g. Paris and Winograd, in progress). Teachers are well aware of the significance of this issue, and student disinterest plays a prominent role in teachers' discussion of why students fail to learn.

To understand the role of will better, it is helpful to consider cognitive theories of motivation in which attributions and perceptions of self-competence play a significant role. These theories suggest that students' expectations regarding success and failure, in hand with the extent to which they value the learning task, determine the amount of effort they are willing to expend as well as the degree to which they will persist in a learning activity.

Students' expectations regarding success and failure are derived from their previous experiences with learning tasks. Children who have experienced repeated failure often develop an attitude of helplessness and passivity with regard to learning (Seligman, 1975; Torgesen, 1982). They attribute failure to their lack of ability and do not acknowledge the role of effort in academic success.

One of the principal goals of strategy training is to alter students' beliefs about themselves by teaching them that their failures can be attributed to the lack of effective strategies rather than to the lack of ability or to laziness. By providing students not merely with a backlog of success experiences but with experiences in which they see the effects of strategic effort, it is possible to change students' expectations for success and failure and to help them sustain strategy use (Borkowski *et al.*, 1986).

[Jones *et al.*, 1987]

7.3 Comparing two sets of guidelines for strategy training

In this task you will compare the two sets of guidelines.

(a) Which of the guidelines described above are similar to those underlying the action plan presented here? Which are not?
(b) Should the different guidelincs be included in developing procedures for strategy training? If yes, what new objectives do they suggest?

The kind of learning that is basic to language training and learner training is the same. In both cases, learners are helped to acquire procedural knowledge — knowledge about how to do something. Would you expect the principles underlying the procedures you use to teach linguistic rules to be similar to those advocated for the teaching of strategies? In order to test your hypothesis, complete the following task.

7.4 Comparing guidelines for learner training with guidelines for language training

Think about a language skills class you often teach.

(a) Make a list of the guidelines you use to devise tasks and select materials for teaching the skill.
(b) Are these guidelines similar to those outlined for teaching strategies? If so, how? If not, how are they different?

Usefulness of the guidelines

The action plan presented in this chapter demonstrates one set of procedures for implementing strategy training based upon the guidelines suggested by intervention research in fields outside language learning. To evaluate the usefulness of the guidelines it is necessary, first, to determine whether the action plan works. Can it be replicated? Can it be adapted to other uses? In either case, what is the outcome? Will students learn to use the strategy? Second, it will also be necessary to use the guidelines to devise different procedures and to test their effectiveness. The next set of tasks will help you begin this evaluation.

As you complete each task, use the following questions to evaluate your experience:

(a) Did the action plan work? Did your students understand the procedures they were asked to follow? Were they able to do them? What was the outcome? Did the students learn to use the strategy in question?
(b) What problems did you encounter as you implemented the action plan? How did you deal with them?
(c) How should the action plan be revised to take the problems you encountered into account? Does your experience suggest different procedures? New objectives or guidelines? If so, what are they?
(d) Revise the action plan presented in this chapter or devise a new one based on your insights.

7.5 Replicating the action plan

Follow the procedures in the action plan to teach inferencing to a group of language learners you are working with. Evaluate your experience using the above questions.

7.6 Adapting the action plan

The action plan presented in this chapter demonstrated the training of inferencing as a listening strategy for understanding the spoken language in informal everyday settings.

(a) In what other types of settings and for what other purposes would it be appropriate to use inferencing?
(b) Devise an action plan you could use to train students in the use of inferencing in one of the settings you listed in (a). Use the procedures

illustrated in the action plan on inferencing, making any changes implied by the different setting and purpose (e.g. different practice tasks).

(c) Implement the plan and evaluate it.

7.7 Developing an action plan for other cognitive strategies

Choose a strategy from your inventory of cognitive strategies that you would like your students to use for this task.

(a) Determine how the strategy works.
  (i) What steps or mental operations must a learner follow to implement the strategy?
  (ii) For what types of communication tasks is it most appropriate? Receptive or productive tasks? Tasks using the written or spoken language?
  (iii) When and where will learners be most likely to use it?
(b) Use the objectives and guidelines to outline the action plan you will follow in training your students to use the strategy.
(c) Implement your action plan and evaluate it.

The cognitive research upon which the guidelines are based was conducted to seek insights on training in the use of cognitive strategies, not self-management strategies. Of course, one of the guidelines requires that learners monitor and evaluate their use of the strategy under training and that they learn to match it to appropriate problem situations. Therefore, in learning to use a cognitive strategy, students will be getting some practice in the use of self-management strategies.

However, self-management strategies can also be used to regulate a broader range of tasks over an extended period of time. For example, students could be expected to 'manage' their attempts to improve their listening or writing or to acquire specialized vocabulary necessary for a professional or academic task they must complete. In such situations, students will need to learn how to set realistic objectives and choose appropriate resources and strategies to achieve them; they will have to know how to assess their entering and changing level of proficiency; and they will need to be familiar with criteria for evaluating their attempts to use the particular skill.

7.8 Devising action plans for self-management strategies

In the next set of tasks you will help students learn to use self-management strategies to manage their attempts to improve their use of a particular language skill.

(a) Decide whether you will work with one student, a small group, or a class.
(b) Have your student(s) identify one of their language learning needs — a skill they may wish to improve over a set period of time (e.g. to

develop facility in communicating on the telephone; to expand their range of vocabulary in a certain area; to improve their reading skills).

(c) Decide which of the self-management strategies you will first train them to use, i.e. planning, monitoring, evaluating.

(d) Determine how the strategy works.

(i) What steps are entailed in its implementation?

(ii) For what purpose will learners be most likely to use it?

(iii) How can you collect information on whether and how your students use this self-management strategy?

(iv) How can you introduce them to the notion of that self-management strategy? That is, what does evaluate mean? Planning? Monitoring?

(v) What activities can be devised to have them practise the strategy in class? In authentic settings?

(e) Use the guidelines and the objectives (pp. 104–105) to devise an action plan for helping your students gain facility in the selected self-management strategy.

(f) Implement the action plan, evaluate it, and make the revisions suggested by your evaluation.

(g) Devise an action plan to provide training in the other two self-management strategies. Follow the procedures outlined in (d) and (e).

(h) As you implement each plan, evaluate the procedures and make revisions suggested by the evaluation.

Some language skills textbooks include strategy training in a special preface 'to the student' or in a first chapter; in others the training goes beyond an introductory preface. Excerpt 2 is an example. The strategy training guidelines can also be used to evaluate the effectiveness of such materials.

EXCERPT 2

From *Listening Focus: Comprehension practice for students of English*

A rock in the road

Vocabulary preview
The following words and expressions will appear in the talk. Listen and write a short definition for each item.

destroy —
earthquake —
sphere —
dig —
bury —
incline —

Sentence cues

Look at the following sentence patterns. Then listen to each sentence.

a. *They decided that* _____.
b. *I think I can* _____.
c. *No matter how* _____, *they couldn't* _____.

Listening strategy

> This talk is a short story about what happened in a small village after an earthquake. In this story there is a problem. The problem was solved by a young boy. Listen for a statement of the problem. Then listen for how the problem was solved.
>
> Listen for these time indicators: *a hundred years ago, one day, when it stopped, all of this time, the next morning, last night.*
>
> Now, listen to the talk.

> Use this space (or additional paper) for your notes about the talk.

Comprehension questions

Listen to the questions and write your answers on the lines below.

1. _____
2. _____
3. _____
4. _____
5. _____

After you listen

Make a simple drawing that illustrates the story of 'The Rock in the Road'. Your sketch should include the following items: *a mountain, a rock, a village, a road, some people, a young boy, a rope, a shovel,* and *a hole*. The first picture is partly completed.

[Kisslinger and Rost, 1980]

7.9   Using the guidelines to evaluate materials

First determine which strategies the materials intend to teach. Then consider to what extent the lesson adheres to the guidelines we have discussed.

(a)   Is an attempt made to determine whether students already use the strategies that are taught?
(b)   Is the training informed or blind?
(c)   Are students taught to regulate their learning, i.e. to monitor and evaluate their use of the strategies?
(d)   Is the training interactive?
(e)   Are the strategies contextualized?
(f)   Are students provided with training that would facilitate the transfer of the strategies they use?

In the Valuable Readings are names of other texts for English as a second language that use the term 'strategy' in their title, and/or include some practice in the use of some strategies (or refer to the importance of doing so). Choose one of these to evaluate if you wish more practice using the guidelines.

Conclusion

In this chapter, you have worked with and evaluated guidelines for developing action plans that help students learn to use strategies. As you continue to help your students become proficient in the use of strategies, experiment with the guidelines so that you can produce action plans that work for your students and their particular needs.

Valuable readings

There are a number of publications that describe strategy training programs. Outside the field of second language learning, there is the work of Dansereau (1978), who first reviews earlier learning strategy training programs and then describes the development of an experimentally based strategy training program. Several of the articles in the special issue on metacognition published by *Topics in Learning and Learning Disabilities* and edited by Wong (1982) describe cognitive strategy training projects.

Twining (1985) describes a four-stage model for teaching notetaking and Weinstein and Rogers (1985) outline a course for teaching strategies to college students. Knowles' guide (1975) lists procedures and provides resources for helping learners to acquire the skills of self-directed learning. Jones *et al.* (1987) discuss a rationale for 'strategic teaching' and illustrate how this can be applied in content areas.

In the field of second language learning, Hosenfeld *et al.* (1981) describe a curricular sequence for teaching reading strategies. Oskarsson (1980) illustrates different ways of having students assess their language skills. Casanave (1988) describes ESL reading research that applied some of the guidelines presented in this chapter to the training of comprehension monitoring. The publications by Cohen (1990), O'Malley and Chamot (1990) and Oxford (1990) also contain materials for training strategies.

Textbooks that include strategy training

The titles and/or description of purpose of the following texts suggest that helping students develop strategies (or skills) is one of their objectives:

Judd, K.R., and Kalnitz, J., 1986, *World Shakers: Reading strategies and skills*, New York: Holt, Rinehart & Winston.
Levine, A., Oded, B., and Statman, S., 1988, *Clues to Meaning: Strategies for better reading comprehension*, New York: Collier Macmillan.
Ruetten, M.K., 1986, *Comprehending Academic Lectures*, New York: Collier Macmillan.
Salimbene, S., 1986, *Interactive Reading*, New York: Newbury House.
Zukowski/Faust, J., Johnston, S.S., Atkinson, C., and Templin, E., 1982, *In Context: Reading skills for intermediate students of English as a second language*, New York: Holt, Rinehart & Winston.

Note

1. The term 'session' is used to group together procedures that focus on one particular objective. These procedures will not necessarily be completed in one sitting.

Chapter 8

An action plan for beliefs and attitudes

Focus   Imagine a language learner who says that grammar and vocabulary are essential to language learning and who therefore refuses to participate in communicative activities. How would you deal with these strongly held beliefs? Would you try to change them? If so, how?

Process   • An action plan for changing attitudes and beliefs
            • Guidelines for developing action plans to change attitudes and beliefs
            • Evaluating the guidelines

Outcome   Guidelines for changing attitudes and beliefs

An action plan for changing beliefs and attitudes

8.1   Determining the objectives of an action plan for changing attitudes and beliefs

The objective of the following action plan is to persuade students to change negative attitudes they hold towards their role in language learning.

As you read the plan, determine the objective of each session.[1]

ACTION PLAN FOR CHANGING ATTITUDES AND BELIEFS
_____

INTRODUCTORY SESSIONS

Resources
A learner self-report (you can use Laszlo's — Chapter 1).

Session 1

Procedures
(a)   Students read the account to come up with answers to the following questions.
    (i) Was the learner (Laszlo) dependent on a teacher to learn?
    (ii) Was all his learning done in a classroom?
    (iii) What did he do on his own, i.e. without a teacher?
    (iv) Did he find 'his way' useful? Do you think that he liked it?
    (v) What do you think his advice would be if we asked him 'what's the best way to learn a language?'
(b)   After reading the account, students discuss the following in small groups and record their views.
    (i) Do you agree with Laszlo's approach to language learning? Why? Why not?
    (ii) Is your 'way' of learning English like Laszlo's? Use examples to show what you mean.
    (iii) It has been said that the best learners are those who can teach themselves. Do you teach yourself? Give examples from your experience. Do you like it? Why? Why not? If you do not teach yourself, tell why.

(iv) When you enroll in a course to learn English, what do you expect your responsibilities to be? What do you expect the teacher to do? Why?

(c) Small groups share the outcome of their discussion with the whole group.

(d) Students are asked to write their views on the same questions.

(e) The reports of the small group discussions and the students' written answers are collected and analyzed for common themes that provide answers to the following questions.

(i) what are students' views on their role in learning? What do they expect to do? What do they expect the teacher to do? Do they expect to be autonomous?

(ii) What reasons do they put forward in support of their views?

(f) The classification system outlined in the content schema (Chapter 5) can be used to organize themes that do *not* bear directly on the questions listed in (e).

(g) The teacher scrutinizes the whole set of themes for views that suggest the following:

- a negative attitude towards autonomous learning;
- a positive attitude towards autonomous learning;
- learners' reasons for holding these views (e.g. goals, fears, frames of reference, values).

Special notes

Step (c) is optional. Use only if you feel students need more discussion on the topic.

It is also possible to complete the procedures following a different order. For example, students can be asked to discuss the last two questions listed in step (b) at the outset. Then, if their responses are too general, step (a) and the first two questions of (b) can be done.

The information chosen to elicit student views should focus clearly and exactly on the attitudes or beliefs to be raised for discussion. A special stimulus question can also be used to elicit some of the more personal information on students' values, incentives and needs if discussion of the initial stimulus does not elicit it.

The purpose of procedure (g) is for the teacher to get an overview of the extent to which students' prior knowledge and attitudes support the idea of autonomous learning and why. This information will guide the selection of 'new information' to be provided in Session 4 and the structuring of the discussion that accompanies the tasks in the rest of the action plan.

Session 2

Procedures

(a) The teacher presents the common themes outlined in Session 1(e) to the students, who prioritize them to indicate those in which they have most interest.

(b) The teacher uses the prioritized lists to select themes for the core sessions.

(c) Students are asked to share any feelings about language learning evoked by these first activities and/or by the topic they are going to discuss in upcoming sessions.

Special notes

It is important that students be given an opportunity to air their feelings about language learning in general, the topic to be discussed, or other topics related to the session at the outset of the action plan if this has not already happened spontaneously in the first session. The third activity (c) of the session is included to ensure that this happens. Moreover, it is intended to serve as a reminder that a learning atmosphere conducive to the expression of feelings must be maintained throughout all the sessions.

The following session will be based on one theme that can emerge from the data gathering session. That is, students say that they do not really know how to go about learning a language on their own and that it is really the teacher's responsibility to see that they learn.

CORE SESSIONS

Resources
(a) A reading 'Definition of a good language learner'
(b) Comprehension guide for the reading
(c) A 'good language learner questionnaire' based on the reading

Session 3

Procedures
(a) Students are reminded of the theme that they will be considering. In this action plan it is what they can do to help themselves learn without a teacher.
(b) They write a letter to a friend who is about to come and visit/live in a country where English is spoken. The friend has asked them for advice about how to go about learning English.
(c) The teacher collects the letters.

Special notes
If the activities in Session 1 (discussion and writing) have already brought out fairly detailed information on students' prior knowledge on the topic of the core session, the information provided by these letters will be redundant and so this session can be omitted.

Session 4

Procedures
Students read 'A definition of a good language learner' (Table 8.1).

Special notes
The chosen reading should be closely related to the analysis of student views (Session 1(g)).

Session 5

Procedures
(a) Students complete the comprehension guide (Table 8.2)
(b) They compare their answers to the guide with those of another classmate and ask (the teacher and the rest of the class) any questions they have regarding the content.
(c) Once students have understood the main ideas of the presentation, the class discusses whether or not these good language learners were teacher dependent or teacher independent.
(d) After the discussion, they may be told that the language learners described learned on their own, mostly without a teacher, and that they all learned more than one language.

TABLE 8.1

A definition of a good language learner

The following definition is based on the research of Naiman, Frohlich and Stern, *The Good Language Learner*. They interviewed adults who had learned a second, third and sometimes a fourth language successfully. Here are their findings.

The good language learner finds a style of learning that suits him/her
When he is in a learning situation that he does not like, he is able to adapt it to his personal needs. In other words, he believes that it is always possible to get something out of any situation. He is also able to discover how he prefers to learn and chooses learning situations that are suited to his way of learning. For example, Jane knew that it was best for her to take a short course in the language when she first arrived in the country where it was spoken. Then, she was able to get involved with native speakers outside the classroom.

Good language learners are actively involved in the language learning process
Besides regular language classes, they plan other activities that give them a chance to use and learn the language. They know practice is very important. Sometimes they choose an activity because they are already familiar with the ideas. For example, Hiroshi listened to the news first in Japanese, his native language, and then in English. Carmen always went to movies she had already seen and understood so that she could concentrate on the language.

 Good language learners can figure out their special problems and try to do something about them. Monica knew she had no confidence in her speaking ability, and so she hired a tutor and twice a week she spoke one hour to the tutor. They also do things they do not usually do to gain more information about their second language. Tom worked as a truck driver. He used the day more as a language course.

Good language learners try to figure out how the language works
They pay special attention to pronunciation, grammar and vocabulary, and they develop good techniques for improving their pronunciation, learning grammar and vocabulary. One learner looked at people's mouths when they were pronouncing a sound she wanted to learn. Then she tried to imitate them. Others practise 'mock-talk'; they imitate the sounds of the language without using real words. When learning new words, some learners make a picture of the object in their minds. They compare the words with words in their native language to see how they are different.

Good language learners know that language is used to communicate
They have good techniques to practise listening, speaking, reading and writing. Walter made up conversations in his mind. Chou read comic books to improve his reading. Michele wrote letters to pen pals. In the early stage of language learning, the good language learner does not worry about mistakes. He speaks and tries to become fluent. They look for opportunities to speak with native speakers. Adela, for example, used to talk with senior citizens while waiting for the bus to come. They also try to learn the special cultural meanings of words; they try to use and learn language for different social situations.

Good language learners are like good detectives
They are always looking for clues that will help them understand how the language works. Sometimes, they make guesses and ask people to correct them if they are wrong. They compare what they say with what others say to see if they are using the correct form of the language. They keep a record of what they have learned and think about it.

Good language learners learn to think in the language

Good language learners realize that language learning is not easy and to overcome their feelings of frustration, lack of confidence
They learn to laugh at their mistakes; they know that it will take a long time and that it can get very boring. They learn to work with their feelings.

Source: Naiman *et al.*, 1978.

TABLE 8.2
Comprehension guide for a good language learner

1. *The good language learner finds a style of learning that suits him/her*
   What do they do when they are in a situation they do not like?
   What kind of learning situations do they choose?

   Style of learning means
2. *Good language learners are actively involved in the language learning process*
   What kind of activities do they plan to improve their second language?
   (a)
   (b)
   (c)
   (d)

   Actively involved in language learning means
3. *Good language learners try to figure out how the language works*
   What do they pay special attention to?
   What techniques do they use to improve pronunciation?
   How do they learn new words?

4. *Good language learners know that language is used to communicate*
   What are some of the techniques they use to practise listening, speaking, reading and writing?

5. *Good language learners are like good detectives*
   Why are they like good detectives?
   What do they do to help themselves understand how the language works?

6. *Good language learners learn to think in the language*

7. *Good language learners know that language learning is not easy and try to overcome their feelings of frustration and lack of confidence*
   They laugh at _____ .
   They know language learning takes _____ and it can get _____ .
   They learn to work with their _____ .

Session 6

Procedures

(a) Students compare themselves with the good language learner, i.e. are they very different? To what extent are they autonomous?
   (i) The refer to their letter to determine whether the good language learner would agree with the advice they gave their friend.
   (ii) Students complete a questionnaire based on the information from the article to determine which of the good language learner's techniques they use (Table 8.3).
   (iii) When they have finished, they determine which of these specific techniques they use 'always' and 'often' and give examples of how they implement each one.
(b) Students consider how they can use the information on the good language learner to help themselves become more autonomous.
   (i) They make a list of strategies from the good language learner questionnaire that they do not use often or do not use at all.
   (ii) They bring their list to a small group discussion or teacher conference to determine which of the five main characteristics of the good language learner *least* influences their approach. (That is, are they not familiar with their preferred

TABLE 8.3
Questionnaire for a good language learner

Circle the answer that describes how you approach language learning.

A: always	O: often	S: sometimes	R: rarely	N: never

The good language learner finds a style of learning that suits him/her

1.	I try to get something out of every learning situation even if I don't like it.	A	O	S	R	N
2.	I choose learning situations that are suited to my way of learning.	A	O	S	R	N

Good language learners are actively involved in the language learning process

3.	Besides language class, I plan activities that give me a chance to use and learn the language.	A	O	S	R	N
4.	I choose activities because I am already familiar with the ideas.	A	O	S	R	N
5.	I can figure out my special problems.	A	O	S	R	N
6.	I try to do something about my special problems.	A	O	S	R	N
7.	I do things I don't usually do to gain more information about English.	A	O	S	R	N

Good language learners try to figure out how the language works.

8.	I pay special attention to pronunciation.	A	O	S	R	N
9.	I pay special attention to grammar.	A	O	S	R	N
10.	I pay special attention to vocabulary.	A	O	S	R	N

Good language learners know that language is used to communicate

11.	I try to develop good techniques to practise listening, speaking, reading and writing.	A	O	S	R	N
12.	I try to develop good techniques to improve my pronunciation, grammar and vocabulary.	A	O	S	R	N

Good language learners are like good detectives

13.	I am like a detective. I look for clues that will help me understand how language works.	A	O	S	R	N
14.	When I don't know, I guess.	A	O	S	R	N
15.	I ask people to correct me if I make a mistake.	A	O	S	R	N
16.	I compare what I say with what others say to see if I'm using correct English.	A	O	S	R	N
17.	I think about what I've learned.	A	O	S	R	N

Good language learners learn to think in the language

18.	I try to think in English.	A	O	S	R	N

Good language learners try to overcome their feelings of frustration and lack of confidence

19.	I overcome my feelings of frustration and lack of confidence.	A	O	S	R	N
20.	I can laugh at my mistakes.	A	O	S	R	N

Source: Adapted from Naiman *et al.*, 1978.

way of learning? Are they not active? Have they not learned to cope with the affective demands of language learning? etc.).
(iii) Then, learners discuss their reasons for not using the specific strategies listed in (i).
(iv) Obstacles to their use are identified and, to the extent that this is possible, ways of overcoming them are examined and chosen.
(v) Learners also discuss whether and why imitating the good language learner in the way(s) identified in (ii) could help them become better language learners and improve their language skills.

(c)   Students also reflect on self-direction as they experience it in the rest of their life roles.
(i) They list some things they have taught themselves to do in other aspects of their lives, i.e. raising children, driving a car.
(ii) These experiences are discussed with their classmates and their teacher. How successful were they? Why were they successful? Why were they not successful?

(d)   They consider why they should learn their second language autonomously.
(i) Why do they want to learn their second language?
(ii) Which of the strategies used by the good language learner would especially help them to achieve their language learning objectives?

Special notes

After completing (a), some students may find that they are already doing what good language learners do. In such cases, they may be asked to evaluate their experience. What problems have they encountered? How did they deal with them? Were they successful? Why? These students can also be asked to give accounts of their experiences to other students.

The four sets of procedures (i.e. (a)–(d)) are suggestive. They may not all need to be done, for some of them may elicit similar information (e.g. (b)(v) and (d)(ii)). Nor need they necessarily be done in the order outlined.

Session 7

Procedures

(a)   Referring to what they have learned from their analysis and discussion of the good language learner questionnaire (Session 6), students determine which characteristics they need to imitate.
(i) From the list of strategies they do not use often, they select those related to their chosen characteristic(s) and give examples of how they can implement them.
(ii) They list other strategies, not included in the questionnaire, that would also help them become more like the 'good language learner'.

(b)   This information is written up into an essay or a learning contract.[2]
(i) The plan becomes the basis of teacher–student conferences throughout the course.
(ii) Students can also form learning/support groups and their progress in fulfilling the contract can be reported and discussed with their learning group as well.

Special notes

If not knowing how or when to use particular strategies is one of the reasons why students did not use them (cf. Session 6(b)(iv)), teachers will have to make provisions for strategy training.

Session 8

The priorities listed in the initial session are reviewed and students select the topic they would like to be the focus of the next series of core session.

Special notes

Of course, whether or not another series of sessions dealing with knowledge and attitudes that students have acquired about learning would immediately follow will depend upon how learner training is being incorporated into the language training program. Several alternatives are presented in Chapter 9.

This action plan assumes that learners are not willing to take responsibility for their learning because they do not know how. Their lack of strategic knowledge about how to approach language learning shapes their attitudes regarding their role. Therefore the plan intends to help them expand this knowledge as a means of changing their attitudes. The objectives of each session in the action plan are as follows:

1. Gathering data on learners
2. Planning
3. Eliciting prior knowledge
4. Presenting information
5. Comprehending information
6. Elaborating on the information
7. Applying the information
8. Planning

The objective of Session 1 is the *gathering of information* about the learners to be used in determining the content of the core sessions. Students are presented with a learner account to elicit their beliefs and feelings about learning autonomously and their reasons for supporting these beliefs. In Session 2 learners are involved in *planning* the content of the core sessions and choose the topic they will discuss.

Sessions 3–7 focus on the topic that learners have chosen to discuss. The activities in Session 3 will bring to awareness their *prior knowledge* on the topic under discussion. Session 4 *provides information* that will introduce students to new ways of thinking about it, and in Session 5 learners are helped to *comprehend the information*. The objective of Session 6 is to extend comprehension to *elaboration of the information*. Learners relate the new information to previously acquired information and experiences and infer its applicability to their language learning. In Session 7 they *apply* insights derived from the information to their language learning to devise a plan which specifies how they will approach their language learning differently as a result of the information. Finally, in Session 8, they *plan* again, making a decision about the focus of ongoing sessions.

The procedures that make up the action plan are presented in a linear fashion with each session building upon the other and contributing to a separate objective. Needless to say, there is a great deal of overlap between them and the insights and changes that are the aim of each session may not occur in the presented order!

Guidelines for action plans for beliefs and attitudes

The objectives in the action plan are drawn from the Elaboration Likelihood Model (ELM) of attitude change developed by Petty and Cacciopo (1986).[3] The following key theoretical assumptions upon which the objectives are based may be used as guidelines in devising original action plans for changing beliefs and attitudes.

- *Persuasive communication* Attitude change can be brought about through exposure to a persuasive communication.
- *Importance of elaboration* The more learners actively process and elaborate on the content of the communication in an unbiased manner, the more likelihood there is that it will be accepted and bring about change in the desired direction.
- *Motivational factors* The intensity with which the communication is processed will depend on (1) the personal relevance of the content to the learner, (2) the extent to which learners are made personally responsible for evaluating the content, (3) the number of different sources through which the information is provided, (4) a supportive atmosphere and (5) the credibility of the source of the communication.
- *Ability factors* The extent and objectivity of the elaboration will depend on (1) the comprehensibility of the content and (2) learners' prior knowledge about it.

8.2 Interpreting the attitude change guidelines
In this task, you will be able to think about what the guidelines mean.

(a) How are the guidelines reflected in the action plan?

(b) Why should these guidelines 'work'?

8.3 Applying the guidelines to your language learning and teaching
Are there any strong evaluations or attitudes about language learning or teaching that you once held and changed? Did the four assumptions about attitude change described above contribute to a change in those attitude(s)? If so, how?

Change in strongly held evaluations, such as those that language learners hold about themselves as learners and/or about the learning process, can be brought about by exposure to a persuasive communication. A persuasive communication is one which presents information to change a learner's evaluation of a particular topic, object, situation and so on. In the narrower more technical sense, it should consist of explicit arguments for a desired change. However, especially when the topic is of great importance, it is considered desirable that the arguments be implicit. Information for the persuasive communication is based on previously collected information about learners' beliefs and the reasons that underlie them, i.e. their goals, fears, frames of reference and values (e.g. Session 1).

In this action plan, the 'persuasive' communication is a reading presented in Session 4.[4] No explicit arguments to influence students' views on their role in language learning are stated. Rather, the communication consisted of facts that demonstrate (1) what learners can do to help themselves learn a language without a teacher and (2) that learners who do so are, indeed, successful. The argument implicit in the information is that language learners can and should take responsibility for their learning.

This first guideline is based on the formal and rational approach to attitude change which uses a structured communication as the main instrument of change. That is, the information in the communication is carefully chosen and presented in a formal setting (e.g. a college lecture, a television debate, panel discussions). This approach is based on a view of learners as capable of processing information and of acting on the basis of what they have processed. It assumes that when learners are faced with new and convincing information about an object, view, situation, they can be led to re-examine existing evaluations they hold about it and revise or change them completely. The formal or rational approach to attitude change is in direct contrast with the informal or group dynamics approach which views learners as social beings needing other people as a basis for self-knowledge and change and uses the group norm discrepant with the existing attitude as an instrument of change.[5]

The more learners elaborate on the content of the communication in an unbiased manner, the more likelihood there is that it will be accepted and bring about enduring change in the desired direction. Elaboration consists of three substeps or mental operations whereby learners (1) try to elicit relevant prior knowledge about incoming information, (2) scrutinize the incoming information and try to make inferences about its explicit or implicit arguments in the light of prior knowledge and (3) draw conclusions on the merits of these arguments. The conclusions are then integrated into a learner's underlying belief structure and (according to the theory) the resulting change is relatively stable and will influence behavior. Important to this guideline is the amount and kind of cognitive activity devoted to the communication. That is, to what extent and how does a person carefully scrutinize and evaluate the content of the communication? Petty and Cacioppo view the extent of elaboration as a continuum going from no thought to complete elaboration of every argument and complete integration of each one into the attitude schema (1986: 8). In fact, in their research, they have actually measured the number of favorable and unfavorable issue-relevant thoughts sparked by the message content.

For Petty and Cacioppo, active elaboration is the key to bringing about a stable change that can influence behavior. In contrast (they say), when motivational and/or ability factors prevent learners from engaging in elaboration, they can be influenced to change an evaluation by a variety of more superficial cues in the message environment (e.g. the attractiveness of the communicator, the number of arguments, the visual prominence of certain content, external distractions and so on). However, the resulting change will not be permanent.

In the action plan presented here, Sessions 6 and 7 engage the learner in the mental operations that constitute elaboration. They compare themselves with the good language learner; determine why they do not always act as the good language learner does; and consider what other skills or knowledge they have acquired autonomously. They are also asked to determine how imitation of good language learners could help them and to decide which characteristics and related strategies of good language learners they will try to emulate.

The intensity with which learners will engage in elaboration of the persuasive communication depends upon the following motivational factors: personal relevance, personal responsibility, multiple message sources, a positive and supportive atmosphere.

Personal relevance refers to the extent to which learners expect the issue to affect their lives and is referred to as ego involvement, issue involvement or personal involvement. From their review of the more recent theory on attitude change, Petty and Cacciopo conclude that this is the most important variable affecting motivation to process a message.

In describing what is essential to changing attitudes, Katz (1960) suggests a framework of four needs for determining what can be highly relevant to a person, i.e. instrumental, ego defensive, knowledge and value expressive needs. These four needs, he maintains, represent a person's deepest motivations for holding certain attitudes.

Instrumental needs are those that refer to the satisfaction derived from achieving positively valued goals or rewards. For a language learner an instrumental need would be being able to study in a foreign university, getting a particular job or being able to function in a new society. Ego defensive needs are intended to protect the individual from his own unacceptable impulses and from the knowledge of threatening forces from without. Thus, language learners who resist learning another language may feel, as some second language acquisition theory suggests, that the new language is a threat to their personal identity — and that it portends a loss of control.[6]

Individuals also have knowledge needs. They need frames of reference to help them understand the world in general and to explain the events that impinge directly upon their lives. Attitudes supply these frames of reference. In the case of language learners, most come into the classroom with strong attitudes about the roles of teachers and learners acquired while in elementary and secondary school. When what they experience in the classroom does not 'fit' into the frames of reference underlying these attitudes, they may resist a teacher's attempts to help them learn.

A fourth type of need in Katz's framework is to be able to give positive expression to one's central values and self-concept. In the case of adult language learners, integral to their self-concept is a striving towards autonomy, and they value their right to make their own decisions. However, in a classroom this is an attitude which may come into direct conflict with the attitudes based on knowledge needs referred to above.[7]

In sum, according to Katz, attitudes or personal evaluations are formed to service these four needs and it is to the extent that learners see the advocated change servicing these needs that it (the change and the message through which it is presented) will be perceived as personally relevant.

Personal responsibility is another factor which will induce learners actively to engage in elaboration of the message. This means that when people are individually responsible for a cognitive task, they will exert more mental effort than when they share the responsibility with others. This notion can be extended to include personal involvement in decision making. That is, motivation to become actively engaged in elaboration of a particular communication will be more intense when the topic is one that learners have chosen.

Multiple message sources: learners will be more willing to process the information when it (the information) is communicated by more than one person. In addition, greater effects will be achieved when each person or source presents different aspects of the topic.

Supportive and positive atmosphere: learners are more likely to attend to the content of a communication and explore its significance for their lives in an atmosphere which provides opportunities to deal with resistance, fear, anxiety and other feelings engendered by the communication situation. These feelings can obstruct objective or unbiased processing if they are not dealt with. A supportive atmosphere would further emphasize the importance of the change and provide encouragement for those who experiment with its implications.

The factors that determine the intensity with which learners may be motivated to engage themselves in processing a 'persuasive communication' are taken into account in several sessions of the action plan. To be *personally relevant*, the information that forms the heart of the 'persuasive communication' must be a response to needs, such as those defined in the preceding discussion (i.e. instrumental, ego defensive, knowledge, value expressive). The data gathering in Session 1, specifically the discussion of the reasons underlying learners' views on their role in language learning, should reveal something about their goals, fears, frames of reference and central values as these relate to their language learning. These insights into their needs should then guide the selection and structuring of the information (or persuasive communication) that is to be presented in Session 4.

In Sessions 2 and 8 learners are made *personally responsible* for making decisions regarding the topics they will discuss, and in Session 7 they draw up a plan of specific behaviors that they will experiment with in order to become more autonomous. Activities in Sessions 3−6 make learners *individually responsible* for processing information that will implicitly argue against beliefs that support any negative attitudes they may have regarding autonomous learning.

One aspect of a *positive and supportive atmosphere* is taken into account in Session 2, where learners are given an opportunity to air feelings if they have not done so already, spontaneously, in the first session. While learners may have many practical reasons for not using the strategies that good language learners use, if negative feelings are an underlying cause this procedure will allow for these concerns to emerge. The teacher−student conferences and class discussions based on students' learning contracts (Session 7) are intended to lend support to attempts at change.

In this action plan, *only one main source of information* (Session 4) is provided.

Ability factors − the extent and direction of the elaboration that learners engage in will depend on the following ability factors: comprehensibility, prior knowledge.

Comprehensibility refers to how the message is presented. Is it vivid and clear? Are the arguments (implicit or explicit) strong? That is, will they engender the elaboration of favorable thoughts, i.e. thoughts that support the desired change? Is the information believable? Does it deal with content with which learners are familiar? Learners should also be given opportunities to hear the information more than once and be led to think about, mentally rehearse and overtly state the new ideas and supporting arguments several times.

In this particular action plan, the content was a summarized statement of the characteristics of good language learners based on research. Each characteristic was specified with detailed examples (Session 4). All the activities in Session 5 are intended to provide learners with the opportunity to view, review and rehearse the material.

Prior knowledge refers to the organized structure of knowledge that learners have already acquired about a particular topic. Interpretations of how this prior knowledge can influence new learnings and change evaluations vary. Some researchers have found that a well-organized schema can make learners less open to opposing views and lead them to generate arguments that oppose the new information and thus further solidify their original position. Moreover, when the new information is seen as too discrepant to their original positions, they may even reject it. This is the view presented by the research summarized by Petty and Cacciopo.

According to other views (notably Sherif and Hovland, 1970) information that is discrepant from existing frames of reference need not always elicit rejection and lasting opposition. Whether it does so or not will depend on the perceived distance or discrepancy of the new information from the listener's original position. Moreover, when attitudes are changed in full awareness of the frames of reference that have supported an original position, the resulting reorganization will tend to have a better chance of lasting than one that takes place without such awareness.

This particular action plan has been devised according to the latter belief — that existing frames of reference need not always bias processing and can be changed if learners are made aware of them. Procedures to help learners become aware of the frames of reference they have acquired regarding autonomous learning are included in Session 1. Raising awareness is the specific purpose of Session 3, and in Session 6 learners will be helped to remain aware of their pre-existing views when they contrast what they have learned about good language learners with what they themselves do and/or believe.

Evaluating the guidelines

Most manuals that deal with the do's and don't's of programming for adults refer to the difficulty of changing adult attitudes. In *Teaching and Learning in Adult Education* (1964), Harry Miller maintains that changing attitudes that deal with an adult's personal and social world causes them discomfort because they are solidly anchored to significant early experiences and such changes will often involve a new set of behaviors — something adults would prefer to avoid. In *Permanent Education: Some Models of Adult Learning and Adult Change* (1974), Huberman states that, the more stabilized an attitude is in a person's life history, the less probability there is of changing it. While Mezirow (1985) does not use the term 'attitudes', he does discuss dependency-producing psychological assumptions which seem to function in much the same way as attitudes. Once aquired, he says, these assumptions fade from consciousness to reappear as anxiety and resistance when they are questioned in later life. In sum, the task and challenge of bringing about change in evaluations or attitudes should not be underestimated.

Certainly, the information-based action plan suggested by the ELM of persuasion is not without its limitations. It assumes that human learners are always rational and, therefore, capable of being influenced if only they process 'persuasive communications' properly. However, experience testifies to the fact that this is not always the case. In this section we shall evaluate the guidelines. How do they compare with other approaches to changing attitudes and beliefs? How useful are they?

Alternative views on changing beliefs and attitudes

The processes underlying the guidelines that shaped the action plan have been acknowledged as essential to the dynamics of personal change by approaches utilized in quite diverse social contexts and for very different aims. One example is the 'laboratory method', which uses the group as the social context and instrument of change. A second example deals with the diffusion of innovations and is taken from the literature on organizational change.

Laboratory method

Referred to as T-(training) Group and Process Analysis, the purpose of the laboratory method is 'to influence attitudes and develop competencies towards learning about human interaction' (Schein and Bennis, 1965: 4). An example of how group dynamics may be used to change attitudes, it is utilized in group approaches to change in many walks of life. Its basic educational strategy is to bring together a group of people who spend anywhere from eight to forty-eight hours together in an instructional face-to-face group. The data for learning are the experienced behavior, feelings, perceptions and reactions of the group members while they are together. According to Joyce and Weil, who have applied the laboratory method to educational settings (1972), learning focuses on four content areas: increased self-knowledge, interpersonal learning, understanding of group dynamics, and self-directed learning skills for improving one's interpersonal and organizational behavior. Using Schein and Bennis's textbook on the laboratory method as their source, Joyce and Weil also list three levels at which learning can occur in response to new information: (1) increased *awareness* of any aspect of the four content areas listed above, which leads to (2) *changed attitudes* towards oneself, others, the group and (3) *new behavior* or improved social skills competence.[8]

Innovation in organizations

In each of the three approaches to the diffusion of innovation in organizations described by Havelock and Havelock (1973), i.e. the Social Interaction School, the Research, Development and Diffusion School, and the Problem Solving School, there is a stage that is referred to as 'diffusion and adoption'.[9] During this stage, dissemination of the innovation brings it to the attention of prospective clients — awareness is raised. Interest is elicited by the provision of more information about the innovation, and clients mentally apply it to their present and anticipated future situation. Sometimes there may even be a trial adoption to allow for more concrete evaluation. Then a decision for adoption is made.

Let us consider, for example, how these processes may apply when an educational institution makes a decision to adopt computer-assisted instruction into their curriculum. General awareness of this innovation is created through the media, professional publications and, perhaps, interchange with institutions that have already adopted computer-assisted instruction. Professional conferences and workshops will elicit further interest on the part of individual teachers and program administrators and provide opportunities for evaluation. Finally, a decision is made to adopt it and resources are set aside for the necessary equipment and training.

The processes involved in the change process of both the T-Group model and the organizational model are outlined in Table 8.4. Although the specific aims and social contexts of these two approaches may be quite different one from the other, they both employ a strategy that concurs in the processes that are basic to bringing about change of strongly held evaluations or attitudes: raising of awareness, change in attitude (interest/evaluation) and the taking on (or adoption) of new behavior implied by the new attitude.

8.4 Analyzing the action plan for the basic processes in attitude change

(a) To what extent are the processes outlined in Table 8.4 implied by the guidelines for attitude change (pp. 118−25)?

TABLE 8.4
Basic process in attitude change

T-group	Diffusion of innovations
Disconfirming information	Dissemination of innovation
↓	↓
Awareness	Awareness
↓	↓
Attitude change	Interest and evaluation
↓	↓
New behavior	Adoption of innovation

(b) How are they incorporated into the action plan presented in this chapter? Consider the objectives and specific procedures.

Usefulness of the guidelines

The action plan for changing beliefs and attitudes presented in this chapter is based on guidelines drawn from theory and research in the literature on attitude change. To evaluate their usefulness it will be necessary, first, to determine whether the action plan works as it is. When implemented with your students, what will the outcome be?

Second, the action plan focused on strategic knowledge and on attitudes learners may hold about their role as learners. Can the same objectives and guidelines be used to develop action plans that focus on the other kinds of metacognitive knowledge presented in Chapter 3 and on other strongly held evaluations about language learning? What will the results be?

The following tasks will help you to begin the evaluation process. They are suggestive. You may wish to devise some that are more appropriate to your interests and situation. As you reflect on your experience with each one, consider the following questions.

(a) Did the sequence work? Did your students understand what they were expected to do? Were they able to do what was asked of them? What was the outcome?
(b) What problems did you encounter as you implemented each session? How did you deal with them?
(c) What revisions do you suggest, if any? Does your experience suggest different procedures? Should some objectives or guidelines be changed or added? Why?

8.5 Replicating the action plan
(a) Use the action plan illustrated in this chapter to introduce the idea of autonomous learning to a group of students you are presently teaching.
(b) Evaluate it using the above questions.

Research in second-language acquisition, referred to in the discussion of person knowledge (Chapter 3), has shown that the following can influence the acquisition of another language: age, language aptitude, intelligence, personality, motivation, sociocultural factors, cognitive style and learning style. False notions or lack of knowledge about these factors may also influence learners' attitudes about their capability to learn autonomously.

8.6 Devising an action plan to change person knowledge

In the next set of tasks, you will use the attitude change guidelines to develop an action plan that will help your students to examine and change, if necessary, the beliefs they hold about one of these personal factors and the attitudes about autonomous learning that these beliefs support.

(a) Determine which of the above factors will be the focus of your action plan.[10]

    (i) Which one do language learners know little about?

    (ii) About which ones do they often hold erroneous beliefs?

(b) Before devising the procedures, analyze your chosen factor to determine the following information.

    (i) What are its defining characteristics?

    (ii) What is the relevance of this factor for language learners in their role as learners? What is its relevance in other aspects of their lives, if any?

    (iii) How can knowledge about this factor affect a learner's approach to language learning?

(c) Use the guidelines and objectives to devise an action plan.

(d) Implement and evaluate your action plan using the questions outlined at the beginning of this section (p. 132).

In previous tasks in this chapter, the intent was to influence learner attitudes towards their role and capability as language learners and to that end information to change learners' strategic knowledge (Task 8.1) and person knowledge (Task 8.6) was provided. The next set of tasks will focus on learners' knowledge about the nature of language (task knowledge) as it may influence their attitudes regarding 'the best way' to learn a language — what they actually do to learn.

8.7 Devising an action plan to change learner beliefs about language

Choose a reading on one of the following topics: (1) the nature of language; (2) the nature of communication; (3) one of the communication skills.

(a) Devise procedures to gather data on what learners already know about the concepts presented in the reading.

(b) Use the information to decide which aspects of the topic learners need to examine and change, and devise an action plan to help them do so.

(c) Before devising the plan, analyze the chosen topic for the following information:

    (i) What are its defining characteristics?

    (ii) How can knowledge about this factor affect a learner's approach to language learning?

(d) Use the guidelines and objectives to outline the procedures of the action plan you will use to help your students understand this concept.

(e) Implement your action plan in the classroom and evaluate it using the questions listed at the beginning of this section (p. 132).

Conclusion

In this chapter you examined guidelines for devising action plans to change language learners' attitudes towards autonomy and expand their knowledge about language learning. The tasks have suggested ways of applying these guidelines to the development of new action plans — a process of experimentation and evaluation that will need to continue until you produce an action plan that works for your students and their particular needs.

Valuable readings

The Elaboration Likelihood Model of persuasion (Petty and Caccioppo, 1986), which has formed the basis for the action plan described in this chapter, provides a comprehensive framework for organizing, categorizing and understanding the basic processes underlying the effectiveness of *persuasive communications*. Though the theory deals explicitly with persuasive communications as the main instrument of bringing about change in beliefs and evaluations, the writers maintain that the basic principles of the model may be applied to other attitude change situations.

For another view on attitude change, see Abelson (1986) who proposes that values may provide a much more realistic and effective approach to attitude change than reasoned argument and logic. Some of the basic concepts presented in the article will be similar to those presented in this chapter. The perspective, however, is quite different and stimulating.

Alternate approaches to attitude change are suggested by the social-therapeutic language teaching methodologies (i.e. Counselling-Language Learning, Suggestopedia, Problem-Posing and Values Clarification) described by Oller and Richard-Amato (1983). Using different techniques and in some cases based on different assumptions about what facilitates human learning and action, these methodologies all seek to change learner attitudes that can inhibit second-language acquisition.

For examples of learner training materials that focus on learner beliefs and attitudes as they apply to language learning in general, see Sinclair and Ellis (1989), Brown (1989) and Rubin and Thompson (1982). Discussions and tasks suggested by these materials would lead to increasing learner awareness of various aspects of their language learning. As noted earlier (Chapter 5), the projects described by Acton (1984), Carrell (1985) and Casanave (1988) include instruction on aspects of task knowledge that are task specific.

Notes

1. As noted in Chapter 7, the term 'session' is used to group together procedures that focus on one particular objective. These procedures will not necessarily be completed in one sitting.
2. A learning contract is a formalized agreement drawn up between a teacher and learner which stipulates the learner's objectives and the methods whereby these objectives will be achieved and evaluated. Guidelines for developing a learning contract are outlined by Knowles (1975) and Dickinson (1987).
3. The action plan is based primarily on the work of Petty and Caccipo because, to my knowledge, it is a unique attempt to bring coherence to the apparently conflicting research findings of much of the earlier research on attitude change in terms of a theory. That is, their theory incorporates the findings and theoretical insights of the earlier rationalist theories and insights from more recent research, including their own many studies which date back to the late 1970s and which have continued on through the late 1980s. In addition, as a theory which places emphasis on the mental elaboration of persuasive communication as the key variable for bringing about stable change in attitudes, it was considered theoretically compatible with the book's emphasis on learners' cognitive involvement in their language learning.

   For information on the earlier rationalist theories see Hovland *et al.* (1953) (reinforcement theories), Sherif and Hovland (1970) (social judgment theories), Festinger (1957) (consistency theories) and Katz (1960) (functional theories).

4. Together with Rubin's article 'What the good language learner can teach us' (1975), Naiman *et al.'s* research on *The Good Language Learner* (1978) laid the groundwork for much of the future research in learner strategies. Included in the study were the results of interviews with thirty-two adult language learners who had successfully learned several languages. These findings were summarized into five characteristic approaches of successful learners to their language learning and referred to as strategies by the researchers. It is this summary that is utilized as the 'persuasive communication' in the action plan in this chapter.

5. For information on the theory underlying the group dynamics approach, consult any compilation of theories in social psychology (e.g. Deutsch and Krauss, 1965) for a discussion of field theory.

6. The idea of a 'language ego', introduced by Guiora *et al.* (1972), points to this kind of ego defensiveness. According to Guiora *et al.*, learners develop a language ego in the acquisition of their native language. Learners with weaker egos, it is hypothesized, will feel threatened by the new language and will resist learning it. Their language 'ego boundaries' are less permeable. Others, less threatened and capable of greater empathy, will acquire the language more quickly or better. The notion of ego defensiveness in the face of language acquisition is also a key notion in Curran (1976).

7. This idea of the conflict between adult learners' desire for autonomy and their acquired frames of reference about the teacher's role proposed by Knowles (1976) has already been referred to in Chapter 4.

8. See Joyce and Weil (1972) for a description of how the laboratory method can be applied in education. The chapter also lists important references on the T-Group model.

9. For other references to literature dealing with change in organizations, see Griffin and Liebermann (1974), Kirkpatrick (1985) and London (1988).

10. Students need not hold completely negative attitudes toward autonomous learning to benefit from this action plan. For those students who already have positive attitudes towards autonomous learning, an action plan that intends to revise erroneous notions they have acquired on the listed factors or to provide them with brand new information about it would serve to strengthen these positive attitudes.

Chapter 9

Settings for promoting learner autonomy

Focus   What are different ways of promoting learner autonomy on a program level? How can learner training be incorporated into a language curriculum?

Process   • Six program settings
       • Learner autonomy and the language curriculum

Outcome   An understanding of different ways of incorporating learner training into a language training curriculum

Six program settings

9.1   Analyzing six program settings for promoting learner autonomy
The following descriptions illustrate how training to promote learner autonomy has been included in the curriculum of six language training settings.

Read through each description (1) to identify the communicative needs of the learners, i.e. why the students are studying another language, and (2) to determine the decisions made regarding the following aspects of each program curriculum.

- *Learner training syllabus*   What is the *content* of the learner training? Will the students learn to use strategies? Will their knowledge about the language learning process be expanded? Will their attitudes towards autonomous learning be changed? Is the learner training *a part of* the language courses offered to the students or is it a *separate* offering? Is the learner training content appropriate to the communication needs of the learners?
- *Learning arrangements*   In what *group arrangements* is the learner training offered (with whole classes, small groups)? Where does it take place (e.g. classroom, self-access center)?
- *Decision making*   Who makes the *decisions* about the language skills that are the focus of the learner training? About the content of the learner training? About the tasks used to practise the skills? About where the practice takes place?
- *Teacher role*   What is the primary *role* of the teacher? Does she function as an instructor? Facilitator of learning? Resource person? Learning counsellor?

SETTING 1

PROJECT FOR EXPERIENTIAL LEARNING OF ENGLISH AND FINNISH IN ELEMENTARY AND INTERMEDIATE LEARNING IN FINNISH SCHOOLS

Belonging to a small linguistic community, Finnish people need to learn foreign languages. Languages are their 'gateway' to international communication. Therefore, within the compulsory education system (ages 7–16), every Finnish learner is obliged to learn the basics of at least two foreign languages, plus an optional third one (grades 8 and 9).

A four-year pilot project in experiential teaching of Finnish and English was launched in 1984 at the Department of Teacher Education, University of Tampere, Finland, under the auspices of the National Board of General Education. Four experienced classroom teachers and four experienced English teachers from four different schools, working with a total of ninety students, participated in the in-service training.

As defined by the initiator of the project, Viljo Kohonen (1987: 50):

> Experiential foreign language learning is . . . personality development enabling the learner to become increasingly self-directed and responsible for his own learning. This process means a gradual shift of the initiative to the learner, encouraging him to bring in his own contributions and experiences. Instead of the teacher setting tasks and standards of acceptable performance, the learner is increasingly in charge of his own learning . . .

The project was motivated by the following considerations.

1. Educational goals set by recent Finnish school laws
In a comprehensive school law (1983), educational goals were defined in terms of learner characteristics, i.e. schools should aim to educate pupils so that they are well balanced, responsible, autonomous, creative, cooperative and peace-loving.

2. The need to test and develop the English syllabus
Revised in 1982, the syllabus defines the general aims of foreign language teaching as helping learners acquire the following:

- the useful basic skills needed in everyday situations;
- a positive attitude to language study;
- the ability to maintain and develop their skills after school.

3. The possible change of the commencement of the first foreign language from grade 3 (age 9) to grade 4

4. The shift from ability grouping to heterogeneous groups
The shift from ability grouping or tracking in mathematics and foreign languages in 1985 to heterogeneous groupings increased the importance of self-directed learning as a way of coping with learner differences.

5. Present emphasis on language training
At present the main emphasis in the schools is language training and only a few teachers are involved in learner training. The purpose of the project was to include learner training as one of the main objectives of foreign language education and to pilot the pedagogical possibilities of doing it in practice.

Materials to be used to promote autonomous learning

Materials were prepared by Viljo Kohonen (1987). The educational goals and subject matter aims were listed as follows.

1. What kinds of personal development should be promoted and facilitated?
   - positive self-concept, self-esteem, positive view of oneself as a language learner
   - self-direction, responsibility, initiative
   - self-control, concentration, imagination
   - creative, intuitive thinking, inference making
   - cooperation, respect for others
   - awareness of planning, monitoring, and assessing one's own learning
2. What kinds of knowledge and skills should learners be helped to acquire?
   - pronunciation, spelling, vocabulary, grammar
   - functional competence, purposeful language use
   - sociolinguistic competence, acceptable language use
   - strategic competence, making predictions, guessing, risk-taking

The content of learner education included the following.

1. Self-knowledge as a learner:
   - Who am I as a person?
   - How do I see my role as a learner?
   - How do I feel about myself?
   - How self-reliant am I?
   - How responsible do I feel for my own life and learning?
2. Task knowledge, i.e. a personal map of the learning task or metalinguistic knowledge of language and communication:
   - What does language consist of?
   - What does it mean to 'communicate' in the foreign language?
3. Strategic knowledge:
   - How do I attempt to solve problems?
   - How do I learn language?
   - What strategies are there for learning vocabulary, reading, listening, speaking?
   - What strategies do I use?
   - Could I improve my learning efficiency by learning new strategies?

His general 'design of learning' consisted of the following.

1. Themes and topics: Topics and themes relevant to the learner's needs and interests are chosen for the learning and practice of language skills. These topics must be connected to the learner's situation and expand gradually to the surrounding society and international connections. To a great extent, these themes and topics are presented through stories, oral and written.
2. Design of activities: The promotion of learner independence is stressed in designing class activities. Teachers are encouraged to evaluate their activities as follows:
   - Who analyzes the needs?
   - Who defines the objectives?
   - Who decides when, where and how often learning is to take place?
   - Who chooses the materials?
   - Who chooses the work techniques?

- Who decides on levels and criteria for evaluation?
- Who monitors the learning programme?

Learner education was done through the following types of activities.

1. Talks with learners in groups and individually:
   - Why do I study English?
   - What do I want to achieve (own aspirations)?
2. Small projects — joint planning in small groups
3. Individual tasks — learners may
   - collect words on topics of personal interest
   - make questions on textbook lessons
   - make vocabulary games
   - modify textbook stories
   - peer edit written work
   - keep a personal learner diary
4. Learner contracts — these are binding agreements between learners and their teachers and learners and themselves. The following items are taken into account when drawing up a contract:
   - What to do — objectives
   - What materials/resources to use
   - What activities to engage in
   - When work is to be completed
   - How to demonstrate completion of task
   - How assessment is to be done

Teacher preparation

Student teachers are introduced to autonomous and experiential learning while receiving their graduate training. They participate in a series of workshops and seminars offered by the Department of Teacher Education. School-based education relying on teachers' own expertise and experience is also contemplated, and currently the work is moving towards using cooperative learning in staff development and language classes.

SETTING 2

LANGUAGE TRAINING PROGRAM IN THE SECRETARIAT OF THE UNITED NATIONS

The United Nations Language Training Program, located in the Secretariat of the United Nations in New York City, is a training service offered by the Office of Human Resources Management. It trains staff members of the United Nations and diplomats attached to the missions of the United Nations in the six official languages — Arabic, Chinese, English, French, Spanish and Russian. Upon recruitment, staff are expected to have a working knowledge of at least one of the two working languages of the Secretariat, English and French. They are encouraged through various incentives to learn additional languages of the organization by taking one or more of the available language courses. In the case of English, here in New York, language study is not only undertaken for professional reasons but also in order to cope better with the English speaking environment. Finally, many staff members pursue language study because of their interest in the culture or to further their own proficiency. The English curriculum consists of seven levels; the French and Spanish of eight; the Russian of nine and the Arabic and Chinese of nine and ten respectively. They all concentrate on the four language skills with a special emphasis on reading, listening and grammar.

Autonomous learning within the program

The decision to incorporate autonomous learning into the curriculum was made by the administration of the language training program to meet the needs of advanced learners who wish to continue with their language learning after completing the most advanced courses. Before the decision, some faculty members had attended workshops on how to promote learner autonomy or had done background reading in the subject, and insights from these experiences were shared at program-organized seminars.

English guided self-study

In the first phase of program development for autonomous learning, described here, guided self-study workshops were developed and offered to students who had reached the most advanced levels in English. The workshops were organized according to skills — a reading/writing section and a listening/speaking section — but the main objective of the workshop was to enable students to learn these skills autonomously. There were from five to twelve participants in the workshops and they met together with a teacher for a period of ten or eleven weeks. The following excerpts from orientation materials (Vaughan, 1987) illustrate the content and tasks of the guided self-study workshops for students of English.

United Nations Language Training Program
Guided Self Study in English   Fall 1987

Reading/writing section

This is not a 'regular' class in which a teacher leads students through a set of materials. In Guided Self-Study, each of you make your own evaluations of your needs and start to work out strategies that will help you attain specified goals. My role as the teacher is twofold: that of resource person, providing some materials or giving you suggestions as to where you can find them; and that of discussion guide for all the students as a group. The class meets once a week for ten weeks, but it is up to each of you to decide whether or not the goal or goals you have set for yourself can be attained partially by coming to class and discussing language learning strategies with other students.

Having finished Level VIII, you have crossed a major hurdle in your learning of English. Obviously, your English is far more than adequate. Nevertheless, I assume you have signed up for this course because you are ambitious enough to want to develop greater expertise and proficiency in the language. You no longer need language classes *per se*, but you would like some guidance as to the most efficient way to keep moving ahead in your skills. (Please let me know if my assumptions are wrong!)

As you assume the role of teacher (teacher of yourself), you need to focus on some of the questions teachers and administrators of programs try to answer before proceeding with a class:

1. *What does the student need to learn?*
    (a) What are your strengths in reading? Your weaknesses?
    (b) Which of the problem areas do you want to tackle first?

To help you answer these questions, let us focus on why you want or need to improve your skills in reading. Rank the following in terms of importance for you and add/delete as relevant:

- To read newspapers or magazines
- To read documents at work
- To read scholarly books (e.g. for university courses)
- To read for pleasure
- To read faster
- To improve my vocabulary
- To keep up on current affairs
- To understand American culture better
- To help my writing
- Other (please specify) . . . .

Look at your list. Consider the top three choices. Which of these would you like to tackle first? Put this answer in 1(b) above. Now, let us move on to the next question a 'teacher' might ask.

2. *What materials will be most helpful to the student?*
To answer this question, consider materials you enjoy working with. Are you the kind of student, for instance, who enjoys a programmed approach — short passages with difficult words defined and questions at the end to test your comprehension? Or do you find that constricting? Do you prefer to read articles that interest you in newspapers and then look up words you need in dictionaries and discuss the content of the articles with friends? What materials have you most enjoyed in previous English classes? What English reading material do you pick up for fun now?

   You will learn fastest from materials that appeal to you personally. However, it may be that the materials you most enjoy are not the ones that you need to work on (see your answer to 1(a)). If that is the case, then move on to Question 3.

3. *What strategies of learning will help the student learn even the difficult materials?*
This is where you can get creative. In the past you had to rely to a large extent on your teacher's decisions about how you would learn something. She might have spent forty-five minutes on vocabulary definitions for instance, when you would have benefited more from working with others in a small group. Now, you choose what strategies will be most appropriate to the task in front of you. (To give you some ideas you may not have thought of before, we will be reading Joan Rubin's *How to be a Successful Language Learner.*)

   First, think carefully about your goal. Say, for instance, that it is to be able to read and understand UN documents quickly and easily.

(a) What are your problems with the documents? Be as specific as you can. (Is it a matter of vocabulary, or is the syntax a problem?)

(b) What strategies have you tried so far? (Have you tried outlining paragraphs or summarizing, or making alphabetical vocabulary lists that you can keep handy?)

(c) On what occasions have you been successful in reaching your goal? (Perhaps when you also discussed the document with a colleague? Or when you took it home and read it several times over a weekend? Or when you read it quietly away from the distractions of the telephone and office conversation?) You need to become aware of the kind of environment in which you learn best.

There are other questions that teachers ask as well as the above three. Teachers have to figure out a good way to evaluate the progress of their students, for instance. You also will need to work out a way of evaluating yourself. And teachers have to be flexible enough to alter the goals they have set for students when necessary. As your own teacher, you must look at yourself, your abilities, your weaknesses, with an objective eye. Do not expect more than you know you can do. But do not expect less!

In the next ten weeks, you should set yourself and work toward a reasonable goal (or several goals, if you have the time). The purpose of the class and of the teacher is to help you achieve these goals. Whether you do or not is up to you.

Participants are asked to choose a goal which is achievable in ten weeks. It must be specific and limited. They complete the following sheet and return it to the guided self-study teacher two days before the next session. The teacher reads and plans the lesson accordingly. This helps her decide on plans and material throughout the sessions.

NAME . . . .

Guided Self Study   Reading

GOAL (be specific):

MATERIALS NEEDED FROM TEACHER:

MATERIALS I WILL PROVIDE:

INITIAL STRATEGIES FOR REACHING GOALS:

USE OF CLASS HOUR
_____ discuss my problems and successes in attaining my goals with the other students
_____ work in small groups or in pairs on texts either provided by the teacher or brought by students
_____ have short sessions with the teacher to assess my progress and particular problems
_____ use the class hour to read texts quietly

_____ hand in written assignments once a week and have them corrected/commented upon by the teacher

_____ other _____

French guided self-study

The objectives of the autonomous learning components organized for advanced students in French were outlined as follows in the self-study manual provided to the students (translated from Guerchon and Muir, 1987):

1. to provide advanced students of French with an opportunity for a systematic and individualized study using available materials;
2. to facilitate a reflection on their manner of language learning with a consideration of the value of trying alternative strategies;
3. to give advanced students who cannot follow a course the possibility of continuing their linguistic study autonomously.

Rather than meet as a workshop, as did the students of English, the French students consulted with the teacher individually (1) to discuss their problems, (2) to work with aural or written materials they had chosen themselves or (3) to get feedback on work they had accomplished on their own.

The manual with which they were provided outlined the course objectives (as noted above) and general information about available resources (e.g. audio, video, textbooks) and cultural events. The second section (1) introduced them to the idea of learning strategies and their utility, (2) included excerpts from *How To Be a More Successful Language Learner* (Rubin and Thompson, 1982) and a self-assessment questionnaire and (3) discussed the appropriate use of a dictionary.

Excerpts from the student's manual illustrate three kinds of questionnaires that students were expected to complete as part of their planning for autonomous study: a self-assessment questionnaire (Table 9.1), a questionnaire to determine their objectives (Table 9.2) and a questionnaire to determine the allocation of their time (Table 9.3).

Audio and video materials to which students were referred had been developed prior to the initiation of the self-study. These materials had been recorded at the United Nations and treated international themes. Written documents related to students' professional needs were also readily avialable. At the same time, students were encouraged to find and use materials related to their needs themselves.

The self-study in both English and French has now become a permanent feature of the program curriculum. Moreover, what teachers developed and applied in the self-study component, which was separate from the language skills curriculum, is now being carried over into the language skills classes at all levels of proficiency.

SETTING 3

PARSIPANNY ADULT AND COMMUNITY EDUCATION CENTER

The Parsipanny Adult and Community Education Center (ACEC), located in New Jersey (USA), is a multi-faceted adult education program developed to service the needs of adult learners. It is sponsored by government, local and tuition funds. Its ESL program is designed to develop the linguistic and coping skills of adult immigrant students who may or may not be attending college. These students vary in their educational and

TABLE 9.1
Auto-évaluation des compétences et objectifs pour l'apprentissage du français

Compétences	Très bien	Bien	Mal

A. *Ecoute:* Pouvez-vous?

- Dégager l'information principale de déclarations publiques, annonces, discours, reunions, exposés, faits en votre présence.
- Comprendre en substance les informations à la radio, ou à la télévision, ou un enregistrement sur magnétophone.
- Suivre une conversation dont le sujet vous intéresse entre des francophones parlant à vitesse normale.
- Comprendre des expressions d'humour, d'ironie, ou du langage parlé.
- Comprendre une conversation téléphonique sur des sujets généraux ou connus.

B. *Lecture:* Pouvez-vous lire?

- Des rapports et documents de l'ONU dans votre domaine de travail.
- Des articles de journaux et périodiques sur des sujets qui vous intéressent.
- De la correspondance liée à votre travail (lettres, télégrammes, messages, annonces, formulaires etc.).
- Comprenez-vous le point de vue de l'auteur d'un article?
- Si oui, à la première lecture?
- Lisez-vous à la même vitesse que dans votre langue maternelle?

C. *Ecriture:* Pouvez-vous?

- Composer des notes et lettres brèves sur des sujets connus.
- Rédiger des comptes rendus sur votre expérience, vos voyages, vos travaux.
- Ecrire sans faire d'erreurs grammaticales.
- Ecrire sans faire d'erreurs d'orthographe.
- Ecrire sans vous référer à un dictionnaire.
- Ecrire sans traduire de votre première langue.
- Ecrire aussi vite que dans votre langue.

Source: Guerchon and Muir, 1987

professional backgrounds, but it is clear that they all need English to function adequately in their new culture. The learning center offers English courses that attempt to meet these needs. They are directed towards learners who range from knowing no English at all to learners who have reached advanced levels of proficiency. Course objectives focus on language in social and vocational settings that are a part of the immigrants' daily life, e.g. reading classified ads, answering the telephone. Individual lessons plans may also focus on a particular function (e.g. persuasion), a grammar structure (e.g. the passive voice) or aspects of English phonology. Students are placed in the program according to their proficiency levels. Skills are taught in an integrated fashion and practised in contexts appropriate to the learners' needs.

TABLE 9.2
Objectifs de l'apprentissage

Classez par ordre d'importance (1 = plus important) les raisons pour lesquelles vous voulez améliorer votre français:

- pour être capable de lire des documents liés à votre travail
- pour pouvoir lire des journaux comme *Le Monde* ou tout autre publication du même niveau de langue
- pour pouvoir écrire des lettres et mémoranda sur des sujets concernant l'ONU
- pour pouvoir écrire des rapports sur votre travail
- pour pouvoir écrire n'importe quel texte
- pour pouvoir écouter et comprendre la radio et la télévision
- pour pouvoir écouter et comprendre des conversations informelles entre amis ou collègues
- pour pouvoir réussir l'Examen d'aptitude Linguistique
- pour pouvoir écouter et comprendre des discours et conférences
- pour pouvoir prendre des notes pendant des réunions ou des conférences
- pour voyager pendant vos congés
- pour partir en mission
- pour obtenir un poste plus intéressant

Source: Guerchon and Muir, 1987

TABLE 9.3
Disponibilité pour votre étude

Combien de fois par semaine pouvez-vous?	De temps en temps	0 fois	1 fois	2 à 3	Plus
• Lire un journal (en français)					
• Lire un livre (en français)					
• Lire des documents (en français)					
• Voir un film					
• Voir une émission de télé					
• Parler avec des amis francophones					
• Parler avec des collègues francophones					
• Parler avec de la famille francophone					
• Faire des exercises sur la langue					
• Ecouter une émission de radio					
• Ecouter des chansons					
• Ecouter des discours					
• Autre?					

Source: Guerchon and Muir, 1987

Autonomous learning in the program

While the language skills syllabus had been developed to focus on the communicative and linguistic needs of the students, the program director felt that what could be done to meet these needs in the classroom was limited and that learners equipped with the skills of learning would be able to further their communicative competence independently by taking advantage of the opportunities available in their social environment. Therefore, included in a teacher education grant solicited from the State Department of Education was a component which would provide for the special training of a select core of teachers in the methods appropriate to promoting learner autonomy. The following excerpts from program documents illustrate how learner training has been integrated into the program.

Collecting data for learner profiles

When students register at the center, they are interviewed to determine their attitudes towards language learning, the extent to which they use English and their personal goals. The interview is recorded for review by the teacher at a later date. A survey form (Table 9.4) is also administered to gather information for the teacher and to make students start thinking about how they learn best.

TABLE 9.4
How I think I learn best

Use the following scale in commenting on the following:

1	2	3	4	5
never	rarely	sometimes	often	very frequently

1. I learn step-by-step.
2. I learn best by acting a situation out in diaglogue form.
3. I learn best by seeing something first.
4. I learn best by listening to something first.
5. I learn best by using a combination of senses.
6. I learn best by using a variety of techniques depending on the situation.
7. I think my mood or how I feel determines how I learn best.
8. I learn best in one-to-one situations.
9. I learn best when doing small group work. I like to have somebody with me to work with.
10. I learn best by working alone at my own rate.
11. I learn best as part of a large classroom group.
12. I generally participate actively in small-group discussions.
13. I generally participate actively in large-group discussions.

Source: C. Broder, K. Brown, B. Foerster and R. Kaufman, Parsipanny Adult and Community Education Center

Integrating strategy training in the language training syllabus

The following excerpts of the objectives of lesson plans for the intermediate level illustrate further how cognitive and self-management strategies have been integrated into the planning (from C. Broder, K. Brown, B. Foerster and R. Kaufmann, Parsipanny Adult and Community Education Center).

Intermediate level

Lesson 3 — pronunciation practice with idioms

Objectives
- To recognize and produce /   / in stressed and unstressed positions
- To introduce common spellings of /   /
- To practise phrases and idioms with the unstressed words 'a, of, to'
- To provide practice in the following strategies: selective attention and self-monitoring

Lesson 4 — using the telephone/taking messages

Objectives
- To provide practice in giving and receiving messages on the telephone
- To enable students develop proficiency in oral spelling and reciting numbers

- To enable students develop proficiency in aural comprehension of letters and numbers
- To provide practice in one self-management strategy: self-assessment

Lesson 6 — classified ads

Objectives
- To increase vocabulary relating to classified ads for cars
- To practise reading abbreviations
- To share knowledge of good consumer practices
- To practise inferring meaning from context

Introducing strategies
In a separate lesson used at the outset of a course students are introduced to the notion 'strategy' through a game entitled 'take a number'. The game gives students multiple examples of language practice they can engage in outside the classroom. At the heart of each there is a strategy. The game is also intended to make students start thinking differently about the rules that govern appropriate behavior in the language classroom, i.e. their and the teachers' roles and the settings where language learning can take place. Five of the twelve activities that constitute the game are described below together with procedures for using the game in class and the rules (from R. Kaufmann).

Procedures for using the game in class

1. Introduce the game and rules to the class. Explain to the students that the objective of the game is to learn ways to learn more English. Review the rules. Review the point values of the tasks.
2. Discuss the concept of 'learning strategies' with the students. A strategy is a 'trick' to help one learn more easily. Practise the trick in class by playing the game. Then, practise the trick outside class to help you learn more English.

Activity	*Language skill*	*Strategy*
Make a friend	Listening, speaking	Global practice

Find someone who speaks American English. Talk and listen to him or her for five minutes.

Write it down	Vocabulary building	Cooperation, resourcing, mnemonic

Look around the classroom. Find five things whose name you do not know. Ask someone for the name or look it up in a dictionary. Write down the name on paper.

Turn it on	Listening	Inferencing, monitoring

Turn on the tape recorder and listen for two minutes. Tell:

(1) Who is talking? A woman or a man?
(2) What kind of program is it? Music, news, talk show?
(3) Write down any words you understand.

Put it back	Vocabulary practice	Imagery

Imagine a room in your house. Take out all the furniture. Put it back naming each piece.

Add it up   Vocabulary building   Mnemonics

Without a pencil, add up these numbers in your head: one, nine, thirty-five, ten.

Rules

1. All players roll the die in turn and move the number of spaces on the board indicated on the die.[1]
2. Pick the card with the same number as the space you land on.
3. All players do what their card says to do.[2]
4. Roll the die again.
5. If a player lands on the same number as before, he/she may pick another card or perform the same task again.
6. Play continues for fifteen minutes.
7. Each card is worth a certain number of points. The winner is the person who has the highest number of points at the end of fifteen minutes.

Recommended number of players: 1–4.

Point values

1.	Make a list	2 points
2.	Make a friend	5 points
3.	Write it down	3 points
4.	Turn it on	3 points
5.	Keep in touch I	2 points
6.	Take a guess	2 points
7.	Tell me again	3 points
8.	As a friend	2 points
9.	Put it back	4 points
10.	Keep in touch II	3 points
11.	Add it up	1 point
12.	Look for clues	3 points

SETTING 4

ESCUELA SUPERIOR DE ADMINISTRACION Y DIRECCION DE EMPRESAS

The Escuela Superior de Administracion y Direccion de Empresas (ESADE), located in Barcelona (Spain), is a business school with a language academy which is fairly independent in status. The academy services students enrolled in the business school, who take classes to fulfill their language requirement, and students who enroll only for language classes in the academy itself. They study English, French and Spanish for academic, professional and social purposes. During a year the language academy handles approximately 4000 students in classes which average eleven students. In addition, there are approximately 900 students in the business school who receive classes from teachers of the language academy.

The language syllabus at the Academy covers seven levels of proficiency from beginning to advanced, each level consisting of approximately 100 classroom hours. In addition to these courses there are 'special' courses (in self-expression, media, exam preparation etc.).

Autonomous learning within the program

In fall 1986, ESADE administrators decided to experiment with greater learner independence and choice in the learning process, and so to explore the possibilities of creating self-access facilities. The director gave responsibility to two teachers who visited four self-access centres in England and read as much as possible about independent learning to develop a long-range plan. In the fall of 1987 a pilot self-access room was opened under the direction of these two faculty members. The self-access room is considered part of the language school and its coordinators are responsible to the person in charge of language classes.

During its first year of operation, the center was opened to students at the pre-first certificate level, and since that time the self-access team has been constantly expanding its offerings. It has handled approximately an average of 120 students per week from both the language academy and the business school. Students from the language academy come on a drop-in basis or to do specially prepared course tasks during class time. Others sign up for a tutorial course which gives them unlimited use of the self-access room as well as one-hour meetings with a tutor on a bi-weekly basis. All students from the business school, whatever their degree program, use access on a drop-in basis. In addition, students from the undergraduate business school who have completed their first cycle language requirements can choose self-access from among several optional courses.

Both language learning and learner training, as provided in the ESADE self-access room, are virtually teacher independent. In this setting, teachers serve primarily as providers of resources and language learning experts. Just as access to language learning materials is intended to be self-selected, the strategies which students might want to use are also intended to be independently chosen.

The self-access coordinators have brought together materials which focus on reading, listening, grammar, functions and exam preparation. These are assigned a number according to the approximate correspondence with the seven levels of proficiency that correspond to the language school courses. In addition all pertinent materials are assigned a topic (e.g. health) and a subtopic (e.g. dieting) so that learners can easily find materials related to their specific interests. To serve the needs of the business school students, a special 'business' category was established. Students may choose to work with any of four types of media — printed materials (including articles, books and exercises), audio tapes, videos and computers. Worksheets with exercises and answers on the back are available to accompany the reading, audio and video material.

The following handouts have been developed to help students self-direct their way through the materials in the self-access room.

A. First Steps to Self-Access
B. How to Use the Self-Access Room
C. A Plan of Study
D. Learning Skills

E. Cassette Information
F. Reader Information
G. Video Information
H. Exam Information

Learner training is provided in two different ways

Specialized *materials* providing information on learning strategies, metacognitive knowledge and attitudes needed for autonomy are available to the student. Learning strategy messages are sometimes included in the answers to language exercises. A second option, currently being evaluated, offers students the self-access option with a *tutorial* which explicitly and systematically introduces students to the learner training materials in the room and allots time to discuss the significance of self-access.

Alternative 1: Materials

Separate materials providing training in the various components of the learning strategies and knowledge needed for autonomy have been developed. The following excerpts illustrate their content and the approach to learner training used in the ESADE self-access center.

TABLE 9.5
Attitudes questionnaire for self-access

Not every learner can benefit from a self-access program, and even those who can may need to use it in different ways. This questionnaire will help you decide if self-access is a good idea for you and will raise some issues related to language learning.

Please respond to each of the following statements by writing a number from 1 to 5 in the box next to it, using the following explanation:

5 — agree strongly
4 — agree
3 — neither agree nor disagree
2 — disagree
1 — disagree strongly
(Try to answer quickly — an immediate response is generally best.)

☐   1. I need to learn English immediately.
☐   2. One problem with studying English is that classes are at fixed hours.
☐   3. Cassettes, videos and computers can be used best by individual students.
☐   4. A big problem in most classes is that students have different levels.
☐   5. I prefer to study with people who want to learn English quickly.
☐   6. If I had the right materials, I'd prefer to spend some time studying alone.
☐   7. Listening comprehension is an important skill that I need to practise.
☐   8. Contact with teachers should be used mainly for speaking practice.
☐   9. The best way to learn a language is through teacher explanations.
☐ 10. One important part of learning English is reading about interesting topics.
☐ 11. Teachers sometimes don't teach what students need to learn.
☐ 12. Grammar exercises and written homework are not necessary.
☐ 13. There isn't enough time in the classroom to assimilate all the information.
☐ 14. I enjoy learning in a group with other students.
☐ 15. Students usually don't have enough choice about what and how they study.
☐ 16. If I didn't have to learn English I wouldn't.
☐ 17. It's not the student's responsibility to decide on the course content.
☐ 18. I need to improve my listening comprehension.
☐ 19. A lot of grammar can be done without a teacher.
☐ 20. I haven't got enough time outside class to study.
☐ 21. The only skill I need to practise is speaking.
☐ 22. You cannot learn without teacher supervision.
☐ 23. I have no serious problems in reading and writing in English.
☐ 24. I think I am a competent student with good study habits.
☐ 25. Reading is one part of the language I don't practise enough.

Source: Barnett, 1989

1. First steps to self-access
Students are first asked to determine their attitudes towards learning autonomously.

(a) They complete an attitudes questionnaire (Table 9.5). Students also analyze the questionnaire to determine whether or not they will benefit from self-access by looking at how their answers reveal the following:
- the extent of their motivation
- their willingness to accept learner responsibility
- their ability to work outside the classroom
- their need to practise specific language skills

(b) They are given an explanation of self-access in terms of the following questions:
- What is the aim of self-access?
- Does self-access mean there is no teacher?
- What kinds of skills can be practised in self-access?
- When should I start?
- What does a 'plan of study' mean?
- Does self-access always mean working alone?
- How do I begin to use this room?

2. A plan of study
A second handout introduces them to the decisions involved in planning for self-access study (Table 9.6).

3. Learning skills
Learning skills materials provide training exercises to let students see how strategies can be used to improve their use of the various language skills. Table 9.7 illustrates how this is done for reading.

4. Information sheets
These are sheets that accompany each medium through which the student may learn/practise language skills. Besides providing students with information about how the materials are organized, these sheets include brief references to task ((a), (b), (d)) and strategic (c) knowledge:

(a) factors to take into account in selecting language skills materials;
(b) explanations about two broad kinds of reading, i.e. to learn the language or to get information;
(c) explanations about reading strategies;
(d) differences between listening with and without verbal clues (i.e. the audiotape versus the video).

5. Learning hints included with exercises
Learning hints, for example, may encourage students to evaluate their work by referring to the answer sheet that is provided. These hints also make them reflect on the difficulty they had in completing the task and alternative ways of approaching it.

Alternative 2: Tutorial
Supervisors of the self-access room have noted that one of the biggest problems is to get users who come to the center to use the learner training materials. There is lack of awareness of their significance and even, perhaps, resistance towards using the materials. Most students tend to go directly to materials related to the language skills

TABLE 9.6
A plan of study

A good plan can be an essential step to good learning. Before filling out the one we have prepared for you on the next page, read these comments about the different sections so you can complete it as well as possible.

1. OBJECTIVES

If you define them well your work will be clearer. An objective such as 'I want to improve my vocabulary' is vague; it will not help you very much. But something like 'I want to be able to understand non-specialist magazine articles without using a dictionary' gives you a very clear idea of what to do.

Are you going to concentrate on listening? Grammar? A test area? Reading? Or one of the other major areas? What topics are most interesting or useful for you? What are you good at? What do you need more work at?

As you think about these 'needs' be realistic about the time you have and how long it will take to accomplish the objectives you set: if you are too ambitious you may only end up frustrated.

2. SELECTING MATERIALS

After you have defined your objectives, you should probably think about what materials you will use; if you need to understand the news, will you go to the video, cassette tapes, magazines? Also what is the best order to use the materials you've chosen?

3. SELECTING A METHOD

One thing is WHAT you study, another is HOW!! Will you always work alone? Will you take notes? Will you use the worksheets we've provided? What techniques will you use to help you understand and remember? (And will you need to learn some new techniques or strategies?)

4. KEEPING A RECORD

A simple record of what you do can be VERY useful. For example:
Date: April 8   What: 5.B.86 (article on pollution)
Why: to practise reading for main idea
How: read once quickly; wrote a 100-word summary
Comments: need to improve technical vocabulary (power station, etc.)

5. EVALUATION

Periodic evaluation — thinking about what you have done, testing yourself even — will help you decide how to improve your learning. Then you can make another PLAN.

Now look at the Plan of Study on the next page. On the back we show you one example of how it could be filled out.

PLAN OF STUDY

1. My objectives for the next ... weeks are:

2. Considering reading, writing, listening, grammar, vocabulary and exam practice as separate skills, I should concentrate on the following to accomplish my objective:

3. The topic areas I will concentrate on are:

4. I will use the following materials:

5. I will work in the following way:

6. I will keep a record of my work by:

7. I will evaluate my work by:

Source: Barnett, 1989

TABLE 9.7
Reading

4.1   Look at the computer disk 6.C.12. Go to the file called 'strats' and do the exercise. In it you see questions BEFORE you see a text and are asked to find the answers in the short time the text is flashed on the screen.

4.2   Go to reading 6.B.24; read the questions before you start and then spend no more than ONE MINUTE looking at the text before you answer them.

These two activities are simply an example of two broad reading strategies. 4.1 is a scanning exercise — it asks you to find specific information in a short time. 4.2 is a skimming exercise — it asks you to get the general idea of a text in a short time. Neither of these are what most people call 'reading', but we do things like this all the time. When you want to know the time a movie starts you do not read the entire entertainment page; you scan it until your eyes hit upon the name of the cinema or of the film. If you aren't sure if you want to see the movie or not, maybe you'll look at a review in the paper, skimming it to see if the critic liked it (but not reading it for details about the production, the actors or the plot).

You can train yourself to 'read' in English by developing skimming and scanning strategies. These will help you do any sort of reading.

Source: Barnett, 1989

they need — looking for a spoken explanation and materials to practise. Once this has happened, it becomes hard to break into their routines to suggest more useful ways of working in the room (Barnett, 1989).

Therefore a second option, which is presently being evaluated, offers students a self-access option with a small group tutorial. Students who enroll for this option meet once fortnightly for a tutorial session of one hour and unlimited time in the self-access room. In order to evaluate the effects of teacher direction on self-access room use, some of these tutorial groups (experimental groups) focus on orienting learners to training materials and different self-access options. They then discuss the assigned tasks and reflect on the use of strategies, their applicability to learner needs, the validity of computer activities and the techniques for using videotapes and other similar topics.

Other groups (control groups) use their meeting time to practise speaking skills about topics having absolutely nothing to do with their work in the self-access room. They may speak about prison reform, exams or any topic which interests them, the teacher playing the role of conversation stimulator and occasionally providing corrective feedback.

It is hypothesized that students who are in the directed groups will use the materials more effectively and probably develop more positive attitudes towards self-access than students in the control group. (Results of the study are not available at this time.)

SETTING 5

UNIVERSITY OF TORONTO SCHOOL OF CONTINUING STUDIES

Two kinds of ESL courses are offered by the School of Continuing Studies at the University of Toronto: a pre-university intensive program and a university program in English for Academic Purposes (EAP). The intensive program consists of four levels: elementary, low intermediate, high intermediate and advanced. Twenty of the twenty-five hours that students study per week are dedicated to the core syllabus and five to electives selected by the students. The EAP program consists of two levels: low intermediate and high intermediate.

Some of the students in the intensive program are foreign students who need English for academic and professional purposes; others are immigrants who need language skills for social purposes. Students in the ESP program, also foreign and immigrant, need English to succeed in their academic courses.

Autonomous learning within the program

The program, which stresses communicative competence as one of its main objectives, has for some years adopted a strategy-based approach to methodology, teaching strategies as *options* that students may use to acquire and use their language skills with fluency. Program objectives include (1) awareness raising of strategies that students already use in their native language, (2) facilitating transfer of these strategies to their second language, (3) provision of information and discussion on various aspects of the learning process and (4) providing for students' preferred ways of learning.

In this setting, learning training is integrated into the language training syllabus, and in designing syllabi and developing materials, emphasis is placed on learner diversity. Learners' purposes for learning English, the cognitive skills or strategies that they bring to the process and their preferred approaches to learning are determined as a first step to any syllabus development.

The teacher is viewed as a learning facilitator and is expected to be able (1) to help raise student awareness of their learning strategies, (2) to identify successful strategies that learners utilize, (3) to adapt language training materials for use in learner training and (4) to provide students with feedback that will enable them to determine and correct their own errors, and to develop the facility to monitor their use of English.

To prepare teachers who had no background in strategy-based methodology, workshops were organized and conducted by the director and other faculty self-trained in the field of learner strategies. Classroom research on individual learner's cognitive styles and strategy profiles also served to sensitize teachers to the importance of learner training. As a result, today, most teachers have incorporated some learner training activities into their classrooms, although only a few would explicitly say that this is what they are doing. Program administrators continue to be committed to an ongoing integration of learner training into the language syllabus, and teacher workshops continue to be planned and conducted to the extent that funds are made available.

Learner training has been integrated into all four language skills courses. Strategies and task knowledge appropriate to the receptive and productive skills make up the content of the learner training.

Reading

The following excerpts are from Tyacke and Saunders (1979) and Tyacke (1981).

Objectives
1. To provide ESL readers with a repertoire of reading skills if they have not already developed them in their first language, or to provide them with the knowledge that will enable them to transfer reading skills already acquired in their first language to their second language
2. To provide ESL readers with a set of 'replacement strategies' that they must consciously deploy . . .

3. To develop in ESL students a greater sensitivity to signals which will help in setting up expectations . . . in a specific reading situation

Procedures

1. The following procedures are used to assess student needs:

> First we pass out a sheet of paper which is divided into three columns on both sides. At the head of the first column is written 'What', the second 'Why' and the third 'How'. The students are asked to write down in the 'What' column what they read on a regular basis in their own language. . . . They are then introduced to the notion that we read either for information or entertainment, and are asked to indicate in the 'Why' column what the main function of each text was, using the letter I = inform and E = entertain. . . .
>
> Finally they reach the 'How' column. They are now introduced to the following reading skills: skimming, reading with focus, reading with total comprehension, critical reading and scanning. . . . For an elementary ESL class, however, these definitions have to be adjusted accordingly but most students can grasp the idea if the teacher demonstrates the activity visually. . . . The students are then asked to indicate, as far as possible in the 'How' column, what skills . . . they used to perform the different reading tasks they have described. Next they are asked to turn the page over and fill out the same columns with one major difference. Now they have to indicate in the 'What' column, first what they are already able to read in English, and second what they want or need to read in English. . . .

2. Once collected and analyzed into the categories listed below, the data provided by the students are used to plan course content that is based on their needs.

    (a) Students' reading habits and their level of literacy
    (b) 'Strong' readers to act as group leaders
    (c) Kind of materials needed
    (d) Common needs, group needs or individual needs
    (e) Functions upon which to base exercises
    (f) Skills which have been acquired and those which have not

Specific strategies and related activities

Some of the strategies students are trained to use include prediction, self-questioning, using context clues, categorizing and grouping. They are also made aware of how strategies vary depending on the reading task.

Strategy training involves two main steps.

1. Demonstration

The following is a description from Tyacke and Saunders (1979) of how they might handle this step.

> A simple visual activity can demonstrate to the students how prediction works. The teacher covers a book which the student has not seen and asks the students to guess what kind of book it is. Because of the size and shape, the students are able to eliminate several possibilities. Part of it can then be revealed, possibly the back cover. . . . Then part of the front cover is shown, without the title, and students continue to guess. . . .

2. Practice

Students are then provided with practice exercises that are completed in the class. The following from Tyacke and Saunders (1979) is used to practise 'predicting'.

> Students are expected to list as many words as they can think of that would fit in the blank space using semantic and syntactic context clues as well as their knowledge of the real world. One sentence at a time is written on the blackboard, so that students eliminate or add certain possibilities as they progress.

1. I was really mad because all of the . . . . was missing.
2. It was in a box on my desk.
3. I had baked it myself.
4. It was whole-wheat.
5. I had wanted to have a piece with butter and jelly.

Similar type activities are used in listening comprehension.

Listening

Mendelsohn (1984: 75) outlines the content for a listening comprehension course 'in which a different strategy or aspect of listening is dealt with in each unit: learning to guess; learning to interpret intonation; learning to determine topic, setting, interpersonal relations and mood . . .'. His training model involves three steps:

1. awareness raising — analyzing how something means what it does;
2. specially constructed training activities — to give students training in using the strategies;
3. less structured activities — practice with unstructured real data.

Reading/listening

One of the objectives of strategy training is to help students develop facility in the use of contextualizing, prediction and inferencing. Another objective is to help students gain confidence in their own ability to work out meaning without relying on teacher or dictionary definition.

   The following exercises illustrate practice activities for contextualizing that require that the student write and listen. In this sequence, students are also given an opportunity to evaluate the strategy they are practising (Tyacke *et al.*, 1980):

(a) Prepare a written or taped 'cloze' activity. . . . Students should then write down missing words. If the cloze activity was taped, hand out a written form of the same text so that the students have to read to find the right answer. If the cloze activity was written, play a tape with the missing words included so that he has to listen to find the right answer.

(b) Tape a series of sentences containing weak forms in the same position. Have students write down what they consider to be the full form, e.g., 'Give 'm the tickets. Where're you going? What 'n interesting movie that was'. As follow up, they can check their answers against a written form of the same sentences.

Talking/writing

The following excerpt from Tyacke *et al.* (1980) describes procedures which, at one and the same time, teach functions and the task knowledge appropriate to the productive skills:

Two students, during a class break, are discussing a movie they have seen. This particular context might carry one of a number of functions . . . (a) sociability (students pass the time of day). (b) Maybe one of the students hated the movie, while the other thought it was quite good — persuading/arguing. (c) Maybe one of the students missed the point of an important scene — imparting/eliciting information. The form which each of these conversations takes could be taped, analyzed, and discussed. The next step is to consider the possibility of one of those students writing a letter to the other about the movie they had seen, using one of the functions already discussed. If the writing sample and the taped conversation are analyzed for similarities and differences between the written and spoken modes, information beneficial to the students will emerge.

Besides the strategy training that is integrated into the language skills courses, students are given an opportunity to plan five hours of their twenty-five hour week. At an 'elective fair', which takes place on the second day of the course, students inform themselves about the content of eleven electives and decide which one they will take.

SETTING 6

NATIONAL CENTER FOR ENGLISH LANGUAGE TEACHING AND RESEARCH: LANGUAGE TEACHING SECTION

The Language Teaching Section of the National Center for English Language Teaching and Research at Macquarie University (Sydney, Australia) offers a fifteen-week course entitled *English for Professional Employment* (EPE) three times a year. The course is for permanent residents who have been in Australia for less than five years and (1) have professional qualifications from a non-English speaking country, (2) are seeking employment in their professional field and (3) can communicate in English at a level appropriate to their professional needs. Students who qualify and participate in the course have immigrated from countries all over the world, e.g. Europe, South America, the Middle East and the Far East. They represent a variety of professions including economists, bankers, engineers, accountants and psychologists and range in age from their mid-twenties to late forties.

Initiated by the director of the Center, the purpose of the course is to provide participants with job-related and communication skills and knowledge necessary for them to pursue and achieve their professional goals autonomously and effectively.

Nine of the fifteen weeks of the course are spent on campus; there are five weeks of professional attachment and one week dedicated to debriefing after the professional attachment and graduation. Four days of a typical weekly schedule in the course includes class-based activities in the mornings and 'open mode' in the afternoon. That is, students may do individual work or take part in tutorials and workshops; they may seek a counsellor or meet with guests. On Thursday afternoons there is an action meeting during which students meet in groups to evaluate the week's activities and to come up with suggestions for change and revisions. They also consider what has been done about the previous week's suggestions. Friday is research and development day. Students pursue individual projects.

Autonomy in the program

One of the main aims of the program is to help students develop self-directed learning skills so that they can pursue their goals independently outside the program. However, program content is not exclusively on autonomy *as it applies to language learning* but on autonomy as it applies to the enhancement of interactional and transactional skills, in English, that the students need to acquire for professional employment together with the related professional knowledge. To that end, the following materials and activities that focus on the attitudes, beliefs and strategies necessary for autonomy are used to implement the course syllabus.

Attitudinal scales
The attitudinal scale in Table 9.8 is intended to help learners become aware of their beliefs about the various personal factors that can affect learning, including the importance

TABLE 9.8
Principles of a learner-centered approach

Indicate your attitude to the following statements by rating them from 1 (totally disagree) to 5 (totally agree).

General:

1. Learner behavior is not fixed, but changes in response to both internal and external pressures. People can and do learn throughout their entire lifetime.

1	2	3	4	5	(4.2)
0	0	4	10	9	

2. Learners enter learning activities with an organized set of descriptions and feelings about themselves which influence their learning processes.

1	2	3	4	5	(3.69)
1	2	7	6	7	

3. The past experience a learner brings to any learning activity is both a helpful resource for further learning and an unavoidable potential hindrance.

1	2	3	4	5	(4.3)
0	0	4	8	11	

4. Part of the learner's past experience is organized and integrated into his self-concept and self-esteem.

1	2	3	4	5	(4.3)
0	0	2	12	9	

5. When past experience can be applied directly to current experience, learning is facilitated.

1	2	3	4	5	(4.52)
0	0	4	3	16	

6. Past experience becomes increasingly important as a person grows older.

1	2	3	4	5	(4.35)
0	1	1	10	11	

7. Learners with a positive self-concept and high self-esteem are more responsive to learning and less threatened by learning environments and the process of change.

1	2	3	4	5	(4.04)
0	2	4	8	9	

8. Adult learning tends to focus on the problems, concerns, tasks and needs of the individual's current life situation.

1	2	3	4	5	(4.39)
0	0	2	10	11	

9. Any group of learners will be heterogeneous in terms of learning and cognitive styles.

1	2	3	4	5	(3.91)
0	2	5	9	7	

Source: D. Nunan, National Centre for English Language Teaching

of self-concept. Students are also asked to analyze self-reports of the language learning experiences of other students as a means of clarifying their own beliefs about how best to learn a language.

Lessons in communication skills

The development of communication skills includes providing students with various aspects of task knowledge as it applies to listening and speaking in a formal situation. The lesson below makes students reflect on the differences between two kinds of communication: confrontation and negotiation. It will also help them become aware of some of the substeps involved in becoming a good communicator, i.e. channeling one's emotions; monitoring and shaping the listener's response.

Getting what you want out of communication: preparing for a forum with invited guests

Problems:	What do you want to achieve?
	How can you achieve it? (i.e. What might help or hinder?)
Approach:	Discuss, analyze, role-play and critique.
Discussion:	Negotiation/confrontation — what's the difference?
	How to channel emotion effectively.
	How to ensure your audience follows you.
	How to steer your listener into a specific response.
	What is their (the guests') world like?

(From L. Parkinson and K. O'Sullivan, Language Teaching Section, National Center for English Language Teaching and Research).

Other lessons help learners develop criteria for evaluating a successful communication and students' oral presentations of their research projects provide opportunities to practise applying these criteria.

Participative decision-making

One of the aims of the EPE is to build a strong partnership among students and teachers so that together they can 'build the program'. To that end, the program is organized so as to encourage a high level of participation. Students are given the following opportunities to develop facility in planning, monitoring and evaluating, i.e. facility in the skills of self-direction.

1. Listing needs and expectations
At the outset of a course, small groups are given an hour to brain-storm their needs and expectations as they apply to the various aspects of program content.

2. Action meetings
These weekly meetings, organized and run by the students, reflect the view of the program administrators that the students are responsible for what goes on in the classroom and that they (the administrators) are always ready to negotiate. The agenda includes reports from last week's action, program progress and logistical progress and suggestions for further actions, e.g. requests for special activities and alternatives to pre-planned activities.

3. Weekly schedule
Other than the action meetings which are specifically set aside for group planning and evaluation, afternoon sessions (Monday to Thursday) and research and development day (Friday) allow students to make their own decisions as to how they will use their time.

4. Professional attachment
For five weeks of the course students are placed on a job location where, again, they will be expected to self-direct or manage the application of what they have learned.

5. Debriefing and evaluation
A day is set aside at the end of the course for students to evaluate their experience.

Independent learning center
Working in the independent learning center is one of the options available for the afternoon sessions. In the learning center, teachers are available to counsel students

in the use of learning strategies and in analyzing their needs and monitoring their progress.

Teacher training

No formal teacher training is provided for participation in EPE. Teachers on staff will already have had training at other institutions. Major professional development required to participate in the program is facilitated by having teachers familiarize themselves with the course material and participate in in-house curriculum workshops and ongoing program evaluation. The need to appreciate the teacher–learner role shifts involved in this type of setting remains a concern and a challenge.

Learner autonomy and the language curriculum

These settings are not intended to be a comprehensive sample of all possible ways of including learner training in a language training program. However, they do illustrate the different curricular arrangements that can be made when learner autonomy is included as one of the objectives together with language learning.

> **9.2 Determining the extent of curricular change in each setting**
> In which of the settings was the most change required? As you discuss this question refer to your analysis of the curricular features listed in Task 9.1, i.e. learner training syllabus, learning arrangements, decision making, teacher role.

> **9.3 Selecting your preferred setting for promoting learner autonomy**
> Assume that you are planning to incorporate training for learner autonomy into your program. Which of these settings would you consider most appropriate? Why?

Conclusion

Teachers who learn to use the planning resources and skills described in previous chapters should be well equipped to implement learner training in their classrooms and to introduce it on a program level. The settings described in this chapter provide illustrations of how this has been done in different programs. In this concluding section we shall consider some institutional factors that are also necessary to the success of such program-wide efforts.

Change agent

The first important institutional factor is the change agent. Who will introduce the innovation into the program? Will it be a decision made by an administrator, or an initiative by one or several members of a program faculty, or will it represent a collaborative approach by both faculty and administrators?

   If efforts to extend these activities beyond individual classes are to succeed, it is important that program administrators be involved in their initiation and support. They have the power to command the use of resources necessary to develop learner training and to encourage and facilitate its extension beyond the classrooms of one or two enthusiastic teachers.

At the same time a core of enthusiastic and committed faculty, however small, is also important to the initiation and maintenance of learner training, for a top—down decision that receives no faculty support can fail. It may receive half-hearted cooperation based on recognition that job security may be at stake rather than cooperation based on an understanding of the basic importance of learner training. Moreover, less interested faculty members may be more willing to listen to colleagues than to supervisors. Finally, a group of interested faculty can provide the social support, feedback and motivation so crucial to pioneering new ideas.

Faculty development

Faculty development is a second factor to consider in planning for the adoption of learner training. Often resistance to new ideas is simply a manifestation of teachers' lack of knowledge of their significance or of their behavioral implications. Teachers must be given opportunities to discuss the significance of learner training, to learn what to do to implement it, and then to evaluate it. Faculty development is essential.

Availability of resources

Educational change will not only require informed and competent teachers, but also material resources. Obviously, both the preparation and training of teachers and the material resources will require some financial commitment on the part of the institution — initially and in an ongoing fashion.

Perceived importance of promoting autonomy

A final and most important factor is how the various actors involved in the promoting of learner autonomy perceive its importance. Is it considered an essential program objective? If so, by whom? The teachers implementing it? The language program administrators? The superiors of these administrators? If it is perceived as an essential program objective, then the necessary resources for materials and teacher training will be provided. Teachers within the program will be encouraged to experiment and evaluate, and a way will be found to deal with obstacles and difficulties.

Valuable readings

For further readings and illustrations of how learner training can be incorporated into language training settings, see Dickinson (1987), Holec (1981) and Oxford (1990). Chapter 8 of Dickinson's book includes a description of a variety of instructional systems for self-instruction. Self-access resources are also described. In Part III of Holec (1981), the author discusses how training for learner autonomy can affect our language teaching objectives and the roles of teachers and learners. In Part IV there are short descriptions of experiments incorporating learner training into language programs. Chapter 7 of Oxford's book presents brief descriptions of diverse settings in which language learning strategies are explicitly or implicitly encouraged.

Several of the chapters in Brookfield (1985) show how self-directed learning has been incorporated into a variety of settings such as graduate programs, cultural institutions, health professions and continuing education in the community.

Notes

1. In her version of the board, Kaufman laid out the numbers for each activity (i.e. ① ② . . .) in a circle about the size of an 8″ × 10″ page. At the top of the circle, there were spaces labelled 'start', and to the left of start, 'roll again' and 'free space: 2 pts'.
2. Each language activity is written on a card.

Glossary

This is a list of special terms necessary to talk about learner autonomy which appear in many of the chapters in the book. Most of the terms are used in the literature on learner strategies and learner autonomy, but there is not always consensus on what they mean. I have therefore indicated what the terms are intended to mean in *Learner Strategies for Learner Autonomy*. For a more detailed explanation on each, refer to the index.

action plan a series of procedures including the activities and resources necessary to carry them out; also a lesson plan

attitudes towards autonomy a willingness on the part of learners to take responsibility for their language learning and the self-confidence to do so

autonomous learner one who has acquired the strategies and knowledge to take some (if not yet all) responsibility for her language learning and is willing and self-confident enough to do so

curriculum all those aspects that have to be taken into consideration in planning, implementing and evaluating teaching/learning: learner needs, objectives and desired outcomes, course content, methods and materials, teacher and student roles

integrated learner training is integrated when in the act of learning, strategies, knowledge and attitudes are all taken into account

knowledge about language learning *see* metacognitive knowledge

learner account information or data about language learning obtained directly from a language learner

learner training the learning activities organized to help language learners improve their skills as learners; includes learning to use strategies; knowledge about the language learning process; and attitude development to support autonomous use of the strategies and knowledge; learner education

learning plans a general term which refers to a particular lesson or specific activities and materials that make up the lesson, a series of lessons, a whole course, a program curriculum; also referred to as action plans

learning strategy specific mental steps or operations learners implement to learn

metacognitive knowledge the stable, statable although sometimes incorrect knowledge that learners have acquired about language, learning and the language learning process; also referred to as knowledge or concepts about language learning or learner beliefs; there are three kinds: person, task and strategic knowledge

task the term has two meanings: it refers to the set of procedures learners implement to learn; when students set their own tasks, the term may be used interchangeably with strategy; references to the *language learning task* mean those specific procedures or skills learners must acquire in order to deal with a particular linguistic or communicative need

task based the content for learner training is derived from the language learning task as defined above

References

Abe, D., Stanchina, C., and Smith, P., 1975, 'New approaches to autonomy: two experiments in self-directed learning', *Mélanges Pédagogiques, CRAPEL.*

Abelson, R.P., 1986, 'Beliefs are like possessions', *Journal for the Theory of Social Behavior, 16,* 223–50.

Abraham, R., and Vann, R., 1987, 'Strategies of two language learners: a case study', in A. Wenden and J. Rubin (eds.), *Learner Strategies in Language Learning,* London: Prentice Hall International.

Acton, W., 1984, 'Changing fossilized pronunciation', *TESOL Quarterly, 18,* 71–86.

Allwright , R., 1981, 'What do we want teaching materials for?', *English Language Teaching Journal, 36,* 5–18.

Anderson, J.R., 1981, *Cognitive Skills and their Acquisition,* Hillsdale, NJ: Lawrence Erlbaum.

Anderson, J.R., 1983, *The Architecture of Cognition,* Cambridge, MA: Harvard University Press.

Bailey, K.M., 1983, 'Competitiveness and anxiety in adult second language learning: looking at and through the diary studies', in H.W. Seliger and M. Long (eds.), *Classroom Oriented Research in Second Language Acquisiton,* Rowley, MA: Newbury House.

Baker, L., 1979, *Comprehension Monitoring: Identifying and coping with text confusions,* Technical Report 145, Champaign, IL: University of Illinois at Champaign-Urbana, Center for the Study of Reading.

Barnett, L., 1989, 'ESADE Idiomas', Personal communication.

Bereiter, C., and Bird, M., 1985, 'Identification and teaching of reading strategies', *Cognition and Instruction, 2*(2), 131–56.

Bereiter, C., and Scardamalia, M., 1984, 'Reconstruction of cognitive skills', Paper presented at the annual meeting of the American Educational Research Associaiton, New Orleans, April.

Bialystok, E., 1979, 'The role of conscious strategies in second language proficiency', *Canadian Modern Language Review, 35,* 372–94.

Bialystok, E., and Ryan, E., 1985, 'A metacognitive framework for the development of first and second language skills', in D.L. Forrest-Pressley, G.E. KcKinnon and T.G. Waller (eds.), *Metacognition, Cognition, and Human Performance,* vol. 1, *Theoretical Perspectives,* New York: Academic Press.

Bode, S., and Moulding Lee, S., 1987, *Overheard and Understood,* Belmont, CA: Wadsworth.

Borkowski, J.G., Johnston, M.B., and Reid, M.K., 1986, 'Metacognition, motivation, and the transfer of control processes', in S.J. Ceci (ed.), *Handbook of Cognitive, Social, and Neuropsychological Aspects of Learning Disabilities,* Hillsdale, NJ: Lawrence Erlbaum.

Bransford, J.D., Sherwood, R., Vye, N., and Rieser, J., 1986, 'Teaching thinking and problem solving', *American Psychologist, 41,* 1078–89.

Bransford, J.D., Stein, B.S., Shelton, T.S., and Owings, R.A., 1981, 'Cognition and adaptation: the importance of learning to learn', in J.H. Harvey (ed.), *Cognition, Social Behavior and the Environment,* Hillsdale, NJ: Lawrence Erlbaum.

Breen, M.P., 1987, 'Learner contributions to task design', in C.N. Candlin and D. Murphy, *Language Learning Tasks,* Lancaster Practical Papers in English Language Education, London: Prentice Hall International.

Brodkey, D. and Shore, H., 1976, 'Student personality and success in an English language program', *Language Learning, 26,* 153–6.

Brookfield, S., 1984, 'Self-directed adult learning: a critical paradigm', *Adult Education, 35,* 59–71.

Brookfield, S., 1985, 'Self-directed learning: a critical review of research', in S. Brookfield (ed.), *Self-Directed Learning: From theory to practice,* San Francisco, CA: Jossey-Bass.

Brown, A., and Palinscar, A.S., 1982, 'Inducing strategic learning from texts by means of informed, self-control training', in B. Wong (issue editor), Metacognition and learning disabilities, *Topics in Learning and Learning Disabilities, 2* (1).

Brown, A., Bransford, J.D., Ferrara, R., and Campione, J.C., 1983, 'Learning, remembering, and understanding', in J.H. Flavell and E.M. Markman (eds.), *Carmichael's Manual of Child Psychology,* vol. 1, New York: Wiley. Also Technical Report 244, Center for the Study of Reading, 1982.

Brown, H.D., 1987, *Principles of Language Learning and Teaching,* Englewood Cliffs, NJ: Prentice Hall.

Brown, H.D., 1989, *A Practical Guide to Language Learning,* New York: McGraw Hill.

Brown, A.L. and Baker, L., 1984, 'Metacognitive skills and reading', in P.D. Pearson (ed.), *Handbook of Reading Research,* New York: Longman.

Candlin, C.N., 1987, 'Towards task-based language learning', in C.N. Candlin and D. Murphy (eds.), *Language Learning Tasks,* Lancaster Practical Papers in English Language Education, London: Prentice Hall International.

Candlin, C.N. and Murphy, D. (eds.), 1987, *Language Learning Tasks*, Lancaster Practical Papers in English Language Education, London: Prentice Hall International.

Carrell, P.L., 1985, 'Facilitating ESL reading by teaching text structure', *TESOL Quarterly, 19*, 727–52.

Casanave, C.P., 1988, 'Comprehension monitoring in ESL reading: a neglected essential', *TESOL Quarterly, 22*, 283–302.

Chamot, A., 1987, 'The learning strategies of ESL students', in A. Wenden and J. Rubin (eds.), *Learner Strategies in Language Learning*, London: Prentice Hall International.

Chene, A., 1983, 'The concept of autonomy in adult education: a philosophical discussion', *Adult Education Quarterly, 34*, 38–47.

Cohen, A., and Hosenfeld, C., 1981, 'Some uses of mentalistic data in second language research', *Language Learning, 31*, 285–313.

Cohen, A., 1987, 'Studying learner strategies: how we get the information', in A. Wenden and J. Rubin (eds.), *Learner Strategies in Language Learning*, London: Prentice Hall International.

Cohen, A., 1990, *Language Learning: Insights for learners, teachers, and researchers*, New York: Newbury House.

Collins, A. Brown, J.S., and Newman, S.E., in press, 'Cognitive apprenticeship: teaching the craft of reading, writing, and mathematics', in L.B. Resnick (ed.), *Cognition and Instruction: Issues and agendas*, Hillsdale, NJ: Lawrence Erlbaum.

Costa, A., 1985, 'Behaviors of intelligence', in A.L. Costa (ed.), *Developing Minds: A resource book for teaching thinking* Alexandria, VA: Association for Supervision and Curriculum Development.

Curran, C., 1972, *Counselling-Learning: A whole person model for education*, New York: Grune & Statton.

Curran, C., 1976, *Counselling-Learning in Second Languages*, Apple River, IL: Apple River Press.

Dansereau, D., Long, G.L., McDonald, B.A., Atkinson, T.R., Ellis, A.M., Collins, K., Williams, S., and Evans, S.H., 1975, *Effective Learning Strategy Training Program: Development and assessment*, Technical Report AFHRL-TR-75-41, Brooks Airforce Base, Texas Air Force Human Resources Laboratory.

Dansereau, D., 1978, 'The development of a learning strategies curriculum', in H. O'Neill (ed.), *Learning Strategies*, New York: Academic Press.

Deutsch, M., and Krauss, R.M., 1965, *Theories in Social Psychology*, New York: Basic Books.

Dickinson, L., and Carver, D.J., 1980, 'Learning how to learn: steps towards self-direction in foreign language learning in schools', *English Language Teaching Journal, 35*, 1–7,

Dickinson, L., 1987, *Self-Instruction in Language Learning*, Cambridge: Cambridge University Press.

Diener, C.L., and Dweck, C.S., 1978, 'An analysis of learned helplessness I: continuous changes in performance, strategy, and achievement cognitions following failure', *Journal of Personality and Social Psychology, 6*, 451–62.

Diener, C.L., and Dweck, C.S., 1980, 'An analysis of learned helplessness II: the processing of success', *Journal of Personality and Social Psychology, 39*, 940–52.

Dubin, F., and Olshtain, E., 1986, *Course Design: Development programs and materials for language learning*, New York: Cambridge University Press.

Duffy, G.G., Roehler, L.R., Meloth, M.S., Vavrus, L.G., Book, C., Putnam, J., and Wesselman, R., 1986, 'The relationship between explicit verbal explanations during reading skill instruction and student awareness and achievement: a study of reading teacher effects', *Reading Research Quarterly, 21* (3), 237–52.

Ellis, R., 1986, *Understanding Second Language Acquisition*, New York: Oxford University Press.

Faerch, C., and Kasper, G., 1983, *Strategies in Interlanguage Communication*, London: Longman.

Faerch, C., and Kasper, G., 1983, 'Plans and strategies in foreign language communication', in C. Faerch and G. Kasper (eds.), *Strategies in Interlanguage Communication*, London: Longman.

Ferrer, J., and Whalley, E., 1985, *Mosaic I. A listening/speaking skills book*, developed by Erik Borve for Random House, New York.

Festinger, L., 1957, *A Theory of Cognitive Dissonance*, Stanford CA: Stanford University Press.

Flavell, J., 1979, 'Metacognition and cognitive monitoring: a new area of cognitive developmental inquiry', *American Psychologist, 34*, 906–11.

Flavell, J., 1981a, 'Cognitive monitoring', in P. Dickson (ed.), *Children's Oral Communication Skills*, New York: Academic Press.

Flavell, J., 1981b, 'Monitoring social cognitive enterprises: something else that may develop in the area of social cognition', in J.H. Flavell and L. Ross (eds.), *Social Cognitive Development: Frontiers and possible futures*, New York: Cambridge University Press.

Flavell, J.H., and Wellman, H.M., 1977, 'Metamemory', in R.V. Kail, Jr., and J.W. Hagen (eds.), *Perspectives on the Development of Memory and Cognition*, Hillsdale, NJ: Lawrence Erlbaum.

Gagne, R.M. (ed.), 1967, *Learning and Individual Differences*, Columbus, OH: Charles E. Merrill.

Gairns, R., and Redman, S., 1986, *Working with Words: A guide to teaching and learning vocabulary*, New York: Cambridge University Press.

Gardner, R.C., and Lambert, W., 1972, *Attitudes and Motivation in Second Language Learning*, Rowley, MA: Newbury House.

Gardner, R.C., 1985, *Social Psychology and Second Language Learning: The role of attitudes and motivation*, Maryland: Edward Arnold.

Griffin, G.A., and Lieberman, A., 1974, *Behavior of Innovative Personnel*, Eric Clearinghouse on Teacher Education, Washington, DC, ED 093 857.

Guerchon, M., and Muir, A., 1987, *French Self Study Manual*, United Nations Language Training Programme, New York, unpublished.

Guiora, A., Beit-Hallahmi, B., Brannon, R.C., Dull, C.Y., and Scovel, T., 1972, 'The effects of experimentally induced stages or ego stages on pronunciation ability in a second language: an exploratory study', *Comprehensive Psychiatry, 13*, 421−8.

Hagen, J.W., Barclay, C.R., and Newman, R.S., 1982, 'Metacognition, self-knowledge, and learning disabilities: some thoughts on knowing and doing', *Topics in Learning and Learning Disabilities, 2*, 19−26.

Havelock, R.G., and Havelock, M.C., 1973, *Training for Change Agents: A guide to the design of training programs in education and other fields*, Ann Arbor, MI: Institute for Social Research, University of Michigan.

Heyde, A., 1979, 'The relationship between self-esteem and the oral production of a second language', Unpublished doctoral dissertation, University of Michigan.

Holec, H., 1981, *Autonomy and Foreign Language Learning*, Oxford: Pergamon.

Holec, H., 1987, 'The learner as manager: managing learning or managing to learn', in A. Wenden and J. Rubin (eds.), *Learner Strategies in Language Learning*, London: Prentice Hall International.

Holley, C.D., and Dansereau, D.F., 1984, *Spatial Learning Strategies: Techniques, Applications and Related Issues*, New York: Academic Press.

Horowitz, E., 1987, 'Surveying student beliefs about language learning', in A. Wenden and J. Rubin (eds.), *Learner Strategies in Language Learning*, London: Prentice Hall International.

Hosenfeld, C., 1976, 'Learning about learning: discovering our student's strategies', *Foreign Language Annals, 9*, 117−29.

Hosenfeld, C., Arnold, V., Kirchofer, J., Laciura, J., and Wilson, L., 1981, 'Second language reading, a curricular sequence for teaching reading strategies', *Foreign Language Annals, 4*, 415−22.

Hovland, C., Janis, I., and Kelly, H.H., 1953, *Communication and Persuasion: A psychological study of opinion change*, New Haven, CT: Yale University.

Huberman, A., 1974, *Permanent Education: Some models of adult learning and adult change*, Strasbourg: Council of Europe.

Hunt, M., 1982, *The Universe Within: A new science explores the human mind*, New York: Simon & Schuster.

Hutchinson, T., and Waters, A., 1987, *English for Specific Purposes: A learning centred approach*, London: Cambridge University Press.

Jones, B.F., Palinscar, A.M., Ogle, D.S., and Carr, E.G., 1987, 'Strategic thinking: a cognitive focus', in B.F. Jones, A.M. Palinscar, D.S. Ogle and E.G. Carr (eds.), *Strategic Thinking and Learning: Cognitive instruction in the content areas*, Alexandria, VA: Association for Supervision and Curriculum Development.

Joyce, B., and Weil, M., 1972, *Models of Teaching*, Englewood Cliffs, NJ: Prentice Hall.

Judd, K.R., and Kalnitz, J., 1986, *World Shakers: Reading strategies and skills*, New York: Holt, Rinehart & Winston.

Kahn, R.L., and Connell, C., 1957, *The Dynamics of Interviewing*, Part I, New York: Wiley.

Katz, D., 1960, 'The functional approach to the study of attitudes', in D. Katz (issue editor), Special issue on attitudes, *Public Opinion Quarterly, 24*.

Kidd, R., 1976, *How Adults Learn*, New York: Association Press.

Kirkpatrick, D.L., 1985, *How to Manage Change Effectively: Approaches, methods and case examples*. San Francisco, CA: Jossey Bass.

Kisslinger, E., and Rost, M., 1980, *Listening Focus: Comprehension practice for students of English*, London: Longman.

Knowles, M., 1975, *Self-Directed Learners: A guide for learners and teachers*, Chicago: IL: Association Press.

Knowles, M., 1976, *The Modern Practice of Adult Education*, Chicago, IL: Association Press.

Kohonen, V., 1987, *Towards Experiential Learning of Elementary English I: A theoretical outline of an English and Finnish teaching experiment in elementary learning*, Tampere, Finland: University of Tampere.

Lachman, R., Lachman, J.L., and Butterfield, E.C., 1979, *Cognitive Psychology and Information Processing*, Hillsdale, NJ: Lawrence Erlbaum.

Larsen-Freeman, D., 1986, *Techniques and Principles in Language Teaching*, New York: Oxford University Press.

Leblanc, R., and Painchaud, G., 1985, 'Self-assessment as a second language placement instrument', *TESOL Quarterly, 19*, 673−88.

Lefebvre Pinard, 1983, 'Understanding and auto-control of cognitive functions: implications for the relationship between cognition and behavior', *International Journal of Behavioral Development, 6*, 15−35.

Levine, A., Oded, B., and Statman, S., 1988, *Clues to Meaning: Strategies for Better Reading Comprehension*, New York: Collier Macmillan.

London, M., 1988, *Change Agents: New roles and innovation strategies for human resource professionals*, San Francisco, CA: Jossey Bass.

Markman, E.M., 1981, 'Comprehension monitoring', in P. Dickson (ed.), *Children's Oral Communication Skills*, New York: Academic Press.

Maslow, A.H., 1970, *Motivation and Personality*, New York: Harper & Row.

McKay, S., 1984, *Composing in a Second Language*, New York: Newbury House.

McLaughlin, B., 1987, *Theories of Second Language Learning*, Maryland: Edward Arnold (reprinted 1988).

Mendelsohn, D., 1984, 'There are strategies for listening comprehension', *TESL Occasional Papers, 8*, 63–76.

Mezirow, J., 1985, 'A critical theory of self-directed learning', in S. Brookfield (ed.), *Self-Directed Learning: From theory to practice*, San Francisco, CA: Jossey-Bass.

Miller, H., 1964, *Teaching and Learning in Adult Education*, New York: Macmillan.

Moulden, H., 1978, 'Extending self-directed learning in an engineering college', *Mélanges Pédagogiques, CRAPEL*, 81–102.

Moulden, H., 1980, 'Extending self-directed learning in an engineering college: experiment 2', *Mélanges Pédagogiques, CRAPEL*, 83–116.

Munby, J., 1978, *Communicative Syllabus Design: A sociolinguistic model for defining the content of purpose-specific language programmes*, London: Cambridge University Press.

Naiman, N., Frohlich, M., Stern, D., and Todesco, A., 1978, *The Good Language Learner*, Toronto, Ontario: Ontario Institute for Studies in Education.

Nicholas, H., 1985, 'Learner variation and the teachability hypothesis', in K. Hyltenstam and M. Pleneman (eds.), *Modelling and Assessing Second Language Acquisition*, San Diego, CA: College Hill Press, 77–99.

Nunan, D., 1988, *The Learner-Centred Curriculum*, New York: Cambridge University Press.

Oller, J.W., Jr., and Richard-Amato, P.A., 1983, *Methods that Work: A smorgasbord of ideas for language teachers*, New York: Newbury House.

O'Malley, M., Chamot, A., Stewner-Manzanares, G., Kupper, L., and Russo, R.C., 1985, 'Learning strategies used by beginning and intermediate ESL students', *Language Learning, 35*, 21–36.

O'Malley, J.M., Chamot, A.U., and Walker, C., 1987, 'Some applications of cognitive theory to second language acquisition', *Studies in Second Language Acquisition, 9*, (3).

O'Malley, J.M., and Chamot, A.U., 1990, *Learning Strategies in Second Language Acquisition*, New York: Cambridge University Press.

Omaggio, A., 1978, 'Successful language learners: what do we know about them?', *ERIC/CLL News Bulletin*, May, 2–3.

Omaggio, A.C., 1981, 'Helping learners succeed: activities for the foreign language classroom', *Language in Education: Theory and practice, 36*, Washington, DC: Center for Applied Linguistics.

Oskarsson, M., 1980, *Approaches to Self-Assessment in Foreign Language Learning*, Oxford: Pergamon.

Oxford, R., 1990, *Language Learning Strategies: What every teacher should know*, Newbury House: New York.

Paris, S.G., and Oka, E., 1986, 'Self-regulated learning among exceptional children', *Exceptional Children*, 53 (2), 103–8.

Paris, S.G., and Winograd, P., in progress, 'Metacognition in academic learning and instruction', in B.E. Jones (ed.), *Dimensions of Thinking: Review of research*, Hillsdale, NJ: Lawrence Erlbaum.

Paris, S.G., Newman, R.S., and McVey, K.A., 1982, 'Learning the functional significance of mnemonic actions: a microgenetic study of strategy acquisition', *Journal of Experimental Child Psychology, 34*, 490–509.

Petty, R.E., and Cacciopo, J.T., 1986, *Communication and Persuasion: Central and peripheral routes to attitude change*, New York: Springer-Verlag.

Pimsleur, P., 1980, *How to Learn a Foreign Language*, Boston, MA: Heinle & Heinle.

Prator, C.H., and Celce-Murcia, M., 1979, 'An outline of language teaching approaches', in M. Celce-Murcia and L. McIntosh (eds.), *Teaching English as a Second or Foreign Language*, New York: Newbury House.

Raimes, A., 1985, 'What unskilled ESL students do as they write: a classroom study of composing', *TESOL Quarterly, 19*, 229–58.

Raphael, T.E., and Mckinney, J., 1983, 'An examination of fifth and eighth grade children's question-answering behavior: an instructional study in metacognition', *Journal of Reading Behavior, 15*, 67–86.

Reid, J., 1984, 'Explanation of learning style preferences', Personal communication.

Reid, J., 1987, 'Learning style preferences of ESL students', *TESOL Quarterly, 21*, 87–112.

Richards, J.C., 1985, 'Listening comprehension: approach, design and procedure', in J.C. Richards, *The Context of Language Teaching*, New York: Cambridge University Press.

Riley, P., 1974, 'From fact to function: aspects of the work of the CRAPEL', *Mélanges Pédagogiques, CRAPEL*, 1–11.

Rivers, W., 1979, 'Learning a sixth language: an adult learner's daily diary', *Canadian Modern Language Journal, 1*, 67–82.

Robbins, B., 1981, 'Social constraints on adult language learning', in H. Winitz (ed.), *Native Language and Foreign Language Acquisition*, Annals of the New York Academy of Sciences 379, New York: New York Academy of Sciences.

Robinson, T.H., and Modrey, L., 1986, *Active Writing*, New York: Macmillan.

Rogers, C., 1969, *Freedom to Learn: A view of what education might be*, Columbus, OH: Charles E. Merrill.

Rubin, J., 1975, 'What the good language learner can teach us', *TESOL Quarterly, 9*, 41–51.

Rubin, J., and Thompson, I., 1982, *How To Be a More Successful Language Learner*, Boston, MA: Heinle & Heinle.

Rubin, J., 1987, 'Learner strategies: theoretical assumptions, research history and hypology', in A. Wenden and J. Rubin (eds.), *Learner Strategies in Language Learning*, London: Prentice Hall International.

Rubin, J., 1989, 'How learner strategies can inform language teaching', in V. Bickley (ed.), *Proceedings of LULTAC*, sponsored by the Institute of Language in Education, Department of Education, Hong Kong.

Ruetten, M.K., 1986, *Comprehending Academic Lectures*, New York: Collier Macmillan.

Salimbene, S., 1986, *Interactive Reading*, New York: Newbury House.

Scardamalia, M., and Bereiter, C., 1984, 'Teachability of reflective processes in written composition', *Cognitive Science, 8*, 173–90.

Schallert, D.L., and Kleiman, G.M., 1979, *Some Reasons Why Teachers are Easier to Understand than Textbooks*, Reading Education Report 9, Urbana, IL: University of Illinois, Center for the Study of Reading.

Schein, E.H., and Bennis, W.G., 1965, *Personal and Organizational Change Through Group Methods*, New York: Wiley.

Schoenfield, A., 1982, 'Beyond the purely cognitive: metacognition and social cognition as driving forces in intellectual performance', Paper presented at the annual meeting of the American Research Association, ED 219 433.

Schoenfeld, A.H., 1985, *Mathematical Problem Solving*, New York: Academic Press.

Schumann, J.H., 1975, 'Affective factors and the problem of age in second language acquisition', *Language Learning, 25*, 209–35.

Seligman, M.E.P., 1975, *Helplessnes. On Depression, Development, and Death*, San Francisco, CA: W.H. Freeman.

Sherif, M., and Hovland, C., 1970, *Social Judgement: Assimilation and contrast effects in communication and attitude change*, New Haven, CT: Yale University Press.

Sinclair, B., and Ellis, G., 1985, 'Learner training: preparation for learner autonomy', Paper presented at the 19th Annual TESOL Convention, New York.

Sinclair, B., and Ellis, G., 1989, *Learning to Learn English: A course in learner training*, New York: Cambridge University Press.

Stanchina, C., 1976, 'Two years of autonomy: practice and outlook', *Mélanges Pédagogiques, CRAPEL*, 73–82.

Stanford, B., 1976, 'Dead people are peaceful', in B. Stanford (ed.), *Peacemaking: A guide to conflict resolution for individuals, groups and nations*, New York: Bantam House.

Stern, H.H., 1980, 'Language learning on the spot', *Canadian Modern Language Review, 4*, 659–69.

Thorndike, E.L., and Woodworth, R.S., 1901, 'The influence in improvement in one mental function upon the efficiency of other functions', *Psychological Review, 8*, 247–61, 380–95, 553–64.

Toney, T., 1983, 'Guides for language learners', *ELT Journal, 37*, 352–7.

Torgesen, J.K., 1982, 'The learning disabled child as an inactive learner: educational implications', *Topics in Learning and Learning Disabilities, 2*, 45–52.

Twining, J.E., 1985, 'Generating a note-taking schema', *Journal of Development Education, 9*, 14–16.

Tyacke, M., and Mendelsohn, D., 1986, 'Student needs: cognitive as well as communicative', *TESL Canada Journal* (special issue 1).

Tyacke, M., and Mendelsohn, D., 1988, 'Classroom implications of learner diversity', *Language Teaching Strategies*, vol. 3, Toronto: Faculty of Arts and Science, University of Toronto.

Tyacke, M., and Saunders, J.B., 1979, 'Functional reading using "found" materials', *TESL Talk, 10*, 169–74.

Tyacke, M., Beyers, J., Beatty, C., McDonough, V., and Mendelsohn, D., 1980, 'Reading, listening, talking, and writing: a communicative approach', *TESL Talk, 2*, 59–74.

Tyacke, M., 1981, 'Alice through the looking glass: reading in another language', *Monographs in Language and Reading Studies*, Indiana University.

Van Ek, J.A., 1975, *Systems Development in Adult Language Learning: The threshold level*, Strasbourg: Council of Europe.

Vaughan, C., 1987, *Guided Self Study in English*, United Nations Language Training Programme, New York, unpublished.

Vygotsky, L.S., 1978, *Mind in Society: The development of higher psychological processes*, Cambridge, MA: Harvard University Press.

Weinstein, C.E., 1987, *LASSI: Learning and Study Strategies Inventory*, Clearwater, FL: H & H Publishing.

Weinstein, C.E., and Underwood, V.L., 1985, 'Learning strategies: the how of learning', in J. Segal, S. Chipman and R. Glaser (eds.), *Relating Instruction to Research*, Hillsdale, NJ: Lawrence Erlbaum.

Weinstein, C.E., and Rogers, B.T., 1985, 'Comprehension monitoring: the neglected learning strategy', *Journal of Developmental Education, 9,* 6–9.

Wenden, A., 1983a, 'Learner training for L2 learners: a selected review of content and method', ED 247 760.

Wenden, A., 1983b, 'The processes of intervention', *Language Learning, 33,* 103–21.

Wenden, A., 1985, 'Learner strategies', *TESOL Newsletter, 19* (5).

Wenden, A., 1986, 'What do second language learners know about their language learning? A second look at retrospective accounts', *Applied Linguistics, 7,* 186–205.

Wenden, A., and Rubin, J., 1987, *Learner Strategies in Language Learning,* London: Prentice Hall International.

Wenden, A., 1987, 'Metacognition: an expanded view on the cognitive abilities of L2 learners', *Language Learning, 37,* 4.

Wesche, M.B., 1979, 'Learning behaviors of successful adult students on intensive language training', *Canadian Modern Language Review, 35,* 415–27.

Wiley, T.G., and Wrigley, H.S., 1987, *Communicating in the Real World: Developing communication skills for business and the professions,* Englewood Cliffs, NJ: Prentice Hall.

Willing, K., 1985, *Helping Adults Develop their Learning Strategies: A Practical Guide,* Sydney: Adult Migrant Education Service.

Willing, K., 1987, 'Learning strategies as information management', *Prospect: The Journal of the Adult Migrant Educational Program, 2.*

Willing, K., 1988, *Learning Styles in Adult Migrant Education,* Adelaide: National Curriculum Resource Centre Research Series.

Wong, B.Y.L. (issue editor), 1982, 'Metacognition and learning disabilities', *Topics in Learning and Learning Disabilities, 2* (1).

Wood, P., Bruner, J., and Ross, G., 1976, 'The role of tutoring in problem solving', *Journal of Child Psychology and Psychiatry,* 17, 89–100.

Wright, T., 1987, *Roles of Teachers and Learners,* Oxford: Oxford University Press.

Yussen, S.R., 1985, 'The role of metacognition in contemporary theories of cognitive development', in D.L. Forrest-Pressley, G.E. McKinnon and T.G. Waller (eds.), *Metacognition, Cognition, and Human Performance,* vol. 1: *Theoretical Perspectives,* New York: Academic Press.

Zukowski/Faust, J., Johnston, S.S., Atkinson, C., and Templin, E., 1982, *In Context: Reading Skills for Intermediate Students of English as a Second Language,* New York: Holt, Rinehart & Winston.

Index